The Miracle Mineral Supplement of the 21st Century

Parts 1 and 2

Jim V. Humble

3rd Edition

What this Book is About

I hope you do not think that this book tells about just another very interesting supplement that can help some people after taking it for several months. Not so. This Miracle Mineral supplement works in a few hours. The #1 killer of mankind in the world today is malaria, a disease that is usually overcome by this supplement in only four hours in most cases. This has been proven through clinical trials in Malawi, a country in eastern Africa. In killing the malaria parasite in the body, there was not a single failure. More than 75,000 malaria victims have taken the Miracle Mineral Supplement and are now back to work and living productive lives.

After taking the Miracle Mineral Supplement AIDS patients are often disease free in three days and other diseases and conditions simply disappear. If patients in the nearest hospital were treated with this Miracle supplement, over 50% of them would be back home within a week.

For more than 100 years clinics and hospitals have used the active ingredients in this supplement to sterilize hospital floors, tables, equipment, and other items. Now this same powerful germ-killer can be harnessed by the immune system to safely kill pathogens in the human body.

Amazing as it might seem, when used correctly, the immune system can use this killer to only attack those germs, bacteria and viruses that are harmful to the body, and does not affect the friendly bacteria in the body nor any of the healthy cells. In this book I have, to the best of my ability, stuck to the facts of exactly what has happened regarding the Miracle Mineral Supplement.

This book is the story of the discovery and further development of the most amazing enhancement for the immune system yet discovered. Thus it is the greatest solution to mankind's diseases and ills now known; it is not a drug. I believe if you follow my efforts to develop this data and to make it available to the public, the story will help make it real to you and convince you to give it a try. To that purpose I have provided complete details on how to make the supplement in your kitchen, or to buy most of the ingredients off the shelf. It is entirely possible that you will save someone's life or your own.

The Miracle Mineral Supplement of the 21st Century

Because the Miracle Mineral Supplement functions as a supercharger to the immune system, it is not meant for treatment of any particular disease; rather it is meant to improve the immune system to the point of overcoming many diseases, frequently in less than 24 hours.

My purpose for writing this book is that this information is far too important to allow any one person, one group or even several groups to have control. It is information that the world should have. After 5 years of seeing practically nothing done by a group that could have done a great deal, I finally realized that the information simply had to be distributed to as many people as possible or someone would always be out of the loop of receiving this life saving data. It regularly occurs that there is a great deal of important medical information withheld from the public that could save lives. It is my intention to prevent that from happening with this information.

Foreword

This foreword is written by Dr. Hector Francisco Romero G., a medical doctor in the state of Sonora, Mexico where he has a very successful clinic that treats cancer and many other illnesses considered incurable. He uses the MMS talked about in this book and a number of other non intrusive treatments. He is well known in Sonora for the work that he has done with Mexican Indians. Dr. Romero makes me look much greater than I am, but then how could I refuse his foreword.

Dr. Romero writes: A dear good old friend of mine and respectful philosopher teacher impeller of man of good temper in this desert state of Sonora Mexico used to say: "Those men who live "the University of Life," would leave footprints in this world."

Not just anyone builds up and writes with his own ideas "a book". This is the same case with my friend Jim Humble. This personality is a challenger, a world walker, an anxious person, who has fought all his life to leave footprints with his contributions of investigation to man humanity. He has covered thousands and thousands of kilometers as his investigation has shown in this book, suffering infectious illness of Malaria; an illness which put his life at risk, demonstrating to medical science that it is possible to count with new alternatives treatments. It will give a better quality of life to those sick ones from endemics zones, as Jim says, in latitudes like in the region of Africa, Asia, and South America. In these places there is a lot of mortality due to malaria and other virus infections such as the HIV, causing the death statistics to be very considerable and is higher compared to other places in the world.

His product was investigated and well recognized by the health authorities in an African country. With the MMS, he offers them better hopes and quality of life. Especially, those who have the threats of these man destructive illnesses. Our experience in Mexico with the MMS, in the state of Sonora has been to treat some illnesses that are contagious febrile infections, inflammatory degenerative tumors, prostate cancer, and some other malignant tumors, with good and hopefully results.

For all of these, I pray to god so he can have a great intelligence so he continues helping those towns of the world that have no hope and are forgotten, specially the children that deserve our attention for a life, and a better future.

Copyright notice

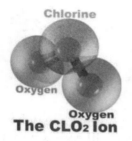

Chlorine

Oxygen

Oxygen

The CLO₂ Ion

Acknowledgements
Thanks to Bill Boynton of Mina, Nevada for his help with the chemistry of chlorine dioxide. Thanks to Clara Tate of Hawthorne, Nevada for her help and inspiration with ideas, suggestions and English.

Table of Contents

Chapter 1

The Discovery

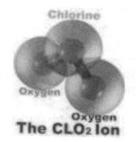

The CLO₂ Ion

The phone was ringing at the other end of the house. It was a long narrow house and there was furniture to get around and a hallway to get through, but in spite of the obstacle course I made it. Bill Denicolo, an old friend, in Chicago was calling. We talked and he asked, "Jim, are you any good at prospecting for gold?"

I was never too modest, so I told him the truth (my truth). "Yes," I said, "I am amongst the best, if not the best". That was enough for him. He was a friend, and being already familiar with my work in mining, he believed me. He continued, "I'm working with a group that wants to do gold mining in the jungle in South America. We need your help and we are paying the going rate, plus you get a share of the profits".

That was it. I agreed to leave in approximately one month. They were willing to use my gold recovery technology. This would require that I ship equipment ahead. It took the entire month to get things ready and to ready myself for the jungle. The most important thing that I took, that relates to this story, was several bottles of Stabilized Oxygen (Please don't get the idea that Stabilized Oxygen is the miracle solution that I am writing about in this book). All water in the jungle is dangerous to drink. In North America, water from fast-moving streams is usually quite safe to drink, but in the jungle it doesn't matter how fast the stream is moving, it is not safe to drink. In fact, one can almost always guarantee that one or more dangerous diseases are present. Despite that knowledge, I did end up drinking from a fast-moving stream while in the jungle, and I did develop typhoid fever.

A number of people had mentioned to me that the oxygen in Stabilized Oxygen would purify water by killing the pathogens present, especially if the water was left setting overnight. I had once sent a single test off to a laboratory after treating some sewerage water with Stabilized Oxygen and the results had come back showing all pathogens dead. I was relatively confident that I could purify my drinking water in the jungle.

I had actually worked with Stabilized Oxygen for some time. A friend of mine that lived a little way outside of Las Vegas used it quite a bit with his animals. He gave it to his chickens in their water to keep them healthy and he used it with his dogs. He even injected it into his dog's veins once when it was sick and his dog was cured in several hours. I often dropped by his home to see how things were going.

Bill Denicolo sent a contract to my house in Las Vegas, Nevada, where I had retired from gold mining. The contract was quite generous. I was to be paid a reasonable salary, and I would have 20% ownership in the operation, provided I located gold in the jungle. I signed a copy of the contract and sent it off, and received an airplane ticket in return. I was 64 years old but in top condition and I would have no trouble navigating in the jungle.

The country was Guyana. The name had been changed a few years earlier from British Guyana to simply Guyana. Guyana is the country just south of Venezuela on the east coast of South America. You probably remember it from the story of Jim Jones and his cult. The entire cult committed suicide at one point or actually a few committed suicides after killing the children and many of the other adults with cyanide. Only a few survived.

I arrived in Guyana on a normal day while it was raining, about midyear of 1996. I was met by several local people who would be part of the mining operation and they led me through the lines at the airport with no waiting. We drove about 30 miles to Georgetown, Guyana's largest city which is also the Capitol. I was taken to a local house where I was to stay until we departed for the interior, where we would prospect Guyana's greatest rain forest and jungle.

At the house I met Mike, a local who owned the claims to a very large portion of the jungle and would also be one of the partners. Joel Kane, who lives in the eastern part of the U.S., was also one of the partners listed on the contract I signed. He was to arrive within two weeks before we departed for the jungle. There was one other partner, who was also supposed to arrive soon, but probably after we departed for the jungle. His name was Beta and he was related to a high official in the government. The high official's name was Moses Nagamotoo, and he was the First Minister directly under the Prime Minister. (Beta's real name was Satkumar Hemraj, but he preferred the name of Beta.)

Beta was not present, but because he was our partner I was invited to the First Minister's (Moses Nagamotoo) house for dinner the second evening that I was there. While at his house the First Minister complained of his back problem that was almost preventing him from doing his job in the government. I explained to him that I sometimes adjusted people's necks and I might be able to help his back. So after dinner he allowed me to adjust his neck, which I did very delicately, making sure that I did not jerk or hurt him. Within minutes his back problem began to subside. We were all amazed and soon he was walking quite easily around the house.

The next day one of the servants called me and asked if I would adjust Mose's daughter's neck, as she was having bad back problems as well. I agreed over the phone, so they picked me up for dinner that night which was the third evening I was there and after dinner I adjusted her neck. Her name was Angela. He had another daughter named Adila, but she did not have a problem. Angela, as amazing as it may sound, was soon walking easily and her back problem seemed to disappear. I did not always have such spectacular results, but sometimes it did happen. I was very glad that I had taken the time to learn to adjust necks. Making such a powerful friend as Moses Nagamotoo was important. I did not realize how important it was at the time, but no doubt it kept me from spending time in prison at a later date.

For the record and future researchers, Sam Hinds was the Prime Minister. Jim Punwasee was the Minister of Mines whom we often went to see and occasionally visited in his home.

The government had a gold laboratory where they bought gold from local miners. The problem was that all gold that came in was completely covered with mercury. They put the gold under a hood and used a blow torch to burn off the mercury before weighing the gold. Well, as everyone knows, mercury fumes are extremely poisonous. Those fumes

were going up the exhaust stack and out into the government courtyard and into the government complex area. Many people had complained of this practice and when they gave me a tour of their gold facilities this was mentioned. I offered to design a simple fume scrubber and they

took me up on my offer. They had very little money for such refinements, so I designed the scrubber from two 55 gallon barrels. It just so happened that I had several thousand ping pong balls stored in a warehouse in Las Vegas. I had them shipped to Guyana to be used in the scrubber. By the time the balls arrived, I was in the jungle, but they simply poured the ping pong balls into the barrel designed to use them, turned on the water spray, and it was working when I returned. It did the job.

As luck had it, with the mercury scrubber, and helping the first Minister and his daughter, I hit it off very well with a few officials in the government there. I had a friend that wanted to move from Russia to Guyana and I mentioned this to the Minister of mining and a couple of days later I got a call from the Minister of Immigration saying that I could call my friend and tell him to visit the Guyana Consulate in Moscow. He said there were papers waiting for my friend there that would allow him to immigrate to Guyana. So you can see, I really did have a little bit of pull. I mention this merely to illustrate my good luck.

In our first expedition into the jungle we would be taking eight men who would carry the supplies and set up camp as we reached various locations. Our workers were called droggers. These men were hired by Mike and they arrived at the house about a week ahead of time to begin putting supplies and equipment together. One of the droggers was the foreman and the others, of course, were workers.

Finally the time for our expedition arrived and neither Joel nor Beta had arrived, but we couldn't wait. The men only made $6.00 a day (U.S. money), but that still cost to keep them around and we wanted to get things done. So the final crew consisted of me, Mike the landholder, and the eight droggers.

The trip into the interior took about two days. First there was about an hour's ride from Georgetown to the town of Parika on the Mazaruni Cuyuni River. We loaded our supplies onto a large truck and four taxies. We arrived at Parika at about 9:00 a.m. and loaded our supplies onto several large speed boats. The river at this point is more than five miles wide. Should you decide to do your own research on this part of the story, you will find that the next leg of the journey took us about four hours at what can be called high speed on that river.

We finally arrived at our next destination, the town of Bartica, which is considered the gateway to the interior of the country of Guyana. There we bought mostly food supplies. There are a number of food stores constructed like warehouses which mostly supply excursions into the interior. Our buyer bought mostly beans and rice. Normally, they buy only rice for such trips, but because I was there, they added several sacks of beans. On other trips I was able to get them to buy more variety of groceries.

We then loaded all supplies into several boats and crossed the river to a port on the other side about one mile away where we transferred our supplies and equipment into two very large trucks. The trucks had wheels that were more than six feet in diameter for driving through the roads consisting mainly of mud there in the jungle. Even those big wheels could not go where there were no roads. The supplies were tied down securely and most of the men then elected to walk on a somewhat shorter route to the next jump-off point into the jungle. I soon learned why they preferred to walk. The road was so rough and the trucks bounced so badly that it took constant attention to just hold on. There was no sleeping during the five hours that the trucks took to arrive at the final jump-off point on the last river leg of our journey.

We arrived after dark as it always gets dark at 6:00 p.m. and gets light at 6:00 a.m. in the jungle near the equator. We slept wherever we could that night. I slept on a bench outside of the small store there. The next morning we again loaded all of our supplies in boats and continued up what was now the Cuyuni branch of the river. Boats in this river are usually loaded to the gills, as the saying goes. The sides of these boats were less than four inches above the water. It wouldn't require a very large wave to come over the side one time and the boat, loaded as it was, would sink to the bottom. However, it just happens that there are almost never any large waves in these rivers. No storms ever happen in the jungle. It rains terribly hard, but very little wind accompanies the rain and so storms simply do not occur. In fact, there are no natural disasters in this area of the world, i.e. there are no storms, no hurricanes, no forest fires, or earth quakes.

We traveled upriver for about four hours and arrived where the real last jump-off point actually was. After we unloaded the boats and they pulled away, the men began loading themselves with supplies. The droggers carried their loads against their backs, but the weight was on their heads. A strap went around the top of their heads and down to the pack against their back. They claimed that this was the least tiring of any method of carrying loads. They carried loads of up to 80 pounds through the jungle and mountains. It was now about 10:30 a.m. We would have to travel up over a jungle mountain to the other side. Well we called it a mountain, but hills are not considered mountains in that area until they are 1,000 feet high. This hill was 997 feet high, and by the time we had climbed to the top, we were certain it was a mountain.

The mountain was totally covered with jungle. In this area, where the humidity is 100%, and sometimes even 110%, it does not matter if it rains or not. One is very soon soaking wet as the perspiration cannot evaporate. All clothes are soaked. Those who bring leather boots will have boots full of water, because either the rain or the sweat will soon fill them. Keeping an eye on what the locals wear, I wore only tennis shoes. Boots offer some protection from snakes, but they become almost impossible to use after a short time because they are soon filled with perspiration. I decided to just be extra careful in watching for snakes.

Some of the men had to make several trips over the mountain in order to get all of our supplies to the other side. It took almost two complete days of travel to arrive at our campsite. This gives you an idea of how far out in the jungle we were. Several days later when two of our men came down with malaria, we were plenty worried. We had been assured that there was no malaria in this area of the jungle and we had not thought to bring malaria medicine along with us. I immediately sent two men running to the closest mining camp hoping that they might have malaria drugs. That would take at least two days, and if they had no malaria medicine it would be at least six days before the men returned. We simply had to accept those facts because it was the best we could do.
We might have tried calling a helicopter, but we didn't have a radio. Radios don't work in the jungle anyway, except for very short distances.

Considering all of the data that I had learned about Stabilized Oxygen, it seemed to me, knowing it killed pathogens in water, that it might cure malaria. I sat down with the men who had malaria and asked them if they would be interested in trying this "health drink" from America. They were very sick and suffering. They lay in their hammocks shivering from the chills, and at the same time with high fever. Their symptoms included headaches, aching muscles and joints, nausea, diarrhea, and vomiting. They were willing to try anything and they did so.

I gave them both a healthy dose of the stabilized oxygen in some water and they drank it straight down. I thought, that's all I can do for now; we'll just have to wait for the runners to return. In one hour the shivering had stopped. That didn't mean much as the shivering comes and goes, but they looked a little better. Four hours later they were setting up kidding about how bad they had been feeling. They got up out of their bunks and sat down at the table to eat dinner that evening. The next morning two more men had come down with malaria. They took the same doses of Stabilized Oxygen and they were feeling okay by noon. We all were amazed. (This is not the whole story, and Stabilized Oxygen does not work all the time.)

I continued with the gold prospecting. I had developed a method of assaying for gold (that means to determine the amount of gold that is present) that was quite simple. I was able to conduct assays myself instead of having to send my assays off to a lab somewhere and wait a couple of weeks for the answer. Soon I had located some gold deposits and we began planning to put up a gold mill in the jungle. This is not a story about gold, so to make a long story short, while putting up a gold mill and doing further gold prospecting, I did quite a bit of traveling in the jungle. Wherever I went, I treated people for malaria (and sometimes typhoid fever). Although the Stabilized Oxygen worked only about 70% of the time, it was enough to make me quite famous in the jungle.

On the way back to town during that first trip into the jungle, we reached a mining operation that was shut down for vacation. There were a number of men who were merely waiting for the mill to start up again. One of the men was sitting at a table looking very sick. I asked him what was wrong and he said that he was waiting for a boat to pick him up. He said he had typhoid fever and malaria at the same time. I mentioned my Stabilized Oxygen which I merely called a health drink and he said he would try it. On my return from town he came running out to meet me. He grabbed my hand and pumped it up and down. He told me that he had gotten better within hours after I left and he didn't have to go into town after all. I left him with a small bottle of drops, as I had done in other places in the jungle.

There were a number of good stories like that one, but unfortunately at that time there were a lot of people it did not help. Still, it was a treatment that got much better results than the malaria medicines used there. People in malaria areas cannot afford to take the malaria preventive medicines as side effects <u>always</u> develop after a time. Visitors can usually only afford to take malaria medicines for a short period. Thus, the locals never take the malaria preventative medicines. They have to depend upon being cured by the standard malaria medicines after they contract malaria, and unfortunately malaria has developed a resistance to those medicines. Visitors can only afford to take malaria medicines for a short period. As it turned out, several of my associates were hospitalized as a result of the malaria preventive medicines.

I visited a missionary clinic near one of the mining villages in the jungle. They had, as I remember, four beds. I offered the "health drink" to them, but they said to me that malaria was a disease visited upon the people of the jungle because of their sinful sex practices and that they did not believe that God wanted them to have a cure for malaria. There was nothing I could do to change their minds. I felt terrible to see those people suffering, but I had to leave. I won't mention the religion involved as I feel that they must have changed their mind about helping malaria victims by this time.

Back in Georgetown I telephoned a friend, Bob Tate, about the Stabilized Oxygen curing malaria. He immediately flew to Guyana. We discussed it and decided to see if we could sell the Stabilized Oxygen in Guyana. We put an ad in the local paper stating that our solution cured malaria. That was a mistake. Immediately the local television station sent reporters over to our place and we were on TV telling about our solution. Then the radio and newspaper reporters arrived. We were famous for about three days. Then the government dropped a bomb on us. The minister of health called us in for an interview. She told us that if we sold our solution to one more person, that we would be in their prison and that we wouldn't like their prison. I had seen the prison and I knew that she was right.

I talked to my friend, the First Minister, Moses Nagamotoo, one evening. He explained to me that two drug companies had called the Minister of Health and threatened to quit shipping drugs to the local hospital if she didn't do something about the person claiming to be able to cure malaria. He explained that there was nothing his government could do at this time to help me, but he mentioned that he suggested to the Minister of Health that she give me some latitude.

At that point I made an even bigger mistake. Although we removed our ad from the newspaper, I continued to sell the solution to more people who needed it. My partner, Bob Tate, had already gone home, but I was still planning to do gold mining in the jungle. We were just about ready with our mining supplies when I got word that they were going to charge me with a crime and that it would be better if I were gone or were somewhere else. I found that people in Georgetown are more afraid of the jungle than are people from Las Vegas. They seldom chase people in the jungle. I immediately made the trip up the river and the supplies followed me a few days later.

This is the basic story of the discovery that Stabilized Oxygen sometimes cures malaria; however that is only the beginning of my story. I did not consider it a Miracle supplement, yet. I stayed upriver for slightly over six months working on the gold recovery mill. That part of the operation I financed myself because Joel Kane was very slow in arriving and never provided additional money. When he finally arrived, after he saw some of the gold that my mill was recovering, he wanted complete ownership, and offered me 3% instead of the 20% in the contract. When I did not agree, he had Mike the owner of the land and the droggers that Mike had hired tear down my working mill and carry it off into the jungle. I know that's what he did, because he told me so. According to the contract, if he did not use my technology he did not need to give me 20%. The problem for him was that the new technology that Mike, the landowner, implemented didn't work. Thus not only did I lose my investment but he lost his as well. He was a millionaire and really didn't care, but it was a little tougher on me.

When I came back to town after those six months, all the Health Ministry problems had blown over and I left for the USA. I lost my investment money, but I had the knowledge of what the Stabilized Oxygen could do and it was very exciting. I no longer cared about the gold. I couldn't wait to get home to begin a testing program to find out why the Stabilized Oxygen only worked part of the time.

I went back to Guyana a couple months later when another company hired me to help them improve their recovery of gold. I was still working with the Stabilized Oxygen. One night, I was careless and allowed myself to be bitten hundreds of times by mosquitoes. It really wasn't planned, but when the mosquitoes started biting, I just let them bite. Several days later I began to develop malaria. The very first symptom is just that you have light indigestion at a meal. It's not very pronounced, only a slight feeling of nausea that passes in about 15 minutes. You don't feel the real nausea until the next day. Since I did get sick, I decided that I might as well check out my own medicine. So I decided to wait until I got a blood test at the hospital in Georgetown before starting any treatment. That was almost a fatal mistake. The bus that runs from that part of the jungle to Georgetown did not come and I know that almost always people who wait too long for treatment end up dead. I waited a couple of days for the bus, but it didn't arrive and I was getting very sick. Still, I wanted to be absolutely certain, with a blood test, that I had malaria. I was going home soon and I would not have any chance to do further testing of this kind in the US.

I didn't tell anyone I was performing a test on myself. My employers, seeing how sick I was, felt responsible for getting me back to town. So when I agreed to pay for part of the cost for an airplane to pick me up, they agreed instantly. In that part of the jungle they do have a radio and a nearby landing strip. The plane finally came the next day (now my fourth day of being sick). I rode a bicycle to the landing strip. By this time I was very sick. When I arrived at Georgetown, they put me in a taxi and took me straight to the hospital.

At the hospital I waited several hours for a blood test. I was definitely showing the malaria symptoms. The doctor told me that my blood tested positive for malaria. I was an outpatient, so he just gave me a small bottle of malaria pills. Of course, I did not take the pills; instead I took a large dose of my own medicine. Within hours I was feeling better. It worked for me. To top it off, I went back to the hospital and had another blood test taken that now showed negative for malaria. I was elated! I was the first patient to have a blood test both before and after taking the Stabilized Oxygen. I believed I had discovered a cure for malaria.

I planned to leave Guyana right after I tested negative for malaria. I was riding my Honda motorcycle that I bought when I first arrived in Guyana around the city. As I rode along the street I met an old friend from Canada who was there to do some diamond mining. I stopped and we shook hands and sat down at a sidewalk café to talk. As we were talking, he noticed a friend shuffling along the street. He called out and the friend came over. We were introduced and he was invited to sit down. He looked very tired and just a little sick. I asked him what was wrong and he said malaria. He said that the drugs that the hospital was giving him didn't seem to be helping much. I said, "Well, you just happened to come to the right place."

I explained what I had just found out about curing malaria and said, "If you will wait just several minutes I will ride home and get you some solution to take". He agreed to wait. When I returned, I mixed a drink and gave it to him in a glass furnished by the sidewalk café. We continued to talk. After about half an hour he said, "You know, I feel a little bit better, it must be my imagination". All in all, we sat there about two hours after he took the solution. In that small amount of time all of his symptoms were gone. I gave him a small bottle of the solution, and later that night he came to where I was staying and got another bottle from me.

My plans at that time were to complete the research and then turn the information over to the world. I was sure I could get it out to the world one way or another.

Chapter 2

Further Development of the MMS

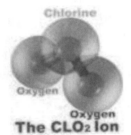

Chlorine

Oxygen

Oxygen

The CLO₂ Ion

I arrived back in the USA in the last part of 1997 and moved to Walker Lake, Nevada, where my partner, Bob Tate, had moved my portable laboratories. The plan was to set up and manufacture my own special mining equipment in order to make a living while also investigating the Stabilized Oxygen that I had used in the jungle. Unfortunately, during my exchange of Guyana money for American money before departing Guyana, a large sum of money was stolen from me as I had no experience with the money system there. Therefore, our funds for investing in the mining equipment manufacturing business were very limited. I sold my 40 foot ocean going houseboat for a small sum, which helped a lot.

We worked our mining equipment business for about a year but then Bob began to develop the terrible illness known as Lou Gehrig's disease and was unable to do much work. The sales of the equipment began to falter for many reasons. The magazine in which we advertised made a big mistake with our advertising and then refused to give us credit for the mistake, which cost us thousands. Eventually I ended up living on my Social Security income. However, at times I did get to do an assay or two, which helped.

With my son's help furnishing me with a computer and using the Internet, I began writing to various pen pals in Africa. Finally, I made friends with a man in Tanzania who took people on safaris to Mount Kilimanjaro. His name was Moses Augustino. I realized that he was mainly interested in making friends with people in America because he hoped to come upon some kind of an opportunity. Had I been in his shoes I might have done the same thing. He soon asked me for $40. I realized that to him $40 was a lot of money, and actually at that time, $40 was quite a bit to me as well. But since I wanted him to try the Stabilized Oxygen on some malaria cases in Tanzania, I sent him the $40.

The $40 paid off! According to my instructions, he began giving my solution to malaria victims that he knew in his area. Soon people were getting well fast, but again not everyone. He had a doctor friend, whom he told about the Stabilized Oxygen. At that time we called it the "Humble Health Drink". I sent his doctor friend two bottles and I received an email back from the doctor saying that he couldn't see how salty water would help a malaria case. I emailed him back and said, "Just try it and you will see." Well, the fact is, he did try it and he was amazed. He began to treat all of his malaria patients with the solution. The problem was there wasn't much malaria in this particular area. If there had been as much there as there was in the South of Tanzania, he would have treated hundreds of people, and it might have been a different story, but he only got a few cases of malaria each week. I thought you might like to see the two letters that they sent to me at my request. They are included on the next two pages.

FURAHA DISPENSARY,
P.O.Box 11293,
Arusha-Tanzania,
EAST AFRICA.

TO WHOM IT MAY CONCERN,

I'm working as a Clinician, I own a small dispensary in Arusha town, this town is situated northern part of Tanzania, this is the biggest country in East Africa after Kenya and Uganda.

I have been working in this field for 7 years now.

One of my usual responsibilities is to provide medical care to patients who come to my office for seeking medical advice and examination.

Most of the patients who come often in my office always suffer from Malaria and Water-borne diseases e.g. Typhoid, Bacillary Dysentry etc.
Malaria is one of the dangerous disease which attacks our people, and there has been various measures which are taken to combat this disease, for example in recent years our government has launched new medicine to combat this disease called SP (Sulfadoxine 500mg combined with Pyrimethamine 40mg). Eventhough I always witness resistance with high motality rate.

I first knew about Humble Health Drink (HHD) in May/2001, I have been giving this drink as Health Drink, I have been using this drink to many patients who comes to my office, but I discovered that among those patients who had taken HHD; those who were suffering from Malaria, amazingly all malaria symptoms disappeared within 2-5 hours but they continued to be weak for 6- 24 hours, after such period they appeared to be back normal, I have been giving them weak solution which is called Humble Health Drink Phase 1.
But also I discovered that there were few cases where Humble Health Drink Phase 1 appeared to fail to eliminate Malaria parasites, I then gave them solution which is called Humble Health Drink Phase 2, here a weak organic acid is mixed with stronger solution of Humble Health Drink and 48 hours is allowed to pass before consumed by the patient.

Within 2-4 hours after Humble Health Drink Phase 2 is administered; amazingly all all symptoms disappeared completely, here again I noticed patients to be back to normal 8-24 hours, and after such period most of patients appeared to resume to the normal.

For most cases there were no failures in treating malaria when I used Humble Health Drink, I have been visiting all patients who used both Phases and come to discover that all Malaria symptoms disappeared totally.
Since the day I first used Humble Health Drink up to the moment, I have successfully managed to treat 30 patients and some of them I managed to keep their records.
I would like to welcome anyone who would like to contact me by using my phone numbers given below or to visit me in Tanzania.

Sincerely,
Kittu J. Thomas.

Kittu J. Thomas,
P.O.BOX 11293,
Tel: +255 742421996 / +255 744306581
Arusha-Tanzania.

Nature Beauties Safaris Ltd.

P.O.Box 13222 Tel/Fax255 272504083,
E-mail: nature.beauties@habari.co.tz,
WEBSITE: www.nature-beauties.com
ARUSHA-TANZANIA-EAST AFRICA.

TO WHOM IT MAY CONCERN,

My job is conducting safaris in the country of Tanzania to our famous tourist attractions as it is known that this country harbour famous attractions in Africa e.g Mount Kilimanjaro, Serengeti National park, Ngorongoro crater, Lake Manyara national park (famous for its tree climbing lions), Tarangire national park, Selous game reserve, Zanzibar Islands etc.

I have been working in this job for three (3) years now, my responsibility in these trips is to Guide tourists who most of them comes from USA & Europe, I explains about Animals, Birds, Plants, African Cultures etc.

I first learned about Humble Health Drink in March/2001, as I have traveled around Tanzania I gave various people who had Malaria this Humble Health Drink, what is now called Humble Health Drink Phase 1.

Within 2 and 4 hours all symptoms of malaria disappeared, I noticed that when the symptoms had disappeared that they still seemed weak from the disease for 8 to 24 hours, but all appeared to be back to normal within that time.

There were a few cases of where the Humble Health Drink Phase 1 did not seem to help malaria patient. I then gave them a second mixture now designated Humble Heath Drink Phase 2. In this case a weak organic acid is mixed with a stronger solution of the Humble Health Drink and a certain amount of time is allowed to pass before the health drink is consumed. Within 2 to 4 hours after Phase 2 is consumed all malaria symptoms appear to be gone. Again the patient seems to be slightly weak, and the weakness seems to disappear within 8 to 24 hours .

I have had no failures when giving the Humble Health Drink to malaria patients. That is to say, all patients appear to have no more malaria symptoms when I have used one or both of the Humble Health Drinks, Phase 1 and Phase 2.

I have kept written record of all people who had malaria and who were given this Humble Health Drink. I have the name and address of each person. In all there were twenty one (21) people who had malaria and who benefited.

Anyone is welcome to call me at the phone number given below, or to visit me in Tanzania.

Sincerely,
Moses Augustino.

Moses Augustino,
P.O.Box 13222,
Tel: +255 0744290223,
Arusha- Tanzania,

Picture: Moses Augustino and his wife about year 2000. Moses was the first man to cure someone in Africa of malaria using the MMS.

They treated many people after these letters were written and I did get more data concerning the Stabilized Oxygen (Humble Health Drink).

Meanwhile, I was working to find out what chemical the Stabilized Oxygen really was and how it was made. I needed to find out why it wasn't 100% effective. I learned that Dr. William F. Koch first started working with this solution in Germany back in 1926. He used it in conjunction with mentally retarded children, because he believed that the Stabilized Oxygen produced nontoxic oxygen identical to the oxygen produced by breathing. Dr. Koch used his formula for the next 10 years believing that this formula somehow increased oxygen to the brain of the retarded children. Unfortunately, that was not the case. The problem was that either the chemistry was not modern enough for Dr. Koch to understand exactly what the formula was doing, or he just didn't understand chemistry well enough.

The formula found its way to the U.S. around 1930. Over the years those who could finally dig out the actual formula began to add it into various products thinking that it was a form of oxygen that the body could make use of. Researchers concerning Stabilized Oxygen since that time have continued to make the same mistake. The fact is that what is now called and has been called Stabilized Oxygen for the past 80 years contains no oxygen that the body can use. In order to be useful to the body, oxygen must be oxygen in its elemental state. That means no charge. In other words, oxygen cannot be an ion form of oxygen. The oxygen that is in Stabilized Oxygen is oxygen in an ionic form with a minus two charge. Saying that the body can use the oxygen in Stabilized Oxygen is like saying that the body can use the oxygen in carbon dioxide. Do you see? Carbon dioxide has two ions of oxygen with the same minus two charges. If you breathe only carbon dioxide you will die. The oxygen in Stabilized Oxygen merely becomes part of the water in the body. Water is made up of oxygen and hydrogen. In that condition, oxygen and hydrogen do not destroy any pathogens at all. I was later amazed to find that several universities had also made this same mistake. Of course, at that point I did not know any better either. I just knew the solution needed to be improved.

When you take a breath of air you are taking millions of oxygen atoms into your lungs. When you breathe out, guess what? You are breathing oxygen out in the form of carbon dioxide. The amount of oxygen going out is the same as the amount that came in. But going out it is carbon dioxide. You see, the dioxide is oxygen, but it is spent oxygen (so to speak). The thing that the oxygen does that keeps the body alive is it oxidizes things in the body. Oxidation consists of the oxygen atom accepting electrons which destroys poisons and neutralizes chemicals and releases heat energy. In the process carbon dioxide or carbon monoxide or some other combination is created. When the oxygen accepts the electrons, it is no longer an oxygen atom but it becomes an oxygen ion with a minus two charge. If it already has a minus two charge, as it does in Stabilized Oxygen, it cannot oxidize anything and thus it is of no value to the body <u>as oxygen</u>.

So if it isn't oxygen that comes from the so called Stabilized Oxygen, that kills the malaria parasite, what is it? You know, finding the formula for Stabilized Oxygen was a hard thing to do back in 1998 if you had a limited knowledge of chemistry. Everyone who had the formula wasn't telling and even when they sold it, they would not put the ingredients on the label. I did find one company that gave instructions for using Stabilized Oxygen. They said that after you put the drops into a glass of water it became unstable and thus you should never wait more than one hour before drinking the mixture. I thought that was interesting. So I put 10 drops into a glass of water, waited for about eight hours and then smelled it, like chemists often do. I thought I smelled chlorine. I realized that if water did make the Stabilized Oxygen unstable, it was because the water had made it less alkaline (more neutral). I had been using 10 drops, but by that time I was getting the idea that I would have to use more drops. After adding 20 drops of Stabilized Oxygen to a glass of water, I decided to add a little vinegar because it is a food that contains an acid called acetic acid which I knew would make it less alkaline than even water would. I waited for more than 24 hours this time and then I could detect a much stronger smell of chlorine.

By that time, my friends in Africa trusted me to some small extent, so they were willing to give it a try. They started using the improved formula of 20 drops of the Stabilized Oxygen in a full glass of water with one teaspoon of vinegar. After waiting 24 hours they then gave it to several of those who were not helped with the original first dose. It worked in every case when they used the vinegar and waited 24 hours.

To test my mixture, I bought some chlorine measuring sticks used for swimming pools, and guess what? After a few hours, the mixture began to measure a slight amount of chlorine and after 24 hours it measured at least 1 ppm (part per million) of chlorine. That really wasn't the total answer, but I was getting closer. I didn't realize it at first, but the sticks were measuring <u>chlorine dioxide</u>.

Next, I put a lid on the glass containing the mixture and found that it developed the same strength of chlorine in two hours as it did in 24 hours without the lid. That is, of course, so long as I also used the vinegar. The reason was that the chlorine was not going off into the air nearly as fast. I transmitted this data to Tanzania and they began to use this new procedure. They added the teaspoon of vinegar, used a lid and waited for two hours before giving it to the malaria victims. It worked every time. They were not having any failures.

This all sounds easy now, but I did more than 1,000 different tests over a period of one year to figure out all these "simple" things. My money was very limited and swimming pool test strips were expensive, as well as the various chemicals that I needed to do the testing. I must admit that I didn't do anything really smart or brilliant, I just blundered along with my slight knowledge of the chemistry of metallurgy. There was also the fact that I was a research engineer in the Aerospace industry for almost

25 years. I set up tests for A-bombs and that sort of thing. So I did have some experience at doing tests. I tried a dozen or more acids and a hundred combinations.

The two-hour wait was okay for the doctor, but for my friend Moses Augustino it wasn't very practical. He was always on the move and would run into cases of malaria on his travels. He needed a method of giving people doses within five minutes or so, as he simply could not wait two hours all the time. Stabilized Oxygen is stable because of its very high alkalinity (i.e. the opposite of acidity.) When a few drops are added to a glass of water, the alkalinity of the drops is neutralized by the water and ions in the drops become unstable and begin to release chlorine. At least that is what I thought at the time. So the question is, how do we get this to happen faster?

The research waited for the purchase and testing of different acids, which I finally accomplished. After trying all the mineral acids and various organic acids, I found that vinegar, which is 5% acetic acid, which is an organic acid, worked the best. Then I made a mini breakthrough which was simple. Instead of using a glass of water, I used no water at all. I just put 20 drops of stabilized oxygen and 1/4 teaspoons of vinegar in a clean, dry, empty glass. I swirled it around to mix it. That worked, and it worked in only three minutes! I checked the mixture with the chlorine strips and it showed a reading of over 5 ppm (parts per million) in only three minutes' time. When I added 1/2 glasses of water, it diluted the mixture out to less than 1 ppm, but the taste was terrible. The Stabilized Oxygen mixture with water doesn't taste too bad before the chlorine is released, but afterwards it's pretty bad. Some people don't seem to mind the taste. However, most people do, especially children, and they are the main ones who need the solution.

I tried various juices to see which ones might work the best. There were two problems. First I needed something that would taste okay, but I also needed something that would not change the amount of chlorine. After trying many juices and tasting a lot of drinks I settled on just plain old apple juice, the kind with no vitamin C added. I transmitted this information to my friends in Tanzania and they used it for a few months. Then something happened and I never heard from them again. I worried that my friend Moses may have been injured on one of his trips to

Kilimanjaro as he simply dropped out of contact. The doctor explained to me that he had not heard from him either. The doctor also mentioned that he was going to move. I never heard from either of them again, although I sent numerous e-mails. They gave me a great deal of help and I miss their e-mails.

You may be wondering at this time what the formula for Stabilized Oxygen really is. I did finally dig out the formula for Stabilized Oxygen. I am sure that a lot of researchers would have found it in 1/2 hour; but living on a desert lake with a very limited income, it took me a while. Anyone in the world can find the data now-a-days, but let me save you some trouble. The formula is $NaClO_2$. The name is <u>sodium chloriTe</u>. That sounds like salt, but not quite. Table salt is $NaCl$, and the name is sodium chloriDe. Notice the difference of the next to last letter. One is chlor<u>ite</u>, and the other is chlor<u>ide</u>. So let me tell you the real story that all the other researchers seem to have missed.

Let me mention now that the chlorine I smelled was actually chlorine in the air above the solution, but there was no chlorine in the solution. I discovered that what is in the solution is Chlorine Dioxide which is much different than chlorine. Sodium chlorite (Stabilized Oxygen) is highly alkaline, that is the opposite of acid. When it is neutralized it becomes unstable and begins to release, not oxygen, but chlorine dioxide. But that is where the oxygen comes in. The formula for chlorine dioxide is ClO_2. That's one ion of chlorine and two ions of oxygen, but the body cannot use that oxygen. It has already lost its ability to oxidize. The chlorine ion however, in this case, has a powerful ability to oxidize. Chlorine dioxide is a powerful explosive. It cannot be contained as it will explode and destroy the container. It is always generated where it is used because it cannot be moved. Even a particle as small as one ion of chlorine dioxide will explode when it hits the right thing, namely a pathogen in the body or some other item more acidic than the body.

An explosion is merely a fast chemical reaction, releasing energy, which is usually some kind of oxidization. When a chlorine dioxide ion meets a pathogen it accepts five electrons of charge and instantaneously results in an instant oxidization, which is the explosion. The result of this explosion (the result of this chemical reaction) is that the chlorine ion is completely neutralized. The two oxygen ions that were a part of the chlorine dioxide ion are already neutral which for oxygen is a minus 2 state. That means that the oxygen ion cannot oxidize anything; it can only become a part of the water in the body. The body cannot utilize it for any kind of oxidation. The chlorine ion becomes a chloride which basically is just table salt which has no particular power either. Both the oxygen and the chlorine now do not have any charge that will create any kind of oxidation. So you see it's the chlorine dioxide ion (the combination of chlorine and oxygen) that does the work and it has a great deal more ability to oxidize pathogens than oxygen.

Another fact is that several deep breaths of air will supply more oxygen to the human body than the stabilized oxygen is expected to supply. Since the formula was supposed to produce oxygen identical to the oxygen in the respiration process, what would be the point of taking the Stabilized Oxygen when you could just take a couple of extra breaths? Anyway, it's a moot point. The fact is, what the researchers believed was happening was not happening. The oxygen just becomes a part of the water in the body and/or possibly becomes part of a carbon dioxide ion, but it cannot be used by the body for anything else.

The Chlorine dioxide supplies electrons. It does not supply oxygen. Basically, the chlorine dioxide ion is the oxidizer, not the oxygen. Check your chemistry book. Oxygen is not the only oxidizer. Any reaction in which electrons are transferred is considered oxidation. If the researchers that worked with Stabilized Oxygen had been able to understand modern chemistry, they may have been much more successful with their research. There is a lot more to it than this initial explanation and I intend to go over it thoroughly as I cover the story of the development of the Miracle Mineral Supplement. It's written so anyone can understand it.

At this time I moved a few miles to the town of Mina, Nevada, where I continued writing emails to other people in Africa.

Thirty miles away from where I lived in the town of Mina, is the town of Hawthorne, Nevada. There I met J. Andrew Nehring, a man that ran a small hobby shop. He had just returned from the Mayo Clinic where he had been operated on for cancer of the pancreas. He was continuing to be tested at a hospital in a nearby city. Unfortunately, the tests were still positive for cancer. He had been scheduled for exploratory surgery in approximately 60 days at the Mayo clinic. While visiting a mutual friend, he heard me talking about my solution. He asked me about it and wondered if it would help his cancer. Since many people had already tried Stabilized Oxygen on cancer and had what seemed to be some success, I believed that the addition of vinegar might make it much better for cancer as it had for malaria.

We both agreed to try it. I had not yet noticed any side effects. IT IS NOT A DRUG. So he began taking the solution using vinegar as the activator. Within two weeks his cancer readings began to reduce. The high reading was 82 (whatever that meant). At the next visit to the hospital the reading was 71. A month later the reading was 55. Two months later it was 29 and so on until the reading was less than five. The doctors at the hospital didn't know what happened, but as soon as the readings began to go down, they canceled the appointment at the Mayo clinic. They wanted to see what might be happening. When the reading reached three, they said there was no point in further testing. This is just one of a number of cancer stories in the past 10 years in which the cancer just went away while taking the MMS.

So at that time, my plan was still to get this information to the world one way or another. I developed a plan where I would put some of the story on the Internet to be distributed throughout the world. The way I planned to do this was to have the information in an e-mail ready to send out to the world. I wanted it to be distributed similarly to the way viruses are often sent. When a person received this MMS information it would have a tiny program that would allow the person who received it to easily send it out to every email address on his computer. But of course he would be in total control. A person would only have to push one button and the complete information concerning using and making the MMS would go out to every email address on his <u>computer that he so designated.</u>

Do you see how fast that could propagate across the world? It would go fast, but there are disadvantages. A book is even better, because not nearly the amount of information in a book could be put into emails.

I sold the one thing that I had, a special process for recovery of gold. I received $17,000 for the process. I searched around on the Internet and finally found a company that claimed they could develop such a distribution program. I started working with them to get the program done. I paid $5,000 up front and several thousand as the program progressed and a large sum at the end. The program never worked. So I never got a working program and I had spent my money. Just to be fair, let me tell you the name of the company that refused to furnish me with a working program after I gave them $14,000. It was Danube Technologies, Inc. in Seattle Washington.

They said when I made the final payment they would send me the working program. Their first proposal to me was dated 9 April 2001. My final payment to them was 11 November 2001. The program never came close to working. They claimed it did. They also said that the program was illegal. They would not do anything more. Now, 6 years later I am finally selling this book.

I know you think that with such a great Miracle Mineral Supplement, philanthropists like Opra Winfrey and Bill Gates would stand in line to give me money to carry out our mission, but not so. It takes a while to get it figured out, but finally you realize it is all based on money or the desire for prestige. Oprah wants to know what is going to bring her TV program the biggest audience because that is what brings in the money, and Bill Gates gets no prestige for helping the little guy. His millions go to the big pharmaceutical laboratories which in turn bring him powerful friends throughout the world. To invest in something that works but reduces the income of the pharmaceutical companies would be unthinkable. He said over the phone he would not back us until we had FDA approval. That takes a hundred million dollars and he knew we would never have that.

I sent many letters to these people and dozens of other organizations. It wasn't, for the most part, that they wouldn't believe me. For a hundred years the medical people and the pharmaceutical people with their billions of dollars have stood shoulder to shoulder using the laws enacted by congress to hold the alternative medicine people at bay. They have made them look like quacks and charlatans, but the fact is that millions of Americans have discovered that they are not. Despite medical warnings, every year more and more people discover answers in the alternative medicine area and now it is a many billion dollar business. You can't possibly think that millions of Americans are so stupid that they would prefer quacks and charlatans if they were not getting real help with their health problems. It may surprise you to know that 55% of the American public now use alternate medicine and have quit going to the family medical doctor. That's why they are so frantic to get all supplements under the control of medical people.

And now, since the first edition of this book, the FDA has announced its intentions of shutting down at least 50% of the alternative medical businesses. The new law enacted by congress gives the FDA the right to require that all supplements be tested to prove their efficacy. That means that the FDA can stop any supplement at any time and require testing. It could cost up to $100,000,000 for a single supplement. While more than 900,000 people die from drugs each year, the health industry does not average one death a year. But should someone even report being sick from a health supplement the FDA can and does stop every supplement of that kind in the country. In several cases, even though nothing was wrong, the supplement was never allowed back on the shelves. Now with this new law, just from what they have said they are going to do, it is obvious that the FDA intends that nothing but drugs will eventually be available to those who are sick.

Please tell your friends about this book.

Chapter 3

Stabilized Oxygen, MMS, and a Contract

Chlorine

Oxygen

Oxygen
The CLO₂ Ion

As stated in the previous chapter, I moved to the small town of Mina, Nevada, in 2001, where I lived on a gold milling property at no cost. Dick Johnson, a friend, did this to help me out with my research. It gave me a few extra dollars to help with my research and investigation of the Stabilized Oxygen. During the first year there I met Arnold, a man of many talents. I have changed his name, in this case to protect the guilty, because I am not going to say very many good things about him, though I will say a few.

The Stabilized Oxygen mixture has been renamed several times since I began to make the solution in my kitchen. It is not easy to get the chemical sodium chlorite, but if you keep at it you can get some. (I'll tell you how to get it in Book II. It is available in many chemical supply houses.) I began making the solution much stronger than the Stabilized Oxygen that is sold on the market. For many years Stabilized Oxygen was 3.5% sodium chlorite. At this time my solution, which I have named The Miracle Mineral Supplement (MMS), is 28% sodium chlorite. That's eight times stronger than regular Stabilized Oxygen. When I am making trips into the jungle, it means I can carry eight times as much "healing power" as the original Stabilized Oxygen formula.

Let me explain what has happened. The researchers over the past 80 years have done their tests using from 5 to 20 drops, at the most, of the 3.5% solution. As I started helping people with malaria and other problems, when a few drops didn't work, I just gave them more. In all the research I have been able to read concerning Stabilized Oxygen, no one increased the drops beyond 25 drops and very few ever used that many. Where did the old idea go that if 10 drops is good, 40 drops is 4 times as good? The only precaution that I took was that I always tried the heavier doses on myself first. Generally, I was dealing with people who wanted to get well, and they agreed to try it after I had tested it. I didn't go from 10 drops of stabilized oxygen to 120 directly, but I finally wound up at 120 drops and used a second 120 drops one hour later. I did it a little at a time until I found out what it took to handle a problem. It is not a drug; it is a mineral supplement. I am an inventor, not a doctor. I don't even know what the Hippocratic Oath says; I am not trying to do what doctors do. My goal has been to invent a way to help the immune system overcome malaria ever since I thought it was possible and I did accomplish that. In my opinion, I have never put anyone at risk and I have helped over 2,000 people personally. Over 75,000 people have overcome malaria with the help of people I trained. The people treated were "cured" with no deaths reported in the bunch. Normally over 300 deaths could be expected. When I say "cured" I'm referring to the fact that they got up, smiled, put their clothes on and went back to work. They have not relapsed, as far as we can tell.

Did we do double blind and triple blind tests? No. The money was not available. Bill Gates told us over the phone that he would not help until we were FDA approved. Usually, FDA approval costs millions, but those people in Africa that went back to work feeling good didn't care if we had FDA approval or not. When I phoned the FDA they said that if I was using it in Africa they had no say over there so they would not comment, but if I wanted to get it approved for treatment of malaria in America, then that would be another story. They didn't care if it was not a drug. The minute I said treatment of any disease, it then becomes a drug and you must have all of the countless tests and laboratory evaluations. That's anywhere from $50,000,000 upwards.
The country of Malawi has accepted MMS as a mineral supplement that can be given to anyone, including those who are sick. They have shown a bit of reasonable logic. It isn't likely to happen here in the U.S. The doctors and pharmaceutical companies have lobbied congress to the tune of billions of dollars to have all the laws written in their favor to produce money for them. In the U.S. every year over 900,000 people die from medical drug related causes. However, when just one single person died in one year from an amino acid found in a health food store, the FDA ordered all of that amino acid to be removed from all health food stores in the U.S. in spite of the fact that it has helped more people than most drugs. Now, years later, that amino acid is still not allowed. The drug companies and the FDA are always ready to pounce on anything that might eat into the profits of pharmaceutical companies. In this particular case that amino acid was replacing a drug. It was costing the drug companies money.

So long as one is using a mineral supplement in the attempt to make people feel better, there is no criticism. So long as one is using a mineral supplement attempting to make people healthier, there is no criticism, but the minute one attempts to treat someone for some specific condition with the same supplement that has been used for 80 years, then that is a different story. You must be a doctor, you must do clinical trials, and you must have 100 million dollars for double blind tests and triple blind tests, and dozens of other requirements. No one offers to furnish the money; they just tell you what you are required to do. How dare you try to treat someone for a disease! That's for doctors and pharmaceutical companies only.

There are many people in America who realize that drugs only treat the symptoms, not the causes of a disease. Why would a company even bother to research treating the symptoms of a disease instead of attempting to find a cure for the disease? Does anyone ever ask that question? Well, a lot of us do, but not the FDA. The answer is this, so long as you are treating the symptoms, you won't cure the disease and you can go on selling that drug until the person dies.

Several wealthy people offered to pay for distributing the MMS throughout the country of Haiti. They wanted to eliminate malaria in Haiti. But when we approached more than 15 clinics there, we found that they were controlled by doctors in the U.S. The doctors in the U.S. were totally determined that we could not give a single person our mineral supplement. Haiti went without the supplement and thousands still have malaria. In any case, it only takes 15 drops of Miracle Mineral Supplement (MMS) for the first dose given to a malaria patient followed an hour later with another 15 drops. This is because the MMS is eight times stronger than regular Stabilized Oxygen. If you were using regular Stabilized Oxygen, you would need 120 drops at first and then another 120 drops in 1 hour after that.

Has anyone been hurt? No. Thousands of people later there are only thousands of happy, well people with none claiming any lasting, negative side effects. In actuality, there are a few instant reactions in about one out of a hundred people, but that's not a side effect. The reaction normally lasts less than 30 minutes. Look it up in a medical dictionary or on the Internet. Side effects are the effect that a drug has on healthy cells that are not a part of the disease. Instant reactions are the result of the body adjusting because the MMS is affecting diseased cells or disease causing germs. There are no effects on healthy cells.

We know that the MMS (28% sodium chlorite) generates chlorine dioxide (that's CLO_2) when mixed with vinegar. The reason why it produces chlorine dioxide when mixed with vinegar is because the acetic acid (in the vinegar) causes the solution to be neutralized or, better than that, causes it to be slightly acidic. The MMS solution is normally extremely alkaline. When it is made acidic, by adding the vinegar, it becomes slightly unstable and it begins to release chlorine dioxide. By measuring the drops and the acetic acid we know that it creates about 3 mg of chlorine dioxide in approximately three minutes. Then when we add apple juice (or other juice without vitamin C) it dilutes the solution so that there is about 1 ppm of chlorine dioxide in the total apple juice mixture. The MMS solution continues to generate chlorine dioxide but now at a much slower rate.

About chlorine dioxide: Chlorine and chlorine dioxide have been used to purify water and kill pathogens in hospitals and for many other antiseptic uses for more than 100 years. Lately chlorine dioxide has been used more and more frequently, especially to purify water. It is also authorized by the FDA to be used to clean chicken, beef and other foods. Research has proven chlorine dioxide to be much safer than chlorine, as it is selective for pathogens when used in water and it does not create compounds from other constituents in the water, which chlorine does. Simple chemistry tells us that without doubt the same situation exists in the body. It has been proven that chlorine in drinking water creates at least three different carcinogenic compounds when it enters the body, but no such compounds have been found from chlorine dioxide. The American Society of Analytical Chemists stated in 1999 that chlorine dioxide was the most powerful pathogen killer known to man.

If this is the case, and it is, then you would have thought that the pharmaceutical companies would have said to themselves, "Hmm, if chlorine dioxide is such a powerful killer of bacteria, viruses, and other germs, and since it is used to kill viruses on food throughout that industry, maybe, just maybe it could be used to kill those things in the human body." But no, they wanted a drug that makes you feel a little bit better and can be sold over and over again. No point in using something that's going to cure someone on the first dose!   Pharmaceutical companies should have discovered it 100 years ago, but they didn't. You might say that is just my opinion, my truth, but I am going to have to call it a fact because it is such an obvious truth. There is no excuse why research has not been conducted with a solution that has been used for 100 years to kill disease causing germs. The pharmaceutical companies not only didn't do the research, but they actually refused to test the Stabilized Oxygen many times.

So what happens when you put Stabilized Oxygen in the body? It goes down into the stomach at first.   There are dozens of research papers which state that when it comes in contact with strong stomach acids, it breaks down into oxygen immediately. They haven't however stated the tests that prove this hypothesis. I used stomach acids in a test glass and that result never happened. Even when I tripled the strength of the acid in the glass to three times what would normally be found in the stomach, it never broke the sodium chlorite down immediately. In fact, it never increased the speed of production of chlorine dioxide beyond maybe 100th of a milligram per hour, in other words, practically nothing. And, of course, creating chlorine dioxide and sodium (tiny insignificant amounts of sodium) is all that can happen when the sodium chlorite does break down. There isn't anything else left. That is all that's there. The chlorine dioxide "explodes" when touching various items of lower acidity than the body by accepting five electrons with tremendous energy. It will almost always be things that are bad for the body. Otherwise, it simply bounces off the healthy cells. There is more about this later in the book (see chapter 14). Again chlorine dioxide is the oxidizer here, not oxygen.

Without the use of vinegar, lemon, lime or citric acid, a tiny amount of chlorine dioxide is all that will be produced. Any benefit from the Stabilized Oxygen has to be derived from the tiny amount of chlorine dioxide because there is nothing else except an insignificant amount of sodium. Because there was indeed some benefit from Stabilized Oxygen we know that the chlorine dioxide was doing it. The oxygen that is finally released by the chlorine dioxide is not useable by the body. Because all Stabilized Oxygen sold on the market today is a solution of sodium chlorite, there are no electrolytes of usable oxygen to be derived from Stabilized Oxygen.

With the addition of vinegar the conditions change drastically. At first, with the 20 drops and 1/4 to 1/2 teaspoon of full strength vinegar, the body receives an amount of about 3 milligrams of chlorine dioxide in the mixture when the apple juice has been added to the dose mixture. The solution then continues to generate chlorine dioxide for the next 12 hours within the body.

The red blood cells that normally carry oxygen throughout the body have no mechanism to differentiate between chlorine dioxide and oxygen. Thus, in the walls of the stomach where the blood picks up nutrients of various kinds, when a chlorine dioxide ion touches a red blood cell it is accepted. If there happens to be a malaria parasite present it will be destroyed and the chlorine dioxide will be destroyed as well. If there are no parasites present, the chlorine dioxide will be carried by the red blood cell to some part of the body where oxygen would normally be used to oxidize poisons and other bad things. There the chlorine dioxide is released. The chlorine dioxide has over a hundred times more energy to do the same thing that the oxygen would do but it still won't hurt any healthy cells, more than likely because the immune system has the chlorine dioxide under control.

This is the point where I like to compare the chlorine dioxide ion to a good Tasmanian devil and the disease germs to bad Terrorists. The Tasmanian devil is a small fellow, but is known for his ferocity. The red blood cell is the bus that carries oxygen, and the conductor doesn't care. He will also carry the Tasmanian devil. Taz, the chlorine dioxide, is let off by the red blood cell at approximately the same spot that oxygen would normally be let off. The terrorists are not even worried. They can handle Mr. Oxygen. But this time there is a surprise. The guy that gets off the bus is ferocious. He's much worse than the oxygen that normally gets off. He jumps out and kills every single terrorist that is present that is harmful to the body. So when the red blood cell bus arrives, MEET TAZ.

If the chlorine dioxide does not hit anything that can set it off, it will begin to deteriorate and thus gain an electron or two. This may allow it to combine with other substances, creating a very important substance that the immune system utilizes to make hypochlorous acid. Hypochlorous acid is probably the most important acid of the immune system. It kills pathogens, killer cells, even cancerous cells with this acid. When the body has a deficiency in the important substance from which the immune system creates the hypochlorous acid, it is called myeloperoxidase deficiency. Many people are afflicted with this deficiency and the deficiency may increase during diseased situations because the immune system needs a great deal more of this acid when a disease is present.

There are some suppositions here. In any case we definitely know that chlorine dioxide is made in the body from sodium chlorite and it then kills the hell out of pathogens.
There is one other function that the chlorine dioxide does in the body. It tends to neutralize poisons. Almost all substances that are poisonous to the body are, to some extent, acidic in nature or below the neutrality of the body. The chlorine dioxide will neutralize many of these poisons. We believe that can be the only explanation why a malaria victim often goes from totally sick to totally well in less than four hours. The poisons that malaria generates are neutralized by the chlorine dioxide at the same time the parasites are killed. I gave some chlorine dioxide to a dog that was bitten by a rattlesnake. I gave him a drink of the solution every 1/2 hour. The dog seemed to know it would help him and he drank it right down each time I gave it to him. He was okay in a few hours, which would indicate that the poison was probably neutralized by the chlorine dioxide.

While I was living in Mina, Nevada, I was finally able to order the first whole drum of 100 pounds of sodium chlorite. Actually, the same friend that helped me by providing a place for me to stay in Mina bought the first 100 pound drum of sodium chlorite. He dropped by and took a few pounds to keep for himself as that would ensure that he would never be without it. For the record, his name is Richard Johnson. I began to help some people here in town and some people began to buy the solution that I bottled here in my kitchen. There are a number of people here in town that now has been using the MMS for several years. I have sent bottles all over the world. Many people have used it to help with cancer and every other disease that you can think of that might be caused by bacteria, viruses, molds, yeast or any other pathogen.

Eventually, as mentioned previously, I was approached by Arnold, a businessman who lived in Reno and who also owned a nonworking gold mill here in Mina. He asked me to do some gold assays. We began talking and when I mentioned that I had help people with malaria, he was extremely impressed. We talked on several occasions' times and in time we finally signed a contract. In the contract he agreed to finance making the MMS available throughout the world. He wanted to put up an Internet site in Budapest and sell MMS to the world from Budapest. I found him to be like many other wealthy men who think MMS is great. They want to get others to invest money, but they don't want to invest any themselves. He began talking to numerous people about the MMS and was able to interest many groups which were "humanitarian." He called me and told me about each new group that he was talking to concerning investing in the MMS for malaria in Africa.

Arnold is a great humanitarian. He works to help the homeless in Reno. He always stops to help anyone who might be broken down on the highway. He supplies a truckload of clothes and other items to an orphanage in Mexico each year. Many times when homeless or people down on their luck arrive in Mina he will either give them a job himself or somehow get them a job with someone else here in town. He also helps out at various places in Reno including distributing meals to the homeless at Christmastime. He has been quite helpful to me in many ways and has worked toward getting the MMS distributed in Africa for the last 6 years.

The problem was he never kept any of the agreements in the contract I made with him. Instead, he kept finding people who would "potentially" finance the MMS distribution in Africa for malaria victims. We were always just weeks or months away from getting the money to distribute the MMS in Africa or to get the money to conduct clinical trials to prove to the world that it works.

Arnold began to use the MMS to help people, as he is very compassionate toward people who are sick. He personally gave MMS to many people after overseeing that they knew how to use it correctly. He found veterans who had malaria that kept coming back and provided MMS for them. That was one way that he proved to himself that it worked. However, I began to see that he would not let me talk to any of the groups that he had interested in helping to finance the distribution of MMS to the world. I don't know what his reasoning was, but it seems he is not as effective dealing with people as he thinks he is. Group after group lost interest in the MMS and simply did not continue with him and his ideas. Group after group or person after person came and went away. Living out here in the desert, I never got to talk to any of these people or groups. I was always told about the people or the groups, but never allowed to talk to them. Even when I asked to be allowed to talk to these people Arnold would not discuss it. This continued for five years. He made many mistakes, such as, hiring a young kid to do our web site, who then sued us when we insisted that the web site be done the way we wanted. The kid took us to court and also sent letters to government agencies saying that we were crooked and our MMS solution was a fake. Those letters prevented us from getting a letter from the IRS stating that we were a nonprofit group. At the beginning of the writing of this book (10/1/2006), now 5 years beyond the time he was supposed to get the Web Site done, 10/1/2001 and thousands of dollars later, we still don't have a Web Site. Four additional people that have been hired have all bombed out and took our money and produced nothing. Had I been able to use some of this money that was lost, I could have completed clinical trials in Kenya. Arnold also hired a grant writer who also began to work against us. Arnold was very bad with people while always thinking that he was especially good. I mention this negative stuff only to point out why I had to write this book. It's part of the story and getting the information to the world is and has been my purpose.

I should reaffirm that I do not think that Arnold is a bad guy. But I finally realized that if I stayed with him it would have to be his way or nothing. If I wanted to get this information to the world I had to leave that partnership. It wasn't happening Arnold's way and he would not allow any other way. Thus, I had to get away where I could do it the way I knew it would work.

The year at this time was 2006 and I could no longer justify keeping this information from the world. There were and are millions of people who need the MMS. How could we allow those to die who could be saved? The answer for me at that time was I could not.

I called a friend, Ed Heft, who had a house in Mexico located near on a bay just off of the Sea of Cortez. He immediately invited me to come down and finish the book. He said I could live there at no charge for rent. It was an ideal offer for me. I accepted. So I packed my bags and left about mid November 2006. But I am getting ahead of my story. There were several other important events that took place before I left. See Chapter 4.

UPDATE For 3rd Edition. The continuing story from the 2nd Edition. I will put the update here because there really isn't a good other place for it. So I arrived in Mexico somewhere below the border and stayed in a house right on a bay off of the Sea of Cortez. I continued to write my book. I am sure anyone familiar with Mexico would know where I was, but I'll not name the place for now.

Christmas came and went and I continued to write. Finally the book was finished some time in about March 2007. I had saved enough money from the job Arnold had given me of cleaning up the old gold mill to buy the first 1000 books. The time was also spent in putting together a Web Site. Not a very good one, but as it turned out, it did the job; it sold books.

Only a few books sold as I was not very good a Web advertising, but the book got to a few of the right people and some of them began making the formula of MMS and selling it right away. One company, especially, began to sell large amounts immediately. They knew how to advertise on the Web and they sold thousands of bottles of MMS. For the record their name was Global Light.

My book sold for $14.95 and that helped out quite a bit. I also made two ebooks. I divided the hard book, *The Miracle Mineral Supplement of the 21st Century,* into 2 parts. I made the download of the first part of the book (Part 1) free of charge. Then if they wanted to read the second part it cost them $9.95. That worked fairly well, for every 15 people that read Part 1, one person would purchase and download part 2. And since there was no cost to me for part 2 it was mostly profit.

The selling of MMS is what really started the ball rolling. Of course, I was down here in Mexico and couldn't send books out from here. I had the book company ship the books to Clara Tate who became my secretary in Nevada. She shipped all the books out from there. Soon I realized that we were running out of books. I needed to make the next order right away.

Things started to go better. One company called me up and offered to help by purchasing a large order. I decided to sell the next edition, the 2nd Edition for $19.95. So the purchase of 500 books at ½ prices would give me $5000 dollars immediately, which was all that the printing company required up front. My friend in Canada, Kenneth Richardson, said that he would pay the rest of the cost when the books were ready to be delivered to Clara in Nevada. I couldn't lose, although I had no money to speak of, everything was being paid for. This order for the 2nd Edition was for 10,000 books.

There were a number of people who interviewed me on the radio and on various web associations. The sales of my book increased up to about an average of $350 a day including the ebook and hard copy. I'd like to name all that helped, but there were too many and if I left anyone out it wouldn't be fair and there isn't enough room in this book. One person who I think was especially effective in keeping my book selling was Adam Abraham with his radio show "Talk for food."

Getting the book sales to increase over the amount mentioned above has been tough. It has hung in there at that level for months. I will be working on that. I have been able to use some of the money for helping in Africa, but for the most part, I am saving the money for when I travel to Africa.

I found that I couldn't live on the bay and still get everything done that I wanted to get done. Most of the computer things and other supplies are available in a large Mexican city 60 miles away and I needed to move there.

Meanwhile there were those who encouraged me to get the book printed in Spanish and with the money from the sales of the books I was able to do that. If found a nice lady in town who wanted to help and soon had an agreement with her to start a Mexican company to sell Spanish books and MMS as well. I moved to town and was lucky to rent rooms from the Spanish lady's family.   One room I made into an office for computers, and one room was for me to sleep in. The family was very good to me. I hired the sister of the lady who was working with me to start the Mexican company as my secretary. The mother there took great care of me and my clothes were washed and ironed and my bed was made. I was no longer alone.

The Mexican company that we were making was extremely important as the NAFTA treaty states that any products that are legal in one country is legal in the other countries of the agreement as well. That meant that if we could get the MMS registered and legal in Mexico it would also be legal in the US and Canada. We could circumvent a lot of problems in the US. Also, of course, I would make money here on MMS. I had decided to not sell MMS in the US as that might help get MMS accepted and selling, since people could not accuse me of trying to make money on a snake oil. And that may have helped in the beginning, but it is priced so low that it seems no one cares if I make some money from the sales of not. I won't try to sell any MMS in the US, but a number of companies who are selling MMS have agreed to donate to my African fund.

One more thing, Nexus magazine decided to get my book translated into German and published which they did with an agreement to pay me a royalty.

So, in all this time, with thousands of people cured there have been many people who want to help, but there has been no one with money who has stepped up to the plate and said, "Let me help." Many rich guys have refused when I asked. But it actually looks like the sales of the book will do well enough to produce the money to cure at least one country in Africa. It actually looks like the project will get done. But what continues to amaze me is that with millions of dollars spent on frivolous stuff each year, the world goes blithely marching on not realizing that the human race is marked for extinction and refusing to see the evidence staring them in the face when just a tiny amount of that frivolous money could change things. See Chapter 9.5, the last part, for more information on this.

Chapter 4

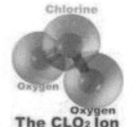

Dr. Flomo

I signed the contract with Arnold in 2001. Arnold talked to numerous people concerning the MMS (which we called OS-82) about helping the people of malaria in Africa. He always had someone that he believed might help provide us with funds so that we could first prove the MMS worked. Then we could ask the world to help us cure Africa. I remained in Mina, Nevada, continuing to write emails to people in Africa. Many didn't believe me and some even asked me not to write them again.

Somewhere around July of 2003, my emails to Africa paid off. I finally got in touch with a doctor in Guinea, West Africa. His name was Dr. Moses Flomo, Sr. I began telling him of the results that we had obtained in Tanzania. He was interested. I sent him a bottle of the MMS and he tried it on a single malaria patient who was well in only hours. He immediately went to the office of the Ministry of Health. Dr. Gamy was the Deputy Minister of Health at that time in Guinea.

This picture shows Dr. Moses Flomo, Sr.
Dr. Flomo was able to deal with one of the doctors in the office of the Ministry of Health who then authorized him to test 25 people. He was to test those 25 people without charge. If the MMS worked he could then begin charging people for the MMS as a treatment for malaria.

Dr. Flomo put a large sign outside his clinic which said, "Free treatment for malaria." Within hours he had more than 25 people signed up and he treated them the same day. He had them agree to come back the next day for testing. The next day all the people who returned were malaria free. He began treating people for malaria for 5,000 fg (75 cents US) on October 1, 2003.

People started lining up outside of his office. He continued treating people for a few weeks. Unfortunately, Dr. Flomo couldn't really see the value of the MMS. He believed that he could make a lot of money from selling herb formulas in capsule form. The malaria thing was only something that he was doing to get me to help him with the herbs. I agreed to help him as long as he was working with malaria. He wanted me to send him some empty capsules, and some herb books, and a capsule filling machine, and other supplies. When I sent his package containing some books and a small semi automatic capsule machine, his post office held it. He got so upset with them that he closed his clinic. It didn't make a lot of sense to me, except he wasn't from Guinea and he thought that was the reason he was being treated badly.

We later found that the postmaster had taken the package and put it on his desk. The next day he took sick and the package remained on his desk for two weeks. An accident happened and the package was essentially destroyed by rain.

Dr. Flomo decided to go out to an America Bauxite Company, the biggest one in that part of the world. He knew one of the doctors in the company clinic. So he took some MMS to the doctor and explained how it worked. They began treating workers who had malaria with the MMS. In all they treated about 2,000 people.   At that time they reduced absenteeism by over 50%. Dr. Flomo began negotiating with them to sell them 150 bottles of MMS for $60,000 US money. That's $400 U.S. per bottle. I had never intended to sell the bottles for more than $26 US, but Flomo insisted that we could use the money to set up a clinic. Since we had never settled on an exact price, I said okay. After all, that was still somewhat less than $1 U.S. per treatment.

At that time, Arnold didn't have complete control of the Malaria Solution. He hadn't yet figured out how to get complete control. I still had some say in how things were handled. Later, Arnold said that the people that were putting up the money wanted him to have complete control. At this time I was able to allow Dr. Flomo to sell the MMS. Later I was not allowed to do such things.

There were some glitches to the Bauxite Company transaction and quite a bit of time passed. I determined the main problem was that Dr. Flomo was making trips elsewhere working on the herb plan that he had. It was quite an extensive plan. He planned to have many acres planted with various different herbs. Dr. Flomo would not allow me to talk to the doctors at the Bauxite clinic. We had to go through him and he was busy elsewhere.

This is a picture of Dr. Flomo's herb clinic.

I decided to tell Arnold about the possible sales. That was a mistake. Arnold then tried to call the clinic at the America Bauxite Company but he couldn't get the right phone number. Then he got in touch with the U.S. Company that owned the Bauxite Company and got the phone number of the president of the America Bauxite company in Guinea. The president said that he would not use our MMS (OS-82) until some university had published a paper stating that they had tested the MMS and that it worked. That ended the $60,000 sale of bottles to the Bauxite company clinic, as the doctors there were informed that they could not use the MMS. Had we not tried to go through the front office, the doctors in the back would have continued to use the MMS. (This was a flub by Arnold. I didn't want to stir things up in the front office of the American Bauxite Company as I realized that things were delicately balanced.) If they had already been using the MMS for six months and the absenteeism had been reduced 50% during that time, no one would have said stop. As it was, the front office was never informed that they had already treated 2,000 people.

I continued to work with Dr. Flomo and sent him 10,000 empty capsules and a number of small capsule machines that could be used to fill the capsule.

He never really got anything more going with the malaria. Guinea is full of malaria. If he had continued to treat people for 75 cents each (a figure people there can afford) he would have become rich in that area. He would have been the best known doctor in that part of the world. He chose to continue to try to sell herbs, which never did work. We would have furnished unlimited quantities of MMS to Dr. Flomo. He could have changed a whole country, but he just had to try to sell his herbs.

Picture: Dr. Flomo and a local herbalist preparing herbal formulas.

If you read chapter 18 you can see his mistake. He was so focused on his own goals; he simply couldn't adjust his vision to see a bigger picture. He wasn't interested in helping the people of that country; he was only interested in making money. He lived in his own world. Still, over 2000 people were cured of malaria as a result of Dr. Flomo's efforts.

MMS is available for your purchase immediately. See the last paragraph of Chapter 8. I have no financial interest in the company that sells it. I just thought you might like to try it before you make a hundred bottles. Chapter 17 explains how to make a hundred bottles.

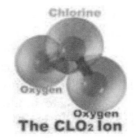

Chapter 5

Kenya East Africa

The CLO₂ Ion

Arnold just happened to know the head man of the missionary group called the Faith Christian Fellowship International or FCF Int. We had decided several months before that we should charge $5 per dose of MMS. It didn't matter that Africans couldn't afford that amount. We were planning on getting the money from one of the humanitarian sources but that still wasn't going anywhere. Finally it occurred to me that with a $5 cost we could offer to make a large donation to FCF Int. I told Arnold and he thought it was a valid idea.

Arnold offered to give them $200,000 worth of the MMS if they would furnish the money to send me to their missions to train their people how to use the OS-82 (That's what we were calling MMS at the time). The name has changed a number of times. Since we had put the price of a dose at $5 we could make $200,000 worth for about $50. Let me just mention here that it was my idea. The 2,000 people treated in Guinea, the 5,000 people treated in Sierra Leone, and the 75,000 people treated in Uganda and Kenya have all been the direct result of my ideas. Yes, Arnold helped, but he didn't come up with the ideas nor did he contact the people in Guinea or Sierra Leone. I did it without any financing from Arnold. And still everything had to be done his way because of course, the donors all wanted it done his way. (That's what he always told me.) I wouldn't have minded doing it his way if it was actually getting done, but it wasn't.

All MMS used in Africa has been bottled in these 4 ounce green bottles.

The offer impressed them and they decided to go ahead and send me to both Kenya and Uganda. For some reason Arnold never allowed me to talk to the head of the FCF missionary group nor any of the other people who might have helped to finance our trips to Africa. However, he had to send me to Africa as he was not qualified to teach the use of the MMS and he knew it. But he was absolutely adamant that things must be run his way and things were always run his way. That, of course, is why I am writing this book. Five years have passed and in my opinion we have gotten nowhere in relation to where we should be. Arnold tries, but he has made many mistakes.

This all happened in 2003. FCF Int. finally sent me in 2004. I bottled hundreds of the bottles of MMS in my kitchen using kitchenware and a very accurate laboratory scale. In fact, to this date 10/1/2006 the only person who has bottled the MMS is me and I have bottled many hundreds of bottles with 450 doses per bottle. It adds up to well over 1 million doses. At the writing of this 2nd edition there are more than 4 manufacturers making the MMS. The bottles that we finally decided upon were tall dark green four ounce bottles with a dropper top so that drops could be dispensed from the bottle as long as there was any solution inside. I was reasonably sure that no other similar bottles would be present in Africa and I was correct. A bottle with the malaria solution could be recognized a block away, as nothing else was similar. So far the other people are still using the same green bottle bought from a company in New York. The company's name and address is given in Chapter 17.

Dr. Opondo with bottles of MMS on the table.

I arrived in Kakamega, Kenya, on January 31, 2004. I was met at the airport by four people who each gave me a hug. There was Javan Ommani the head minister of the mission there, Gladis Ayugu, Hezron Juma, the second in command at the mission, and finally Beatic Iadeche. They were very glad to see me and they were very gracious. I was driven to the Mission where they had a very nice room fixed with mosquito netting and everything that I would need.

Doctor Isaac Opondo came to see me that evening. He was responsible for the mission hospital and he had been told that I was going to be giving people something to help with malaria. He was worried. He really needed to know what I was going to be giving them. I realized that if he didn't like me or the MMS that he could shut everything down and nothing would happen. I would simply be going back home with nothing accomplished. So I began to explain exactly what the MMS was and how it worked. He understood chlorine dioxide because his scientific knowledge included water purification plants and disinfectants. I told him most of the things already mentioned in this book plus other data. He was interested. I have found the exact facts work better than anything else and that is what I gave him.

Finally, Dr. Opondo said, "I have the picture and if you can really get the chlorine dioxide into the body, I believe it will do exactly what you say it will do." Once he had the picture of the chlorine dioxide in his head, he was so convinced that he said, "My wife is sick with malaria. Can I go get her right now?" I said, "Sure." She arrived about 20 minutes later. I mixed an MMS drink for her of only five drops. I considered 15 drops to be a standard dose at that time and I do not remember exactly why I only used five drops. I guess I was worried about making her nauseous. So Dr. Opondo's wife was the first person I helped overcome malaria in Africa. The next morning she was feeling a little better but she was not completely well, and I had told him that she would be well. I was scheduled to start treating at the hospital that morning.

That was actually a problem, but not as bad as you might think. The doctor believed my explanation of the chlorine dioxide and he seemed to have faith in what I had to say. The problem was that the strain of malaria here was more virile than the strain of malaria in South America. In seeing that the doctor's wife was indeed a little better, I knew it was working but that it simply was not a large enough dose. I told the doctor that his wife just needed another dose and he agreed.

That morning when I began treating people at the mission hospital, I put on my white lab smock with the words "The Malaria Solution Foundation" embroidered in gold lettering on the front. I wore my hat, light tan pants and white shoes. I looked like a doctor. I arrived at the hospital at about 8 A.M. and Dr. Opondo set me up in his office. I of course, explained to the people in the office that I was not a doctor. They didn't care. I was the only white man for 50 miles in any direction and they all had a great deal of respect for white men.

I discussed the number of drops to be given each patient with Dr. Opondo. I pointed out that the malaria here seemed to be a stronger strain than that in South America. We decided to use 15 drops per dose. Soon his wife arrived to get her next dose. She received a second dose which was 15 drops and went on home. We gave the patients 15 drop doses all day, but the next day most of them came back, feeling better, but not well. That did it. I decided on 30 drop doses as we needed to get cures with only one dose.

There were too many malaria victims to have to handle each one twice.

The hospital laboratory was overloaded. We simply could not check every sick person's blood for malaria. However, in that area there isn't much question about whether or not a person has malaria. Normally a doctor merely looks at a person and recognizes malaria. But they did take as many blood samples as were practical. All persons who tested positive to malaria by blood sample eventually tested negative after the second dose, or after the 30 drop dose. It usually took about four hours to have all malaria symptoms gone. In a few cases, it would take up to 12 hours for the symptoms to disappear. Although many had other diseases as well as malaria, we never had a failure as far as the malaria was concerned. We cannot guarantee that fact, as

Rev. Ommini

everyone was not blood tested; but to the best of our knowledge there were no failures to kill the malaria parasite.

We treated the ones that were still feeling bad and all were recovered when they returned the next day. Dr. Opondo agreed with me that we should increase the dose to 30 drops. It began to work with only one treatment. This was eight times the dose that was used in South America. This would equal 240 drops of stabilized oxygen sold in health food stores. At the hospital, each malaria victim was introduced to me and those who could speak English would describe their symptoms a little bit. I gave a dose to everyone. I did not try to just help the malaria victims. I knew that the MMS would be good for most any problem that they had. Some would soon throw up worms, and many others said that various difficulties were better.

The Reverend Ommini was head of the mission there and he looked a little tired. He told me that ever since his accident he had not had any trouble with malaria. He walked with a cane and he had some steel braces in his leg. He said that maybe the steel was somehow causing a reaction in his blood that was killing the malaria parasites. I looked in his eyes and face very closely. I could only see extreme tiredness. He was sick and didn't know it. I asked if he was taking pain tablets, and he admitted that he took several each day. I said, "Reverend, please do me a favor and have your blood tested for malaria." All of a sudden it seemed to occur to him; he realized how he really felt.

Picture: Dr. Vincent Orimba talks with a mother about her baby who has just taken some MMS.

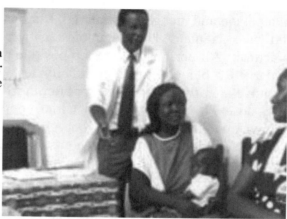

I had actually meant for him to have the blood test the next day, but he took one more look at me and he went to wake up the laboratory technician.   In about one hour he came back with an amazing report. The average malaria patient that showed up for treatment at the hospital had a reading of plus six. Rev. Ommini had a reading of plus 120. He could have dropped dead at any minute. I gave him the biggest dose that I felt would be safe, which was 30 drops. Normally a person with that high of a reading would be sick in bed almost unable to move but the pain killers in some cases will mask the symptoms.

The next morning Rev. Ommani felt much better, but he was sick again by noon. At noon his blood was reading plus six which was a normal reading for a person sick with malaria. I gave him another 18 drops and by the next morning he was proclaiming that he felt great. He looked good. His blood read zero malaria parasites. He was lucky that it turned out this way. It happens many times that people take pain tablets to mask the pain of malaria. They don't realize it is malaria just as Rev. Ommani had not, but he believed in me. They keep taking more and more pain tablets as their headache and the pains in their joints get worse and worse. That is a very dangerous condition as they can be walking around with enough malaria to kill them. When this happens one can just drop dead, which does happen.

Picture: People at church   await   our arrival.   In all there were over 300 at this church.

Rev. Ommani began organizing churches around the area so that people with malaria could come to be treated. Each morning about eight of us would crowd into a mini bus driven by Peter Mwangi, a local pastor who owned the mini bus. The bus was about 20 years old. It was only a bus shell with a motor. Everything else had been stripped out. The door hinges were far beyond wearing out. They just sort of held the door from falling off, but certainly not from rattling. Being the only white person, I had to ride up front, but then so did three other people. Peter was somewhat of a mechanic, so he kept the bus going. But everything in the bus was extremely worn. When an auto gets that bad and something quits working you simply pull it out and throw it away. After all, all you really need is a motor, a chassis, and wheels.

Peter would drive us to several churches during the day and he also helped me by taking pictures. There was usually anywhere from 50 to 200 people at the various churches. They introduced me to the crowd and asked me to say something before we got started. I would talk for a minute or so, stating that it was my pleasure to be there and that I hoped that they would feel better. Then they would stand in line as I began filling the glasses that were furnished at each church.

When there were several hundred people I would ask for extra glasses and they would get some somehow. Then we would line up 20 or 30 glasses and I would begin putting the solution in the glasses. I had a small measuring spoon that held exactly the right amount of solution (30 drops). Then I would add vinegar to each glass. I would then fill each glass with pineapple juice to about three quarters full. We would give the dose to each person. (There was always the three minute wait right after adding the vinegar and before adding the juice.)

Several times when the group heard that I would not be inoculating them they would express disappointment. They felt that if they were not getting inoculated that the medicine might not be powerful enough to help. However, as the day wore on at each church, people started feeling better. Headaches went away, nausea vanished, and/or muscle pains left. The people were quite surprised and pleased so they showed it. It was always a pleasure to see the people getting better and feeling better.

While we were in Kakamega, Javan wanted us to visit one private clinic. We were to spend a full day at the clinic. The name of the clinic was The Bukura Community Nursing and Maternity Home. When we arrived, there was a big, long line of local people who needed help with malaria. We spent most of the day there and then we left them with several bottles of MMS for their use. The head man's name was Vincent Orimba. He treated many people and took their blood readings both before and afterward taking the MMS. Unfortunately, his clinic was one from which the support of the Missions to supply them with MMS was withdrawn as far as supplying them with MMS when they suspected me of being evil. I have included a picture of Dr. Orimba at his clinic. No doubt, that he, like most of the other people in this book, can still be contacted.

While in Kakamega I did not see any other white people. One lady stopped me on the street and shook my hand. She said that she wanted to tell her husband that she shook the hand of a white person today. Probably the biggest laugh I got at the table was when I told everyone that my biggest worry was that these converted cannibals might decide that they would rather have a good meal than go to heaven. All of them past the age of 30 claimed to be converted cannibals, but I doubt that any of them were. They just like to have something to say.

While in Kakamega I did not see any other white people. One lady stopped me on the street and shook my hand. She said that she wanted to tell her husband that she shook the hand of a white person today. Probably the biggest laugh I got at the table was when I told everyone that my biggest worry was that these converted cannibals might decide that they would rather have a good meal than go to heaven. All of them past the age of 30 claimed to be converted cannibals, but I doubt that any of them were. They just like to have something to say.

Picture: Wade Porter and his wife stand on each side of the Author. The others were doctors and nurses. Wade decided not to use the MMS as they decided the Author was evil.

BALL - ⬤ - WORLD MISSION

EMATSAYI MISSION HEADQUATER
P.O Box117, 50100 KAKAMEGA, KENYA   Tel No: 0722-300301

February 11, 2004

We the people of the Ematsayi Mission which is the headquarters of 128 Ball Churches and their pastors, hereby give our thanks and appreciations to The Malaria Solution Foundation for sending Mr. Jim Humble to bring us the Malaria Solution. Over one thousand patients have been treated and reported that they have recovered from malaria including the Bishop Rev. Javan Ommani and his wife. So of the places he visited are: Ematsay Mission Hospital 80 patients were treated and reported back that they have recovered by Dr. Isaac Opondo.

2. Bukura Community nursing Home 3 patients were treated and reported that they have recovered after taking phase two of the treatment led by Dr. Edwin Otieno.

3. Inaya Church clinic, 512 patients were treated some returned the second day for number two of the phase 2 treatments and reported recovered. Led by Rev. Mutuli.

4. Imanga and Naburera Chruch clinics 228 patients were treated and reported recovered under Rev. Javan Masimber.

5. Emangale, Nazareti, Musaga 125 patients treated. They reported recovery of malaria. Led by Rev. Eseri Mahonga.

6. Klialala Church Clinic 50 were treated, reported recovered from Malaria. Led by Rev. Parton Wangila.

7. Mwilala 36 people were treated positive live reports came back. Led by Rev. Charles Ommani.

8. Anyiko Church Clinic 250 patients were treated and reported recovered. Led by Rev. Henry Apondi.

9. Buyonga Chruch Clinic 50 people were treated and reported recovered. Led by Sister Jackline Makokha.

10. Eshirumba Church Clinic 52 were treated and reported recovered. Led by Pastor E. Kabole.

With time running out some with malaria were left before being treated. There has been reported three cases of vomiting and at least one case of diarrhea after taking the Malaria Solution but in all cases the situation settled after getting the second treatment. Sincerely we thank all concerned in this program.

Rev. Javan Ommani   Rev. Hezron Okaba   Alfred Okwanyi
Bishop   Ass. Biship   Chairman

EMATSAYI MISSION HEALTH CENTER
P.O Box1176, 50100 KAKAMEGA, KENYA   Tel No: 0722-300301

February 11, 2004

Jim Humble
The Malaria Solution Foundation

Here I present to you my special observations during the Malaria Campaign using the Malaria Solution Formula.

1- The very 1ˢᵗ day of the introduction a very sick baby of 1 ½ years was brought complaining of convulsions from high fever with temperature of 104 F (40 C). Blood slide microscopic examination was positive of malaria with 4 pluses ++++ indicating very severe infection with malaria fulciparum parasites.

After reseseration the patient was given the malaria solution phase 1. After 4 hours the blood slide microscopic examination was done. The parasites were reduced to 2 pluses (++). At that time phase 2 was given (5 drops of the malaria solution). The following day the blood slide was negative of malaria.

Note: No other antimalaria drug was given. No antibiotic was given. After two days the child was discharged. There had been no temperature above normal nor any other symptoms for 48 hours. The malaria had been cured by the Malaria Solution administration alone without the usual quinine for such serious cases.

2- A female patient aged 34 years had persistent fevers sever headaches in evenings, persistent nausea, loss of apatite, and loss of weight. Microscopic examination of blood revealed malaria fulciparum parasites present. She had not responded to many antimalaria drugs including quinine injections. Malaria Solution phase 2 was given in two doses within 24 hours. By tie third dose all signs and symptoms had reduced. After 5 days the patient was back to work eating well after two months of illness. A check of the blood slide showed negative.

3- Three sick children were administered Malaria Solution after the presence of symptoms of bronchial pneumonia for 2 days. After 6 hours the signs and symptoms had reduced. They stayed in the ward for 48 hours until the symptoms of pneumonia were completely gone. No other antibodies were administered.

4- I smeared the Malaria Solution to warts in the groin region of a male patient of 5 years. Within 5 days the warts were gone.

Cases 3 and 4 indicate that the malaria solution is effective against other diseases.

5- During a mobile clinic campaign one of the female patients was given phase 2 Malaria Solution. She immediately started having severe abdominal pain. I gave her 3 glasses of water which she vomited after each glass. Soon she was feeling better.

Note: On further interrogation I found out that this patient was a known case of peptic ulcer and was on treatment at the moment with antacids.

Conclusion: This patient could have been saved from the reaction from the Malaria Solution if she had told us she had stomach ulcer. In the future we should ask about stomach ulcer.

In conclusion let me say that I am on the look out for other benefit of the Malaria Solution and will give you a feed back as I progress carefully in assessing which other conditions can be treated using the Malaria Solution.

Since the campaign is almost free I find it hard to change a fee for Microscopic blood examination as many patients cannot afford it. That would strengthen the positive results, but as in the case #1 above, finance is a problem.

I am continuing with the Malaria Solution Program.

Sincerely,

Dr. Isaac Oyondo
PO Box 1176, 50100
Kakamega, Kenya
Phone 0722-300301

MINISTRY OF HEALTH

Telegram: "MOH", KAKAMEGA
Telephone: 056-31110
       31131 Ext. 245
       30052 Ext. 3091

When replying, please quote

Ref. No: DIS.10.VOL11/98

**The Medical Officer of Health,
Kakamega District,
P.O.Box 750,
Kaka mega.**

Date: 22nd September 2004

TO WHOM IT MAY CONCERN

RE LURAMBI COMMUNITY BASED ORGANIZATION

This is to certify that Lurambi Community Based Organization is a registered CBO based in Kakamega Municipality.

It is mainly involved in HIV/AIDS activities in both the Municipality and Lurambi Division of Kakamega District. It is also involved in activities to improve the status of Women, Children and Youth living in slum and rural areas in regard to HIV/AIDS, Poverty, Food Insecurity and Illiteracy.

Please grant them any support necessary to carrying out these activities.

Thank you.

MEDICAL OFFICER OF HEALTH
KAKAMEGA DISTRICT

Dr. Shikanga O-tipo
MEDICAL OFFICER OF HEALTH
KAKAMEGA DISTRICT

PETER MWANGI GITAU
P.O. BOX 659
KAKAMEGA
KENYA
2/11/2006

TO WHOM IT MAY CONCERN
RE: JIM V. HUNBLE

This is to certify that I, Peter Mwangi Gitau has worked with JIM since 2004. He came to the Ematsayi Ball Mission to treat people for malaria and for all this long, I have been driving him. We visited many churches and treated about 1000 people with Malaria Solution. After that, we went to Uganda to help people there and over 500 people were treated in the Life Medical Centre in Kampala, Uganda.

We left each other and he, JIM sent me some bottles of the Malaria Solution to treat and train people how to use the Solution in Kakamega Town. See pictures and report of those treated on the next page.

I am looking forward to treating as many more people in Kenya and helping JIM in this work as more money and donations are made available to us.
It's my pleasure to have many people treated and get well and reach out to millions with Malaria Solution.

Yours faithfully

P. Mwangi

Peter Mwangi.
0722 860674

February 11, 2004

Location: Ematsayi Mission

I Sila Kombo, give much thanks to God who brought brother Jim Humble to Kenya to give the Malaria Solution. I am happy that when I got the Malaria Solution I was recovered. I would like to ask the office of the Christian Faith fellowship to extend the treatment up to Tanzania country where I am a Bishop having more than 25 churches where the disease (Malaria) kills so many people and I've seen this chance to be of help to us in Africa. Thank you. Good bless.

Yours Sincerely,

Chapter 6

Uganda, East Africa

When I left Kakamega, Kenya, I flew to Nairobi. There I gave a lecture to Wade Porter and his group of doctors and nurses. The lecture with the doctors and nurses was well received; they talked to me for an hour after the lecture. There were much handshaking and friendly words, but for some reason Wade and his wife decided I was evil so that ended their plans to treat villagers in the nearby bush. They would never communicate about it so I had no way to tell them differently. Even stranger than that, the head man at FCF Int. in the US was fired a few weeks after I returned. He was the man in that organization that made the decision to send me over there. Maybe there was no connection; but it seems funny that he was fired and I never knew the reason. Well, anyway, the story continues.

From Nairobi I flew to Kampala, Uganda. I was met at the airport by Solomon Mwesige who was the main pastor of the mission there and the owner of the clinic that was connected to the mission. He drove me to his house. They had a room fixed up for me to stay in. Here in this area, everyone who comes into the house must take off his shoes. I didn't notice that at first, but as soon as I did notice, I apologized and took my shoes off. They were very gracious hosts. Dinner was served every evening with everyone sitting at the table. The food was very good. In Uganda, where they are not fighting, there is plenty of food. In fact, an observer would call it a land of plenty.

Solomon said that I could start using the MMS in the morning at his medical clinic. I was anxious to get started as this would be one more test in proving out the MMS. I arrived at Solomon's clinic, after having breakfast at his home, at about 8 AM on the 14th of February 2004. Patients were already arriving as Solomon had announced in his church services that I would be there.

Picture: Author and nurse look on as mother gives her baby the MMS at the Life Link Medical Center in Kampala, Uganda.

They were charging a small fee for my MMS doses (OS-82 was on the labels of the bottles at that time, but I had long since quit calling it that back in Kenya, because "Malaria Solution" was the only thing any of the doctors or nurses would call it. And that is what we finally started calling it. The people of Africa had actually named it. When I called Arnold I gave him the new name and he immediately agreed.)

I started off using the data obtained at the Kakamega mission in Kenya. I used 30 drops and almost everyone was getting sicker and vomiting after taking the drops. Of course, the next day or even hours later, they were well, but the vomiting was not popular. Something was again different with this malaria than at the other place. All those here who had malaria had enlarged spleens. Somehow the drops were reacting with this strain of malaria differently. probably had something to do with the enlarged spleens. The malaria victims in Kakamega did not have enlarged spleens. Not everyone was vomiting and thus we continued for several days, but the people were beginning to stay away.

Finally, I decided that I had to do something. I had each person take only 15 drop doses, but come back in four hours for a second dose of 15 drops. This worked out OK. The 15 drop doses did not cause anyone to vomit and soon people were again lining up outside for a help. So, once again minor problems had been overcome. All these small things bring about the collection of information that is necessary to give proper instructions to other people.

Picture: Life Link Medical Center in Kampala Uganda.

When I mention 15 drop doses or 30 drop doses all such doses require the addition of ¼ to ½ a teaspoons of vinegar, lemon, lime, or citric acid solution (That's 5 drops of acid for each drop of MMS.). Without the one of these food acids the solution does very little good. The food acids act as an activator that makes the solution work. One must wait three minutes before adding anything else. After the three minute wait, one can then add a 4 ounce glass of juice to mask some of the taste. The juice must not have any added vitamin C. This is the reason for using fresh juice because one can be sure that vitamin C has not been added. Almost all bottled or canned juice has vitamin C added as a preservative. Vitamin C is very good for you, but in this case vitamin C prevents the MMS from being effective in the body. So only use fresh juice.

These food acids have a very important role. They cause the sodium chlorite solution to give up chlorine dioxide ions on a linear basis and it also protects the sodium chlorite from giving up too many ions at one time. This is important as one does not want the entire amount of chlorine dioxide to be released as soon as the solution reaches the stomach. The acetic acid or citric acid is necessary for the proper function of the solution in the body. Vinegar always contains acetic acid while lemons and limes contain citric acid. One of these acids is a necessary ingredient to the MMS.

Solomon's clinic is called "The Life Link Medical Centre" and the address is PO Box 15081 Kampala, Uganda, Phone 077 479017. He had a microscope and technicians who could determine the malaria parasite in the blood. During the time we were there we treated at least 50 patients who checked positive for malaria before treatment and who tested negative after treatment. However, most of the 500+ patients that we treated didn't care. They only wanted to feel better. And that was the result. They always felt better after they took the first and second doses. The fact is that at least 95% of them had malaria; we just did not have time to test everyone's blood. Still, we did have 50 verifications of people who were cleared of the malaria parasite.

Shortly after I arrived at the Life Link Medical Centre I met one special pastor from the DRC Congo. His name was John Tumuhairwe. He was interested in the MMS and after he accepted a dose he immediately began to help the people as they came in. He was very enthusiastic concerning the MMS and he talked to me extensively about going to the DRC Congo, but, I didn't have the money or other support to do so. He visited a number of places in Kampala and almost arranged it so that I could visit the army in Northern Uganda where the fighting was taking place. I was willing to go as there was widespread malaria in the army and it would have been a significant contribution to settling the war. That would have been a very good advertisement for the MMS at the time. But John was unable to get things completely arranged while I was there.

Picture: Author gives Ev. John Tumuhariwe his first MMH for reoccurring malaria. Read John's letter at the end of this chapter.

When I left I gave him my last bottle of malaria solution (MMS) which was enough to help about 180 people with malaria. If you read John's recent letter to me you will see that he treated quite a few people in the Congo. Several months later I sent him 10 bottles that he used quite a bit. His letter also tells about using those 10 bottles. The picture shown here was taken as I first gave him some dose of MMS. He, like most of the people named in this book, can still be contacted. As of 10/10/2006 I have just sent him another 10 bottles.

A few of the malaria victims were children. Some of these children would have died without the MMS. Although reactions were infrequent, it was in this clinic that we began to notice that the reactions were often similar. As time progressed we occasionally noticed the following reactions: (1) Dizziness. Some patients reported dizziness several hours after taking the MMS. The dizziness never lasted over one hour. When the dizziness passed the other symptoms of malaria seemed to disappear at the same time. (2) Nausea. The nausea usually occurred within 10 to 15 minutes of taking the MMS and seldom lasted more than 15 minutes. (3) Vomiting. On rare occasions someone vomited as a reaction to the MMS, but not more than once.

Picture: Author mixes MMS doses in the clinic room.

(4) Tiredness. The tiredness was total and throughout the body. It was quite amazing as I experienced this once myself several years earlier when I first took the MMS to overcome some malaria I contracted in the jungle. One feels completely lethargic and has an inability to move. It is not really unpleasant its just a weird sensation that's slightly alarming. It lasts from 1 to 4 hours, no longer. (5) A combination of several or all of these reactions. This is rare, but it did happen once or

twice. There is really nothing that needs to be done for any of the reactions. They all pass and have no lasting effects.

This clinic here had at least six beds. There were several people who recovered after taking the MMS. The doctor there was a black man who had a great deal of compassion for children. He treated them with kindness and appeared to be very concerned. He saved several lives while I was there simply by being able to diagnose correctly. He questioned me very thoroughly about the MMS. I ended up telling him about my friend who had used the "Stabilized Oxygen" to inject the solution in the veins of his animals. And I mentioned that he had injected me a couple of times. In our discussions I finally told him that the strength of the solution that my friend used for injection into the animals was 15 drops in 20 ml of injection solution.

Toward the end of my stay there I noticed the doctor talking to groups of people who met him outside the clinic. After he talked to several groups I asked him about them. He said that the groups consisted of an advanced AIDS patient with his relatives. I didn't ask him what the conversation was about as it seemed that would be impolite. However, the day that I left he took me aside and said that he was going to treat some AIDS patients and that he would use an injection. He said that he was connected to the very large Kampala Hospital and that he would be able to approach AIDS patients that were being sent home to die. You may feel that I would feel concern at this point, but back in Las Vegas I had my friend inject me several times. We first used one drop, then several drops, and then a full dose two different times. There was never any adverse reaction, but the injection did handle a very bad case of the flu. It wasn't that I was worried about these AIDS patients; it was that I was extremely sad that we couldn't treat every AIDS patient that was being sent home plus those AIDS patients in the hospital.

Picture: Most children treated the MMS almost like they thought it was a magical drink. These three did

Again the MMS releases chlorine dioxide into the body. Chlorine dioxide is the most powerful killer of pathogens of all kinds known to man. There is no reason why it wouldn't kill AIDS viruses. It does no damage to the human body in the low concentration used in the MMS. When using direct injection into the blood you cannot use vinegar. The fact is, the blood has the same neutral level as water, thus it dilutes the MMS and causes the release of chlorine dioxide without vinegar over a period of a few hours without vinegar.

At the time I did not encourage the doctor, nor did I discourage him. I could not see that the injection would hurt these AIDS cases and it would probably help. After I returned home I kept in close contact with this doctor as he treated 390 AIDS patients over a period of 8 months. They were patients that had been sent home from the local Kampala Hospital assuming that they would die soon. His emails showed that 6 out of 10 AIDS cases were feeling good and anxious to go back to work or back to their lives within three days. The other 40% recovered within 30 days. None of the cases that he was able to keep track of had a relapse. Two out of the 390 cases died. The ones that were well in 3 days needed time to recover, but it seemed that they were only recovering from an extreme case of weakness. Unfortunately, this doctor's name is one name that I must keep confidential. But, you can see that he had very good results, as all of these patients were slated to die within weeks of being released from the Kampala hospital.

I did not find it hard to believe his reports as he had no reason to lie to me on a constant basis day after day as I was paying him nothing nor even sending him free MMS (I left 40 bottles there). I have been able to treat a number of AIDS patients successfully myself. My friend in Malawi, who runs a business there, has been treating several employees who were too sick from AIDS infection to come to work. They are now all back to work.

The owner of the clinic was also the pastor of a local church. His church was a member of the FCF Int. Missionary group to Africa. It turned out that he had a problem very similar to the other Pastor in Kenya. Solomon Mwsegi was also taking pain tablets for the pain caused by malaria. Both he and his wife were avoiding the idea that they had malaria. The pain tablets will often mask the malaria, not very well but they keep you going. To go on taking them is extremely dangerous as the malaria can kill you without you much feeling it.

Actually when I asked him about it, he said, "I know its malaria. I've just been putting off doing anything about it." He said, "I'll take a double dose right now." I asked if he was sure, mentioning that it was going to make him nauseous. He said, "I know it is, but I want to get it over and I want to be sure the malaria is killed." He had been watching carefully what we were doing and how I was re-adjusting the number of drops. So he took the double dose (of course, with the vinegar activator and the standard three minute wait.) He later told me that he wanted the drops to make him sick as he felt that would be proof that something was really working in his body.

Here is word for word what I wrote in my notes at the time: "Within 20 minutes he was nauseous. Within an hour he could not drive the car. He had diarrhea. At home he felt totally tired like he didn't want to move except to go to the toilet. It started at about 11 AM that morning and at 4 PM when we got home he was better. At 8 PM he was up lying of the couch. He said all sickness was gone, but he was feeling weak. The next morning he was slightly dizzy but feeling good otherwise." From the beginning to the end of this ordeal, he was very enthusiastic about it. When he got sick, he was enthusiastic because he believed the MMS was working. When it was over, the next day he said he couldn't believe how well he was feeling.

His wife was watching the whole ordeal and she was very worried, but she was also afraid of doing nothing because she was well aware that her pain tablets were also masking malaria. When she proceeded to take the dose, her husband (Solomon) stayed with her. She was not as nauseous as Solomon had been, but she stayed sick for most of the second day. Finally, however, she was extremely happy about how well she was feeling. She said it was the first day in over a year that she felt like herself. Evidently, when malaria is masked with pain tablets, it gets very bad and thus the MMS was extra reactive. However, they could have avoided the reaction simply by taking a few days using smaller doses instead of trying to do it all at once. The problem was that they were always extremely busy and didn't feel that they could afford the extra time.

It didn't seem to matter who I was involved with while I was in Africa; the people were willing to trust me. I think that they could feel or that they knew that I would not do anything that was against their better interests. The time spent at Solomon's clinic was very productive in learning more of the ins and outs of the MMS. My driver, Peter Mwangi drove to Kampala and arrived a day later than me. Solomon also furnished him a room in his house. Peter was a great help in the clinic. He helped me mix MMS doses. He took pictures and he learned as much data as he could about the MMS.

Several months later, Solomon accused Peter of raping one of his servant girls. The girl was pregnant. Peter said that it was impossible. He didn't do any such thing. It seems like, since I was in the same house, that I would have heard some kind of noise, or would have noticed the girl crying or something. But I did not hear anything. I observed only a very high integrity from Peter while I was there, so I rather believe Peter when he says that he didn't do it. The thing that seemed kind of peculiar to me was that Solomon continued to fire person after person from his clinic even while I was there. I worked with the people that he fired and they all seemed to be doing a good job. I never understood why he fired any of them, so when he stated that Peter had raped his servant girl, I question that accusation in my own mind, but I did not interfere with Solomon's operation of the clinic.

In any case, we treated over 500 people while I was there. Solomon asked me to help and to remain present because those people who came were expecting a white man. The people there had a great deal more confidence in the MMS because a white man was helping them. Even when I quit giving the solution to people, they were much more confident when I was simply present. Solomon promised that a white man would be there and the people who came were much more confident even if I only stood outside on the front porch.

I finally left Kampala on the 27th of February 2004 and flew back to Reno, Nevada. From there I returned to the desert town of Mina, Nevada.

Life Link Medical Center

Lugujja Church Zone
PO Box 15081
Kampala, Uganda
Phone 077 479 017

February 27, 2004

This paper is to verify that Jim Humble gave Dr. ▓▓▓▓▓ and the staff here instructions and training in the use of the Malaria Solution.

During Jim's stay here from 2/15/04 to 2/28/04 some _400/EH_ malaria patients were treated with the Malaria Solution. Some were given blood tests for malaria and of the blood tests given approximately 40% tested positive. The exact number of patients that tested positive were _25 (EH)_ patients. All patients that tested positive to malaria were given the Malaria Solution. All those given the malaria solution eventually tested negative for malaria on either the first, or second dose, and one person on the third dose.

All other patients not given the blood tests testified to feeling well within 24 hours of taking the Malaria Solution either the first or second time.

Sincerely,

Rev. Solomon Mwesige
Director

Ev John Tumuhairwe.
Katwe RD Buyaya House plot No 53
Po.box71915
Kampala Uganda East Africa.

Dear Humble,

I hope this letter finds you well and strong. This is John Tumuhairwe. Just to remind you, we first met in Uganda at life link, the first time you came to Uganda, with a Kenyan brother who was with you, when you introduced the malaria solution. I had visited Pastor Solomon and I was staying at the Clinic (Life Link), because I used to live in DRC Congo those days. I immediately got interested in the malaria solution and I joined you and Dr. Emma, to start giving the malaria solution, to people.

I also contacted the Ministry of Defence in Uganda, who wanted, to meet you, but we didn't make it I think due to some other arrangements Pastor Solomon had. You gave me a bottle of malaria solution, which I then took to DRC Congo and it did a lot of miracles and wonders to the people I gave to drink.

This was after we treated and HIV positive woman, whose CD 4 count had lowed so much, but she recovered immediately and her CD 4 was risen from 50 to 200.
When I came back to Uganda, I took some malaria solution to the government chief chemist, Mr. Onen, who is new in Japan for one year course. He tested it and gave me a Certificate for it, whose copy I later gave to Pastor Solomon to give to you, but I also sent you a copy by mail.

Later when I started living in Uganda, I asked you to give me permission to use malaria solution which you did and sent us ten bottles of malaria solution , to use with Dr. Emma after you found out, that he had stopped working for Pastor Solomon's Clinic. It is part of these bottles, that I have used to go to the Ministry of Defence here in Uganda. I have been treating soldiers here who are HIV positive and the results have been good. I am also working, with other organizations, and the branch of World Vision International in Uganda to test on HIV positive patients, in their care.

As I mentioned to you later I am intending to rung the first Holistic Healing Centre in Kampala-Uganda. We shall use the humble health drink (malaria solution) as our major treatment.

Yours in bond of love for Christ Jesus.
God Bless you.

Ev. John Tumuhairwe.

Chapter 7

Continuing Story of the MMS

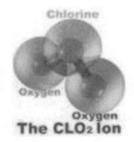

In Mina I continued sending emails to everyone I could think of. I sent emails to the president of the U.S., to Bill Gates, to various people who did humanitarian things, to all of the TV shows that did humanitarian things, such as Oprah. I continued to send out free bottles of MMS as well as I sold the 4 ounce bottles with 325 doses for $20 each or for $5 to anyone living in town. Later when I doubled the strength, I sold the 4 ounce bottles with 450 doses for the same price.

As time passed, people talked to me about various problems I continued to find new uses for the MMS. All of my life I have had trouble with my teeth. Most of my teeth were missing and I wore dentures. My gums were quite soft and my teeth were somewhat loose in the gums. They often got sore and at that particular time they started to hurt and I thought I would have to have one or two pulled. Then I finally decided that I should brush my teeth with the MMS. I used 6 drops of MMS and 1/2 teaspoon of vinegar swirled together in a glass and then I waited the 3 minutes and added 1/3 glass of water and used that to brush my teeth. Again I was amazed. All of the infection and soreness disappeared in hours. Within a week my gums had hardened up. When I finally did go to have a tooth pulled, it took the dentist a full hour to pull the tooth. My gums were so tough and the tooth was so well imbedded into my jaw bone he simply couldn't just grab it with his pliers and pull. It wouldn't come out. I'm not sure I should have had it pulled. It looked perfectly healthy when it was finally out. The dentist was more surprised than I was.

Since that time there have been a number of other people who began to use the MMS for oral hygiene. All that have used it have had the same results, a much healthier mouth. There have been a number of people who were able to fix their abscessed teeth merely by brushing with MMS.

I am sure Arnold was working hard to get the money for our next trip to Africa. My contention was always that if he would provide me with enough money for a round trip airplane ticket and some living expenses then I would travel anywhere. I would talk to the various government agencies and hospitals until I found some place to do clinical trials. Arnold's contention was that we could not go anywhere in Africa until we had an invitation. According to Arnold there was always plenty of money but his insistence that we needed an invitation kept us immobile for years. Peter Mwangi secured an invitation from one hospital in Kenya to go do clinical trials in Kenya. Remember, Peter was my driver in Kenya and Uganda who I trained in dispensing the MMS. We could have done the clinical trials of 100 malaria patients with before and after blood tests for less than $20,000 including my travel expenses. The money was available, but Arnold would not allow me to go to Kenya. Instead, he wanted to help Floyd Hammer and his wife who had various projects going on in Tanzania but who could not get clinical trials for months. It finally proved out that he never did get clinical trials. A clinical trial was what we wanted at the time. We could have had it through Peter, but we were going to do it Arnold's way regardless of the results.

Time after time for over a year, Floyd Hammer was provided money from our Malaria Solution Foundation and he never gave us any information back as to its use. We helped them buy a pickup truck and shipped a large container of food supplies to Tanzania. When Floyd wrote a report to his people in the U.S. he never acknowledged that we helped at all. He talked about treating malaria patients, but he never acknowledged that he was using the MMS to treat the patients. Finally Arnold just said that he wasn't going to send them any more money. But if I could have had that same money, I would have completed the clinical trials in Kenya and would have had the proof that everyone was asking for. I continued to very discreetly say that giving Floyd money was not helping but it took over a year before Arnold would listen.

The other thing that I tried to get Arnold to do was simply hire Peter Mwangi, my driver who was proficient with the dispensation to continue treating and passing out the MMS. He was traveling to hospitals which were willing to try the MMS. He could have been traveling to churches, orphanages, hospitals, and clinics. They trusted him and many were willing to use the solution. In the same amount of time that we fooled around with Floyd, Peter would have helped thousands of people and dozens of places would have used the MMS. Unfortunately, nothing I suggested was considered. Hiring Peter, a local instead of someone from the U.S., would have been ridiculously cheap. We would not have had to pay for his airplane ticket; he would have worked for less than $100 a month. We would have had to pay for gasoline, some operating expenses, and have shipped him plenty of MMS. His expenses were 1/10 that of a foreigner or missionary. He would have gotten done exactly what we wanted to do. Arnold didn't trust Peter but he never met him. I worked with him every day for an entire month. We were good friends by the time I left. On the other hand, Floyd took our money, which was thousands and didn't even say thanks. The money we paid Floyd got absolutely nothing done so far as we could tell.

Arnold kept making mistake after mistake while all the time saying that everything had to be done his way. He hired the kid who finally made such trouble for us that he prevented us from getting a legal nonprofit Malaria Solution Foundation. Arnold hired several people to create our Web Site. After they had worked almost a year on it, it was still a very poor site. Then he hired another man to do our site, paid him up front and never got a thing for his money. All the while our site never got done. It has been six years since Arnold said he was going to get a web site set up. As I write these lines we still don't have one. He sent thousands of dollars to Floyd Hammer and we never received any acknowledgment or data concerning the malaria people helped with our MMS. With the money Arnold continued to lose, I could have had a number of clinical trials completed in Kenya with the proof that we needed to show others. Even though he flunked again, he continued to adamantly insist that everything must be done his way. He continued to claim that the people who were going to sponsor us would only do so if he was in total control. Arnold actually prevented the MMS from being used distributed while all the time proclaiming to be getting it done.
Arnold continued to tell me that although I was on the board of the Malaria Solution Foundation it was going to be operated like a corporation. Basically, he said that he was the president and things were going to happen the way he specified. Arnold and John continued to say that I had no say in the way things were being run. There was no arguing with either one of them. If there was any discussion about the events of the past weeks or past year, they would both get together and tell me my memory was wrong. When there was any discussion and I

tried to say something they would just start shouting. I could not get any ideas across. Everything went quietly so long as I kept my mouth shut. I could have left, and I should have, but there was always the promise that they would have the money to get to Africa to prove out the MMS so that the world would accept it. I kept my mouth shut because that promise always hung there in front of me. To be completely fair, when I finally returned from Africa the last time, Arnold called me with several questions concerning how to do things. He stated he wanted my input, but as things continued he would do things as he wanted regardless of my input. Up to this point, Arnold had been the only game in town for me. Then I realized I could write this book.

I made a contract with the World Health Organization (WHO).

Before my trip to Kenya and Uganda I had written quite a few letters to the World Health Organization which, evidently, didn't want to appear like they were not interested. They returned one of my letters saying that they had a program in which they tested various drugs that might have some effect on malaria. They were interested in the MMS, they wrote. After some discussion they sent me a contract to sign. We negotiated a bit, changed some points, and I finally signed their contract. I sent them a bottle of the MMS. About a year and a half later, after I returned from Africa, I finally got a letter from them stating that they were testing my solution in a separate lab. They had contracted with a doctor to do the testing for them. I was enthused to learn that the doctor was actually of doing the testing. But he tested it on mice and reported it simply didn't work. I was amazed, but he reported that it wouldn't cure mice or even improve their condition. There was nothing more I could say as I wasn't present when the testing was done. So at that time 35,000 human field patients were back to health, but it wouldn't cure a mouse? Sorry, but I don't believe him.

There is a country in Africa that won't even allow WHO to come across its borders. It seems to me that WHO, if they were really interested in helping the world as they claim to be, would have at least given the MMS a comprehensive test. That's especially true after they were informed of the successes in Kenya and Uganda. At that time over 35,000 people had been successfully treated in the field, based on reports that said that everyone went away feeling good. I also informed the doctor of our field work but he was not interested. Had they been even slightly interested they would have invited me over to help them with the testing. The doctor doing the testing didn't have the slightest idea what the MMS is about. He didn't understand it. He didn't understand the vinegar activation and he didn't understand what the chemicals were. He didn't want to know. He preferred to use my solution without knowing what it was. My evaluation of his disinterest is that he just wanted to prove it didn't work and that was that. Let me say it again, he was absolutely totally disinterested in the fact that 35,000 malaria patients had been successfully treated in the field. I talked to him at length on the phone, but again, he showed total disinterest. Obviously, all WHO wanted was a doctor's signature that said that the MMS didn't work.

There was also a doctor in Israel who also tested MMS, and said it wouldn't work. But guess what, he refused to use vinegar to activate the MMS. He said that acetate was the same thing so he used only acetate. Well the fact is that acetate is not the same thing as vinegar. Chemically it's totally different, but he simply would not use vinegar as he obviously believed he knew best.

I thought you might like to see the contract that I had with WHO. The contract is several pages long and there really isn't enough room here to show it, but they (WHO) sent a letter along with the contract. I have included that letter on the next page. If you are really interested in seeing the contract just write me and I will send you a copy of the contract. You could even come by my place and view the actual contract.

WORLD HEALTH ORGANIZATION ORGANISATION MONDIALE DE LA SANTE

Téléphone Central/Exchange: 791. 2111
      Direct: 791. 2665/3193
      Email: pinkr@who.int

In reply please refer to:
Prière de rappeler la référence:

Your reference:
Votre référence:

Mr Jim Humble
P. O. Box 185
1200 Doolittle St.
Mina, Nevada 89422
USA

0 4 APR 2003

Dear Mr Humble,

Enclosed are two signed copies of the Confidentiality Agreement. Kindly affix your signature on each page, return one copy to us and retain a copy for your file.

We should like to clarify that if and to the extent the idea of using the Preparation OS-82 for a new indication (i.e. in this case malaria, leishmaniasis, trypanosomiases, filariasis and/or onchocerciasis) is not in the public domain at the time of disclosure by you to WHO/TDR, and if we cannot demonstrate that this idea was known to WHO/TDR prior to disclosure by you, this idea would not fall in the exceptions of paragraph 3 (a) and (b) of the enclosed agreement.

With best wishes.

Yours sincerely,

Dr Carlos M. Morel
Director
Special Programme for Research and
Training in Tropical Diseases (TDR)

CH-1211 GENEVA 27-SWITZERLAND Telegr.: UNISANTE-GENEVA Telex: 415416 OMS Fax: +41 (22) 791.3111 CH-1211 GENEVE 27-SUISSE Télégr.: UNISANTE-GENEVE

At this time Arnold began pushing his ideas about the MMS. He said that I could not give any more away. We went through that same thing from time to time. He wanted us to keep control of every bottle. I am sure, from Arnold's point of view; he believes that he was the man who got everything in Africa going. He continued to meet people and groups that just might finance us to go to Africa. I continue to live out here on the desert and Arnold continued to not allow me to meet any of the people who might finance us in Africa. I wrote this paragraph today simply because I gave two local people one bottle of MMS each. Arnold found out and there was a long discussion about how I might go to jail because of it. Today I just got a call from Arnold as he was leaving San Francisco after talking to one more prospective donor, another one he would not let me meet.

Out here in the desert, only writing emails to Africa, I was able to get help for over 5,000 people with malaria since March of 2004 by making friends in Africa. Arnold had done nothing during this time except talk about what he is going to do in Africa. Nothing had happened. According to him, he had unlimited money (at least in the millions) to handle Africa and I had just my Social Security check.

One day in the desert, about one year after coming back from Uganda, while working on the roof I fell off and broke my neck. I was rushed to the hospital in the nearby city, but they didn't have the necessary equipment so they flew me by airplane to Reno. Finally, they opened my neck up and put a titanium screw into the 2nd cervical in my neck (the same bone that the actor who played Superman broke). You should see the screw. It looks like a 1-1/2 inch wood screw. I also broke my back at the same time. My back healed quite quickly but my neck refused to heal. The doctor left the bones not quite touching. The screw should have had another 1/2 turn. Six months went by and still no healing. The doctor was insisting that he open my neck back up and put two more screws in place. The Veterans Hospital said that I must have another operation as well, but they had another idea of how to do it. However, they couldn't get to it for another six months. I was left between a rock and a hard place or a broken neck.

Finally a friend in Canada, Michael Haynes, suggested that I look into magnetism. In my search of the Internet I found a group of clinics that were using a new theory of magnetism and that the clinics were having really great results. The cost was very high. After getting as much evidence of the new technology and as much data on the old technology as I could find I bought some of the strongest magnets now available. In fact, they are so strong that they are dangerous. They can squash a finger or cut it off when being handled improperly. The new technology works on the basic concept that magnetism must have a completed magnetic circuit through the body in order to get maximum healing power.

During this time I continued to communicate with as many people in Africa as I could plus sending emails to various organizations. With the magnets I bought; I constructed a steel curved piece that would allow for a completed magnetic circuit through my neck with the South Pole nearest the broken bone. I put the magnets in place for a total of five days and nights sitting up all night to make sure they were exactly in place. At the end of five days my neck began to swell up. I went back to the doctor and had another x-ray. The bone was completely healed. The doctor removed my neck brace. He said that I didn't need it any more. He said he was glad that he decided to wait before giving me the operation. He didn't remember that I was using magnets. He didn't care and he wasn't interested. In fact, he would have preferred to give me the operation. He didn't decide to wait before giving me the operation. I didn't get the operation because I refused it. If he had his way, I would have had the operation.

I don't know what all the magnetic circuit does, but I do know that the extremely strong magnets cause the area to swell with blood and turn red. No doubt the extra blood aids in the healing. The x-rays before and after proved that the bones healed in the five days that I kept the magnets in place. I was mainly relieved that if the opportunity came to return to Africa, my neck was healed and I could go.

If you have problems with getting bones to heal, look into the magnetic side of healing bones.

As time passed, a man from Guinea called; he wanted us to go to that country to help the people there. He said that he was a friend of the first lady and that he could get us approved by the government. He had told the first lady about us, they were anxious for us to come to Guinea. Arnold finally took me to meet him so we talked. Things were being set for us to go. I called this man from Guinea and then all hell broke loose as Arnold told me that I was never to talk to this man again. He would never allow me to talk to anyone that he considered his contact. There was the hollering and screaming that I so hate and cannot take part in. As things turned out, this man decided he was going to dictate the terms of our every move in Guinea, which it was simply something that we could not accept. At least that is what Arnold told me. So we didn't go to Guinea. I can't tell you how humiliating it is to be told that you can't even talk to someone. The date at this time was the first part of 2005.

Chino goes to Sierra Leone West Africa

A very active young fellow by the name of Chino contacted me and stated that he would like to know more about the MMS (We were calling it the Malaria Solution at that time). I met Chino in Beatty, Nevada, about March 2005. I explained how the MMS worked, mixed some doses and had him take it.

Chino explained that his family in Sierra Leone owned a large gold mining concession along the main river there. He explained that the malaria was so bad that everyone in his family had malaria. Many people there had died of malaria. He said that he needed as much of the MMS as I could furnish him. I said I would try to get him as much as possible. We had decided to charge a price that any African could afford at that time, which was about 10 cents. I explained the price and he said that he could get the money. I furnished him with 20 bottles at that time which could treat about 200 persons per bottle or a few more because more than ½ people treated were children. I gave them to him free of charge, but he insisted that he would pay in the near future.

About two months later he visited me in the desert. He had been to Sierra Leone and treated about 1,000 people in the village and the area where his family lived. He said that more people were there waiting for him to bring more bottles of the MMS. He explained that it was not possible to charge anything for the MMS that he gave the people. He said that the minute he began selling doses for any amount of money, the government would come, take the money, and the MMS. That's the way it is in East Africa. The government wants all the money and all the business. If you give the stuff away, there is no money in it and the government is not interested. The only way to make it work is bring it into the country and give it away without charge.

Picture: Chino's relatives in Sierra Leone help him with hundreds of people. The plastic glasses each hold a dose of MMS.

Otherwise the government will take it and sell it only to those who can pay large sums for the treatment. His assessment of the situation was that to furnish it for freely was the only way that the people of Sierra Leone would ever get the MMS. But he said that he had people in the U.S. who would furnish the money. I didn't ask him for money even though he kept saying that he would pay.

Picture: People line up to take a dose of MMS in Sierra Leone. Notice how closely they stand to one another. This was Chino's operation.

I put together 100 bottles with 450 doses each. Then Chino and I traveled to Reno and shipped the bottles to Sierra Leone. He paid for the shipping with a credit card. I asked for no money only that he give us a signed letter from each person that was treated and helped who had malaria. He then left to go back to Sierra Leone to begin helping more people. He later returned from Sierra Leone after helping an additional 5,000 malaria victims. This trip took about three months. He had a camera and his cousin took a number of pictures of the people during the process. When he returned he did not have any letters signed, but he did have the pictures. Later he asked for more bottles. We never refused any of his requests for bottles even though he did not bring the signed letters. I have included pictures of his work in Sierra Leone.

John continued to talk about furnishing the money for us to go to Africa. Arnold said we couldn't go until we had an invitation. Because they had money and kept talking about financing a trip to Africa to do clinical trials done, I kept quiet. They relied on my desire to see the people of Africa helped. Thus, they could take my technology, allow me no say at all, and pay me nothing but expenses for the trip, which of course, was really nothing. They assured the sponsors that no one (me) would be receiving payment for the technology. They said that the sponsors wanted all of their money to go toward helping people in Africa. I couldn't really argue against that. How could I be so selfish as to want some return for my technology? The fact is though; I never knew who the "sponsors" were.

I finally realized that although they were ensuring that the money went towards treating people in Africa, they were also using my technology to become known in the country of Malawi. They were then working towards several different business ventures there including mining and a new rice technology that would furnish rice protein worldwide. I'm not included in any of that. I don't want to be. I figure that if I continue to attempt to get this MMS information to the world, money will eventually come my way. If not, at least I know that this data is too important to have it under the control of any one person. I am not going to allow that to happen. I will see that it is published to the widest audience that is within my ability to reach.

Picture: Chino on the left, gives MMS to a boy that is in this case somewhat reluctant to take it. Most children are very enthusiastic about the MMS, looking at it like some kind of a magic.

Chapter 8

Malawi, East Africa

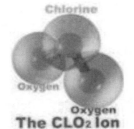

We, meaning the Malaria Solution Foundation formed by me (the author) and Arnold, finally received an invitation, not from the government of Malawi, but from a businessman there. His name is Zahir Shaikh. He is a great humanitarian. Once he learned about us, he wanted to help his people. So with his invitation and money that John furnished, Arnold and I flew to Malawi in February of 2006, along with two other people that Arnold wanted to bring along.

Picture: From left to right, James Christiansen, Jim Humble (author), Zahir Shaikh and John Wyaux.

On the night before we left for Malawi, we were having a farewell dinner. John said to me, but with everyone listening, "I just want you to know that you have to do everything exactly how Arnold wants it, or there will be no money to finance you in Malawi. You are a loose cannon and we can't have you screwing things up." I simply replied, "All right, I'll do it Arnold's way." Talk about "off the wall," everything was already being done Arnold's way. They had already insured that I had no say. It had been told to me again and again. John just had to get this one last dig in for no apparent reason so far as I could see.

There were many things that were not going to work Arnold's way, but he would have to see it for himself as we went along. He certainly wasn't going to listen to me.

I wanted to walk out on the whole thing. It's not a way I enjoy being treated, but we were slated to be helping sick people in Malawi and I just couldn't walk out. (The fact is, if I had walked out, the mission would have failed). Yes, it was John's money that was making it possible, but it was also my years of work pushing the idea and my technology that also made it possible. I had no idea that they considered me a loose cannon, as I had agreed to their demands. When I returned a little over a month later, John apologized because his girlfriend said he should, but that didn't really change anything. Money people have a tendency to not respect people without money. Money, however, was never my thing. I spent 50 years and hundreds of thousands of dollars studying spiritual philosophies and religions. I have something John and Arnold will never have and will never understand. My spiritual studies had enabled me to be sufficiently receptive to new possibilities so I could discover the MMS in the first place.

Zahir Sheikh (see picture) is the businessman who invited us to Malawi. He is an East Indian whose ancestors moved to Malawi many years ago. He took us all around the capitol of Malawi to many government offices helping us get approval for the MMS (which we called at that time the Malaria Solution). Our success in getting the MMS accepted in Malawi was completely orchestrated by Zahir. Every day he would take us around the city in his automobile to visit various officials such as the Chief of Police, the Inspector General, the Health Minister, and so on.

When we visited the office of each official, Zahir would introduce us, Arnold would talk about our mission to bring the MMS to Africa, then he would suggest that I tell them the details of how the MMS really works. At that time I would spend 10 to 20 minutes explaining the basic chemistry of the MMS. The time I took was mostly determined by how many questions that they asked.   I thought this was particularly interesting because before we left on the trip, Arnold was extremely adamant that we should not tell anyone in Malawi about how the solution worked. That was one of the reasons they called me a loose cannon. I tried to point out that our program would not be workable if we didn't tell people how the MMS worked. That was one of the main points of contention.

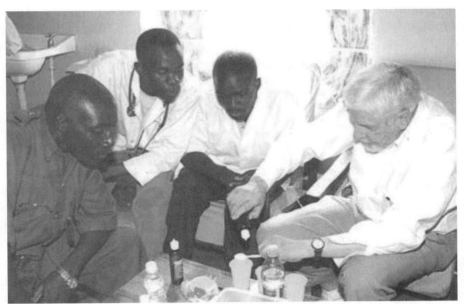

Picture: Three of the prison nurses watch as the Author shows them how to mix the MMS.

I was forbidden to tell them how it worked, but to the very first person we went to see, Arnold said, "This is the inventor and he will tell you how it works." So for months Arnold was stuck on <u>not</u> explaining how it works. But when we were actually there, Arnold immediately saw that we would have to tell them the details. This was one of the many examples that were used to show me that Arnold must have complete control.

I didn't really push the point, because I knew that the doctors and the scientifically trained officials would never allow us to do anything without an explanation of how it worked. At one point Arnold even said to me, "If you start telling them how it works, I will take you down to the airplane and send you home." (That was when we were talking about going to Guinea).

Another point of disagreement was Arnold's insistence that we should not be the ones to administer the MMS that we should only train the people there and then let them give the MMS to the malaria victims. But that simply wasn't practical. I didn't push that point either as I knew Arnold would have to change when he got there. When you bring a solution, you had better be prepared to give it to the people. If you don't, no one will trust in your solution either! As it turned out, we always gave the doses. Arnold was smart enough to see that it had to be that way. To hand the solution to a local and say, "Here you give it" just doesn't work in Africa. They conclude you are afraid to give your own solution.

So as the inventor, when we arrived at different places, I made sure we gave the doses and Arnold quickly saw the advantage. When we went to see an official, I generally would mix doses for everyone including the officials, and believe it or not, every official we saw was willing to drink some. So the very first thing we did in Malawi was to personally give people their doses of the MMS. Then when we finally got out to the prisons or other places, again we were the ones to dispense the doses. In the entire time we were there, I do not believe that we had a single Malawian dispense the doses. Basically, everything went the way I said it would go, but there was no recognition of that. Rather there was just increased determination for everything to go the way Arnold dictated.

Things do change rapidly there. When they see that you are willing to give the solution and that it works, then they begin to ask to be allowed to handle the solution and the situation. One must not show in any way that he is hesitant about dispensing the solution.

While we were in Malawi, Arnold fired the two other people that he brought with us. One was a photographer named James Hackbarth and the other, a friend of Arnold's, named John Wyaux. I won't tell all the details, just the highlights. The most embarrassing part happened in probably the most exclusive restaurant in town. Everyone had on suits and ties and we were the only white people there. Arnold stood up and shouted at John Wyaux. I never really knew why. The whole restaurant went deathly silent when Arnold began to shout. I just sat there looking at my plate, too embarrassed to look up. Finally being so angry, Arnold stomped out of the restaurant, and things settled back down to the normal murmur of conversation. I found out the next day that John had said something to Zahir, our businessman helper, but Zahir never heard what was said. I didn't hear what was said either. In fact, no one but Arnold heard what was said, not even John knew what he had said that set Arnold off. To this day, I don't know what John said, thus I still have no idea why he was fired.

Three evenings later, Arnold was slightly under the influence of alcohol. He entered James Hackbarth's room and fired him because he wasn't taking the right type of pictures, according to Arnold. I admit I didn't like some of his pictures, but I figured all we had to do was explain exactly what we wanted. In any case after that, Arnold told both of them that they could get home the best they could. During the few days they had left, Arnold was extremely rude to them anytime he saw them. Perhaps I should have gone home with them, as no one deserves that kind of treatment, but I wanted the Malawi project to succeed so badly that I was able to compromise my integrity concerning the treatment of my acquaintances. All of my decisions and choices were then, and still are predicated, on the idea that I want the MMS to be in use widely throughout the world.

We had the same problem in Malawi that we had in Kenya. The initial doses that I mixed were too weak. When we were first helping prisoners in our clinical trials at the prison, they were coming back the next day, feeling better but not totally well. So I began increasing the doses. There was one other problem. We were purchasing juice that had vitamin C added as a preservative. The added vitamin C reduces the effectiveness of the MMS by about 75%. I had already proven this fact, but I let it slip by me at first as I had never had a real problem with it before. Once I realized that vitamin C was present in the purchased juice, I started using only fresh juice and also increased the dosage. Then we began to get a 100% recovery rate from malaria.

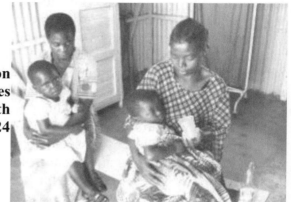

Picture: Two female prison inmates give their babies the MMS formula. Both babies were okay in 24 hours.

Someone had suggested that doing clinical trials in the local prisons would be the easiest thing to do and the easiest place to get permission. We decided to give it a try. We visited the local prison by the name of Maula in the city of Lilongwe, which is the capital of Malawi. The manager of the prison gave us permission to talk to the medical technician. The assistant medical technician's name was S.S. Kamanja. Although he was the assistant, he was always the only one there. He arranged for us to do the clinical trials. We slipped him a few dollars at several different times and he was quite cooperative. Actually, it is only fair to mention that he was quite cooperative even before we slipped him a few dollars, but he was such a nice man that we thought it would be nice to help him out a bit.

We then left the prison to find a lab or hospital that would be able to process blood samples. It was especially important that they be a separate organization. We finally settled on a medical hospital called MARS which was an international organization. MARS stands for Medical Air Rescue Service. Dr. Joseph Aryee was the head man there and he was very responsive to us. We explained what we wanted to do and what our MMS actually did. We mixed our normal drink to show him. He went ahead and drank the mixture as did most other officials in Malawi. He assigned us a medical lab technician whose name was Paul

Makaula. Dr. Aryee said that all we would need to do would be to pay Paul's salary while he was working for us. We agreed on $300 U.S. for six days, plus we agreed to pay his gasoline and other expenses. Dr. Aryee allowed the medical lab technician to use the MARS lab and microscope for the blood tests from at the prison at no charge, which we thought was very generous. He wanted to be of some help.

Throughout the country of Malawi the officials all drank a full dose of the MMS. If it had been a drug they probably would not have taken it. If they were not willing to take the MMS, which is merely a mineral supplement, then they would not be willing to have their people take it. In my opinion, these officials were very courageous to assist us to help their people. They were willing to take the doses of MMS just on our say so.

It is my belief that the reason the Pharmaceutical Medicines and Poisons Board so readily accepted our MMS as a mineral supplement rather than a drug, was that so many officials drank it without hesitation when we told them that it was not a drug. In essence many people really wanted to see the MMS help their country. They wanted it to work and they were willing to cooperate in order to have it work for them.

Back at the prison the next morning, S.S. Kamanja brought in the first 10 men. They were given six drops each, with ¼ teaspoon of vinegar, the three minute wait, and then pineapple juice was then added. Arnold checked each patient for temperature. The first thing we learned was that those ear thermometers simply do not work in Africa. I think it is because ears in Africa, especially in prison, are cleaned differently, or not at all. Luckily we had the plastic strip thermometers that you just press on the forehead. Within about 10 seconds the temperature can be read in the plastic. Finally Arnold was using the strip thermometers on everyone he checked. The strip thermometer worked well and we were able to get the temperature of each patient which was generally quite high. Paul, the lab technician, stuck each patient's finger and took a blood sample and put it on a slide with the patient's name. These slides were then taken back to the MARS laboratory and Paul checked each one on the microscope. We carefully recorded the data from the 10 patients that morning after taking the blood samples. Then I mixed the doses in plastic cups and Arnold handed the cup to each patient.

When we had finished taking blood samples, recording the data, and after giving each of the 10 patients a dose we asked if there were any more prisoners complaining of malaria. Kamanja said that there were 19 more. We said, "Bring them all in and we will dose all of them," which is what we did. We returned that afternoon after 3:00 p.m. to see the results but they were not so great. Most said they were feeling better, but they all still had fevers. The fever had been reduced in only one man. I knew something was wrong. We dosed everyone again including the 10 actually being tested and the other 19 that were just receiving a dose without taking blood samples or having records kept. We again used only six drops.

You probably guessed it, the next morning everyone still tested positive for malaria. It was then I began to remember that in Kenya I had been using 15 drops. We only used six drops in the U.S. for maintenance. I began to get an inkling of what was going wrong. I also remembered the experiments proving that vitamin C reduced the effectiveness of the chlorine dioxide. I began working that evening at getting the correct juice without vitamin C added.

The Malawi prisons are much like concentration camps. The prison is closed in by with only a wire fence with barbed wire at the top. There are armed guards at the corners of the prison in small guard shacks. While we were there, they asked us if we would like to see the women's quarters. Of course, we said yes. The women sleep on the bare floor with only a blanket or two. Arnold said that he would get the women a foam mattress to sleep on. Women who have children have the children stay with them in the prison. The guards get most of the food slated for the prison and sell it elsewhere. Therefore, the inmates have very little to eat. They do raise a few vegetables like potatoes. There is a single toilet for the entire women's dorm with water continuously running down the toilet. Aside from the bare floors, the prison stays fairly clean. The women bathe outside under a water faucet out of the sight of the men.

Picture: Shows 5 pads where the female inmates sleep. Children also stay here with their mothers.

There was one man in the prison that had a high fever, but his blood test came back negative (meaning no malaria present). Since he seemed to have malaria symptoms, we suspected he may have been faking it. However, when we gave him the MMS, his temperature came down to normal overnight and his symptoms disappeared. Paul, the lab man, said that he checked the blood a second time, but no malaria parasites were present. In any case, he got well even if it wasn't malaria. There was also one prisoner who refused treatment. But since he was there, we recorded his name and temperature anyway. Several days later, when he saw all of the other prisoners getting well and he was still sick, he decided that he wanted to be treated also. So, we went ahead and dosed him and he was okay the next day.

I finally realized that the pineapple juice from the grocery store had vitamin C as a preservative. As I mentioned before, Vitamin C prevents the MMS from generating the chlorine dioxide that is necessary. We bought pineapples and a juice maker and made our own juice. In addition to using fresh juice we increased the dose to 18 drops. The next morning, before using the 18 drop doses, we again checked the patients. Of the 10 from which we had originally taken blood samples, the one man that did not test positive for malaria was feeling okay. The other nine again said that they were feeling better, but not well. A second blood test was done. This test showed that the malaria parasites were still present but the parasites looked distorted in several cases. We then dosed everyone with 18 drops and used the fresh pineapple juice. We also dispensed the same 18-drop dose to the 19 additional prisoners with malaria.

The blood tests that our lab man took the next morning all came back negative and all patients reported they were feeling good. The other 19 also reported feeling good, as well. We then selected another 10 cases to check. We had Paul, the lab man, take their blood. We treated them with 18 drops of MMS and used the fresh pineapple juice in their doses. Arnold was very helpful and assisted in everything. He handed out the doses to the patients and took their temperatures while I mixed the doses and recorded the information. The next morning, (24 hours later) their blood all tested negative for malaria. In addition, all of the "old" patients that we treated in the prison were still feeling well.

I had learned in Uganda that the sure way to completely destroy the malaria parasite was to use two doses of 15 drops each, separated by one to four hours. If that had been the way we had started out, there would never have been any trouble here. I have to plead being old with a poor memory. Two years had passed since the treatments in Uganda. I simply had forgotten the details and had to learn them over again. In the U.S. we usually just use six drop doses for maintenance, but we often need to go above six drops to overcome some problems. I had forgotten that we were doing two 15 drop doses in Uganda. I'll never make that mistake again and hopefully someone smarter than me will be doing it next time anyway.

At the end of the prison tests, Dr. Aryee at the MARS hospital reviewed Paul's lab blood tests and gave us a very positive letter. The fact was, that every patient that originally tested positive for malaria in the blood tested negative after MMS treatment and they were feeling fine. It took several extra doses for the first 10 tested, but all eventually tested negative. Let me say that again, all eventually tested negative, which made it 100% successful even if it did take an extra day to get the first group cured.

While in Malawi we also visited several grass hut villages. There we helped with every kind of sickness you can imagine. We dosed the villagers as they came up to us telling us what was wrong. We didn't refuse a dose to anyone. Why not treat as many as we could, it's only a mineral supplement. Most of the people in the village have one disease or another. Their water is not pure. The warm weather encourages all kinds of diseases. They walk with bare feet and the grass and streams have diseases that enter through the skin. The next day when we returned to the village most of the illness had been overcome. A number of people had vomited worms and some had dead worms in their stools. In the future, we hope to go back with enough solution so all of the villages can have what they need.

Let me mention at this point that after Arnold fired the two people he had brought, he was very active in getting things done. He made things happen. I was pretty much just along for the ride at that point. I had no say in how things were done. Arnold dictated everything and he made it work. So I helped at the prison and made suggestions to Arnold. I carried the technical side of things. But Arnold controlled all phases of the operation. I really didn't need to be there except to figure out why the solution hadn't initially worked and then make the necessary adjustments. The fact is, Arnold made the whole operation work and it was successful.

Arnold asked me once, "How would you have done it differently?" Well, I would have done many things differently, simply because no two people do things the same way. But, he asked me if I disagreed with how he did things ...... well; I felt that there was no point in nitpicking. I would not have disagreed with anything except with the way he fired the two guys who he brought along on the trip and the fact that he tried to keep such complete control of the bottles of MMS solution. At one of the villages I wanted to leave a bottle with the chief, but Arnold insisted that we would come back the next day to treat those who needed a second dose. But we never got back, although I suggested it several times. Thus many went untreated, and in any sort of a situation where we didn't keep our commitment it were upsetting to me.

I hope you understand my purpose. I don't just want to help some people in some villages. That is great to do and we enjoyed it, but my real purpose is to first prove out the MMS to the point that the world becomes willing to use it to help destroy many health problems in Africa including malaria and AIDS. When that happens, the world will need to spend less and less money on Africa. Right now, the world spends untold billions of dollars in Africa. Malaria alone is the biggest cause of poverty in Africa. Each year 500,000,000 people are sick with malaria and can't work; millions more have AIDS and other problems. It also takes millions of other people to care for the sick. Everywhere you go in Africa you see nonprofit humanitarian groups working to help the people there. Billions and billions of dollars are being spent in an effort to help Africa, but still it isn't enough. This money will not be needed when these diseases are under control or even eradicated. Those billions of dollars can be allocated to other purposes.

We accomplished a lot in Malawi. We got several agencies of the government to accept our MMS as a mineral supplement, which was important, but we treated less than 100 people while there. After we got the government acceptance and did a couple of 10-patient clinical trials, we went home. In actuality we did a total of three clinical trials. Finally, six months later we also found out that the clinical trials conducted by the Malaria Board of the government resulted in the same 100% recovery from malaria that our tests proved in the prison.

There is the promise to treat the entire country, and I hope we do. Arnold did a very good job. He kept at it until we had our data. We however, did not come close to doing what we had come to do. We were supposed to spend a great deal of time in the villages training the chiefs and others to use the MMS. We only went to three villages in all. We did not train anyone in a single village to use the MMS. That was really what we were there for. We left, I assume because we were out of money, but I never knew why. I wanted to stay and do our job. It was merely told to me that we were going home, so we went home. Our original idea was to treat a few thousand people, but we went home after doing three clinical trials.

We left Malawi for the U.S. on April 27, 2006. I again wound up out in the desert in Mina. Nothing has happened in Malawi since then, only lots of promises. I have been working for Arnold as the foreman of a crew of men fixing up his mill. It is a chance for me to make a few dollars while I am writing this book. John is financing most of the operation there at the mill. (This is not the same John that was fired in Malawi. This is a friend of Arnold's that has been helping with finance for some time.) They are spending hundreds of thousands of dollars on the mill and mining operations. They keep talking about returning to Africa, but it doesn't appear to me that it will happen any time soon because Arnold will have to be in charge of operations here or they will lose money. My single goal is to get the MMS to the world. So I have written this book.

Up to this point Arnold still doesn't allow me to talk to any of the new groups that he finds that are interested in helping our cause. I suppose that he believes that I am as bad with people as he is. Isn't it normal for people to see faults in others that they themselves have? Things have changed. See the update paragraph below.

I have a strong desire to see the entire country of Malawi treated for malaria. Arnold and John continue to say that they will furnish the money, but Arnold does not trust me to go to Malawi alone and he is not ready to go, as I write this book. However, even if they do treat all of Malawi, and start on the next country, they still plan to keep the MMS solution a secret. They want to treat all of Africa while keeping it secret. I must see that the world gets the complete information. Even if organizations and people throughout the world know the secret of MMS, that should not prevent us or others from seeing that Africa is treated for all the problems that the MMS will handle. Hopefully, everyone will understand that. I have furnished as much information as I can in this book so that you, the reader, can save lives. You really can; please try.

To give a little update at this time (2008, March 1) more than 8000 books have been sold and over 11,000 bottles of MMS are being sold each month.

Available MMS for you to purchase immediately. If you don't want the hassle and you would like to try my exact formula, you can order it from my friends in Canada or other places in the US where other people are manufacturing the MMS. At this time they all charge about the same price. Most are putting it in the same size bottle which is a four ounce size bottle (it contains actually 5.5 ounces) for only $20 USD plus shipping which is small. So far they have kept the price down. I want everyone to be able to afford to be well without it being a financial worry to them. There are 450 six drop doses in this bottle. It should last you about one year. That's far more solution than anyone else selling the weak solution of Stabilized Oxygen. So, make it yourself, or buy it. Just get it into as many hands as possible. For information about obtaining this product (MMS) go to the following Web Site http://www.health4allinfo.ca/ or check the Web Site http:www.miraclemineral.org . There I list all of the suppliers that sell MMS that I have checked. See end of chapter 17 for supplies of empty bottles.

I have no personal interest in my friends' operation, but they have agreed to donate $1.00 per bottle to the operation that is distributing the MMS to Africa. So you will be helping the project in Africa with your purchase. Go to Web Site http://www.health4allinfo.ca/ for further information.

One other thing, he has also agreed to furnish enough MMS to supply an entire country in Africa at no cost. Whatever country that requests it first, I assume is the one that will get it.

The next several pages show documents from the Malawi government. The documents give evidence that we were there. You could always give them a call.

MALAWI BUREAU OF STANDARDS

Our file code: BS/LAB/35/4   Our date: 06-04-07

Your file code: Your date:

Address Correspondence to the Director-General

Malaria Solution Foundation
P.O Box 719,
Lilongwe

Dear Sir

MS SOLUTION AND NALI VINEGAR

We submit our Report No. 354/AJ 134 on the analysis of the above mentioned sample which you brought to the Bureau.

Our receipt **No 42483** for **MK2,791.25** being the cost of testing and reporting is attached for your kind attention.

We thank you for using our facilities and look forward to serving you again in future.

Yours faithfully

Patricia N Nayeja
Senior Scientific Officer
For: DIRECTOR-GENERAL

PNN/ljm

A STATUTORY CORPORATION ESTABLISHED IN 1972

Postal Address   Office Address   National Tel : 01 670 488   National Fax : 01 670 756
P.O Box 946   Moirs Road   International Tel : +265 1 670 488   International Fax : +265 1 670 756

PHARMACY, MEDICINES & POISONS BOARD

ALL CORRESPONDENCE SHOULD BE ADDRESSED TO THE REGISTRAR

Telephone: (265) 01 750 108/755 165/755 166

P.O. Box 30241
Capital City
Lilongwe 3
Malawi

Fax: 265) 01 755 204

E-mail:admin@pmpbmw.org
www.pmpb.malawi.net

Ref: PMPB/PR/114

12th April 2006

The Manager,
The Malaria Solution Foundation,
USA.

Dear Sir,

REGISTRATION OF MS SOLUTION

I would like to acknowledge receipt of dietary mineral supplement (MS Solution) and its write-up.

Well, if this product is indeed a dietary mineral supplement, then its not under the jurisdiction of Pharmacy, medicines and Poisons Board to register. But the claims of the label on the bottle suggest that it cures or alleviates certain medical conditions which may include malaria.

The composition of the solution of sodium chloride (NaCl) and water which may have undergone electrolysis to make chlorine dioxide (Cl2O) which may kill pathogens does not show any pharmacological activity. From the documentation, it does not stipulate the pharmacological activity and mode of action on the malaria plasmodium. Similarly, the medical journals do not mention anything concerning this preparation.

Moreover, in Malawi the Malaria Control Programme through its taskforce is the sole authority that can accept or refuse an anti-malarial medicinal product in Malawi. This is to protect the public and the resistance of anti-malarial drugs.

Yours faithfully,

Aaron G. Sosola (Deputy Registrar & Head of Technical Services)
For: REGISTRAR

CC: The Project Manager
     Malaria Control Programme
     Lilongwe

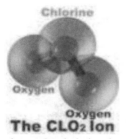

Chapter 9

Understanding the Miracle Mineral Supplement

The CLO₂ Ion To understand the MMS one must understand chlorine dioxide as that is what is generated and what does the job in the body.

Chlorine dioxide is a high explosive. Therefore, wherever it is used it must be generated on site. It cannot be transported as chlorine dioxide. It will instantly destroy any container that one might try to house it in. It cannot even be moved through metal or plastic pipes. Numerous methods have been devised to generate chlorine dioxide and many different chlorine chemicals are used for that purpose. Chlorine dioxide is used for many industrial processes. It is used in paper mills to bleach the paper pulp white. It is used in cloth mills to bleach cloth. Probably the most important use is to purify water and thousands of water purification systems utilize chlorine dioxide throughout the world. In water purification systems it is selective for pathogens and other bioorganisms that might be harmful to larger animals and humans. It does NOT combine with hundreds of constituents with which free chlorine will combine. Free chlorine will combine with several items found in most water systems and will create carcinogenic compounds. Thus, although the initial cost of installing chlorine dioxide systems is higher, in the long run the chlorine dioxide systems save money and they are much safer from a health standpoint.

One of the most popular methods of generating chlorine dioxide is by various methods of treating sodium chlorite. It is a white or slightly yellow flaky substance. Keep in mind that table salt is not quite the same thing. Note the spelling of the last two letters. Table salt is sodium chlor*ide*. We generate chlorine dioxide from sodium chlor*ite*.

Throughout the world today sodium chlorite (the formula is $NaClO_2$) is probably used to generate chlorine dioxide more often than any other method. For the formula for chlorine dioxide we merely remove the Na which is sodium, and we have chlorine dioxide, ClO_2. (Don't worry; you don't have to understand these formulas to understand the basics of what

I am writing here.) There are possibly several dozen methods of using sodium chlorite to generate chlorine dioxide. The FDA approves several methods of just adding swimming pool acid to a watery solution of sodium chlorite for the purpose of making chlorine dioxide which is used to sterilize chicken or beef before it is sold to the public.   The acid generates the chlorine dioxide from the sodium chlorite. In many cases of sterilizing vegetables the chlorine does not have to be rinsed off as the chlorine dioxide soon turns into salt but not enough to make the vegetable salty.

Amazingly enough, in a hundred thousand health food stores in the U.S. one can also find sodium chlorite in a watery form known as Stabilized Oxygen. In almost all cases Stabilized Oxygen is manufactured by simply adding 3.5% sodium chlorite by weight to distilled water, that's 35,000 ppm. You can do it in your kitchen. Just don't use any metal pots and pans, not even stainless steel. Use only plastic or glass or Corning Ware. However, you will be much better off making the Miracle Mineral Supplement with my formula or buying it from someone who is using my formula. I'll tell you exactly how to do that later in this book.

For 80 years hundreds of thousands of people have put a few drops of Stabilized Oxygen into their water or juice and drank it down thinking that it somehow furnished extra oxygen to their bodies. The few that realized that some form of chlorine was generated, mentioned it in passing, but still insisted that the chlorite furnished the body with oxygen.   Somehow during all those years, not one of the alternate medicine groups ever decided to have a good chemist look at the formula, or at least not one of them wrote about doing so. The fact is that simple chemistry shows us that no oxygen is generated that the body can use.

Chlorine dioxide is a powerful chemical and it has many uses. It is an oxidizer, less powerful than oxygen, but with greater quantity available for oxidizing.   Chlorine dioxide explodes when it contacts certain chemical conditions, and is neutral with other chemical conditions. It is selective.   What do we mean when we say it explodes?   Well, an explosion is merely a fast chemical reaction, mainly oxidation that also releases energy. In the formula, ClO_2, there are two oxygen ions. So why do these not get released these so that the body can use them? It's because they have a minus two charge. They have already done their oxidizing before they arrived in this position. They cannot oxidize further. But the chlorine combined with oxygen can. When chlorine dioxide touches a pathogen or a poison that is acidic in nature, it instantly accepts five electrons. It destroys anything that it can draw electrons from and generates heat at the same time (this action is called oxidation even when oxygen is not a part of it). The oxygen atoms are then released from the chlorine dioxide, but they are not elemental oxygen. They are ions of oxygen with a negative two charge. They are at the same charge as the oxygen in carbon dioxide, a gas that will kill you if you breathe enough of it. The carbon dioxide is not a poison. In other words it doesn't do anything to the lungs; it is sort of like drowning. It prevents the lungs from getting the elemental oxygen that they need.

Hydrogen and oxygen mix together becomes water. That's about all that the oxygen can do at this time. It becomes water or it can become part of a carbon dioxide molecule. The chlorine, after the explosion of oxidation, has also lost its charge and it becomes a chloride which is basically table salt, which again has no ability to oxidize as it no longer has any charge. There is nothing else left to cause any kind of a side effect.

The basic idea is simply that oxygen and chlorine must be charged to the correct number of electrons, or they do not do the job of oxidizing. When oxygen is not capable of oxidizing it simply cannot do the job in the body that is required for oxygen. What sodium chlorite really does for us is it gives us chlorine dioxide, a chemical that is selectively to destroy almost all bad things that might exist in the body. Each tiny chlorine dioxide molecule has tremendous power to destroy those things from which it can draw electrons, but it does not have the power to draw electrons from healthy cells or aerobic bacteria.

Chlorine dioxide does not last forever. It has too much energy bundled into a small area. It begins to lose some of its energy after a few minutes in the body and the same thing happens when it is released into public water supplies. In the body when it has lost some of its energy so that it no longer is explosive (unable to oxidize) it can then combine with other substances. There is some evidence that it helps make myeloperoxidase, a chemical that the body uses to make hypochlorous acid that is then used by the immune system to further kill pathogens, killer cells, and other things. Chlorine dioxide is the only chemical known that has these qualities and that can do these things in the body without creating side effects. In public water works or the bleaching of paper pulp in paper mills, the chlorine dioxide is generated on the site where it is used. In the body it is also generated on the site where it is used from sodium chlorite.

How to Generate Chlorine Dioxide in the Human Body

All of those people who used Stabilized Oxygen for all those years didn't realize the benefits were coming from the chlorine dioxide and thus no one ever tried to generate more of it. They believed that the millions of oxygen ions that were connected to the chlorine were available to the body. Thus, they received the little benefit that resulted from the fact that when a few drops of Stabilized Oxygen is added to water it begins to release chlorine dioxide, but very slowly, too slowly to do much good. It releases a few chlorine dioxide ions per hour instead of per minute. There was always some benefit, but not nearly the full potential. For 80 years they missed it.

So if we are going to generate chlorine dioxide in the body, we need to do it about 1,000 times faster than what is now done when one adds a few drops of Stabilized Oxygen to a glass of water or juice. That gives you about 1 ppb (one part per billion) and what you really need is 1 ppm (one part per million), and often even more than that. In fact, sometimes it takes 1 ppt (one part per thousand). But don't worry about those figures; one does not need to know all the technical details to make it work. Just know that to cure AIDS it takes at least a thousand times more chlorine dioxide than Stabilized Oxygen gives you, actually more like 10,000 times.

As it was mentioned above the FDA authorizes adding swimming pool acid to solutions of sodium chlorite in order to generate chlorine dioxide. All of those public water purification plants that use sodium chlorite to make chlorine dioxide also use acid in various mechanical devices that add the acid at a pre established speed to a flow of watery sodium chlorite. In the human body we have a tougher problem because we want to add a lot of chlorine dioxide, but not all at once. We want to allow it to exist for a few hours so that it can be carried around to all parts of the body. But chlorine dioxide deteriorates in minutes and will not exist in the body for hours if you just simply swallow some. There isn't any mechanical mechanism that one can use to add acid slowly to a watery solution of sodium chlorite inside the body.

The Importance of Vinegar or Lime or lemon or Citric Acid

That is where vinegar or lime or lemon comes in. The part that is important is the 5% acetic acid or the citric acid in lime or lemon. (Just recently, 7/1/2007, it has been discovered that pure citric acid works even better than vinegar, lime, or lemon.) When one of these items is added to sodium chlorite it causes the solution to begin releasing chlorine dioxide on a continuous basis for about 12 hours. The addition of six drops of a solution that is 28% sodium chlorite (that's the Miracle Mineral Supplement) to 30 drops of vinegar or lime or lemon will release approximately three mgs (3 milligrams) of chlorine dioxide in three minutes. That's the reason for the three minute wait, but when you add water or apple juice to make about 1/2 glass of liquid the process slows down to one mg per hour. But three mgs is quite a bit for the body. Thus these acids have a particular quality that works to create a continuous supply of chlorine dioxide for about 12 hours. In addition to creating the continuous release of chlorine dioxide they also prevent the solution from releasing chlorine dioxide too quickly when the stomach acids mix with it. As the chlorine dioxide deteriorates new chlorine dioxide is continuously being generated in the body. Adding vinegar or lime or lemon to the sodium chlorite does the trick. If you don't add one of these items, all you have is the same old Stabilized Oxygen health drink, which is interesting, but it really doesn't get the job done.

You can see from the above paragraph that the MMS starts off with three milligrams of chlorine dioxide and then continues to supply chlorine dioxide to the body for about 12 hours. The initial three milligrams is what the body needs. The MMS works best to destroy pathogens when 2 or 3 mg of free chlorine dioxide are in the solution at the time it is swallowed. It has an immediate effect. We have been talking all along about six drops which is a maintenance dose. If you are treating a disease 15 to 18 drops is a full dose. But read the instructions, you usually start off with small doses and work up.

To give you an idea of what one milligram is, consider a standard U.S. dime. One gram is just about exactly 1/2 of a dime. Imagine 1/2 of dime cut into a thousand pieces. One of those pieces is one milligram. That's less than a fly speck. That's how powerful chlorine dioxide is. One milligram of chlorine dioxide begins killing pathogens in the body. Over a period of 12 hours the body will receive somewhere between 12 and 20 mgs, and there will be about two milligrams of chlorine dioxide distributed throughout the body at any one time, because as the chlorine dioxide is generated it is either used up by destroying pathogens or it deteriorates into other harmless chemicals in just minutes. When the chlorine dioxide degenerates, the final chemicals that are left are either chemicals that the immune system really needs, or the chlorine just turns to a chloride making a tiny insignificant amount of table salt and water. Because of this there simply can be no side effects. There is nothing left to cause side effects.

Make no mistake. Chlorine dioxide ions are extremely powerful. They bundle tremendous energy into a small particle. But they only remain that way for a few minutes. They contain too much energy to last for a lengthy amount of time. In the world of submicroscopic energy particles, they are a torpedo with a selective warhead. The chemical makeup of chlorine dioxide gives it that quality and no other chemical has that same quality.

Some people have taken more than 20 times the amount of Stabilized Oxygen (sodium chlorite). Perfectly healthy people may have a small amount of nausea for 10 or 15 minutes from that large of a dose, but if they have any bad conditions in their body, depending upon what they are, they might get nauseous for a period. A few people including myself have tried 25 times the recommended MMS dose, and that will make you nauseous but it does not leave side effects. (This has already been tried and it would be extremely sickening to try it.) The point is, chlorine dioxide is not only not harmful, but it is of great benefit to the body. Getting nauseous is the result of the chlorine dioxide attacking some bad condition in the body. In the case of a liver condition such as hepatitis, one almost always gets nauseous. The reason for this is that the liver begins to expel the poisons as the chlorine dioxide begins to destroy them. <u>But it also cures the condition in record time.</u>

One lady with hepatitis C did just what I told her not to do. Instead of taking two drops at first, she wanted to be certain that she killed it. She took 30 drops, added the vinegar, waited three minutes and added it to apple juice. It made her sick for three days. She then put the MMS aside and did not touch it for eight months. She thought because it made her so sick that it didn't work, but when she finally decided to go to the doctor he could find no hepatitis in her body. Both were amazed. I have given it to many people with one of the hepatitis diseases A, B, or C. I can guarantee that 30 drops will make any hepatitis patient feel very sick, but it will also cure them. However, that is not the way to do it. A hepatitis patient should never start out with more than two drops. In that case, normally they will not feel any nausea, and if they keep slowly increasing the drops until they can take 15 drops twice a day without nausea, they will check negative to hepatitis of all kinds.

Procedure for Taking MMS for Maintenance
Taking the MMS for longevity is important. I wish I could say for sure that it will give you an additional 25 years of life. I can't prove it yet, but I believe it. All the evidence points to that conclusion. Dozens of older people are taking the MMS. All those diseases that normally kill older people simply no longer have the sting. The immune system can be 100 times stronger than normal in older people and then pneumonia and flu and other disease just don't get a foothold that is as long as one is taking the maintenance dose every day.

Younger people can get by with taking the MMS maintenance dose two or three times a week, but older people need to take it at least once a day. When taking it once a day, every day, one can probably get by with taking four drop doses, and be sure to take it with the vinegar and three minute wait and then add the apple juice (see below for exact instructions.) Anyone taking it two or three times a week should always take at least six drops for each dose. Remember, hundreds of thousands of people have been taking this solution for 80 years; all I have done is added a little food acid. No side effects have been reported in all these years, no side effects have been reported in the six years since the vinegar was added. Technically there should be none. It has been proven that chlorine dioxide does not attack healthy cells. (That is in the small quantities used in MMS. A large quantity would kill anyone or anything).

Remember how it was pointed out earlier that the chlorine dioxide deteriorates into constituents that are totally nonpoisonous. Nothing is left behind to build up, as is the case in many conventional medicines. The chlorine dioxide lasts long enough to do its job, and then the part that does not furnish the immune system with needed ions becomes nothing but micro amounts of table salt and water. The chlorine dioxide has just a few minutes to do its thing and then it no longer exists. It leaves nothing behind that can build up.

Initial procedure: Keep in mind that anyone taking the MMS for the first time should start out with no more than two drops for their first dose. The reason is that the two drops will not produce enough chemical reaction to cause bad nausea in those who have some sort of a health condition. If there is some really bad condition in the body, two drops could cause a mild nausea for ten minutes or so. In that case, continue to take only two drops daily or several times daily until there is no nausea. When one has reached the point where there is no nausea from two drops then use three drops the next time. Continue this until you are at 15 drops a day and then drop back to six drops a day. When using for treatment of some serious illness, you will need to progress until you are taking much more than six drops, depending upon the illness.

Keep in mind, that when we refer to drops we always mean that one must add 1/4 to 1/2 teaspoon of vinegar or lime or lemon or citric acid and then wait three minutes before adding 1/2 glass of juice. That's four ounces of juice for those of you who are more scientific. Without the vinegar or lime or lemon, the whole exercise consists of drinking a nice health drink. But nice health drinks don't do the job. And remember, DO NOT use juice with added vitamin C.

So the exact procedure is this: Add two drops of MMS to a clean empty dry glass. Then add 10 drops of lime or lemon (if you use citric acid see the instructions in chapter 10). Swirl the glass by hand to mix the vinegar and drops. Wait three minutes. Add 1/2 glass of apple juice. Drink right away. You can substitute grape juice or pineapple juice as long as they are freshly made juices, meaning don't buy juices with vitamin C added. Do not use orange juice. Orange juice prevents the production of chlorine dioxide.

The reason for using fresh juice is that most juices have vitamin C added for a preservative. It makes the juice last longer and it is good for you, but it inhibits the release of chlorine dioxide. It can even prevent you from getting the results that you want from taking the MMS. If you do use store bought juice make sure that it does not say that vitamin C has been added. If it does say vitamin C added, you can always drink it several hours before or after taking the MMS.

Allowing the drops and vinegar set more than three minutes is not necessarily a problem. The chlorine dioxide in the drops begins to separate and the chlorine goes off into the air and thus the concentrate of chlorine dioxide remains fairly constant for up to 1/2 hour, however tiny amounts of chlorine do remain in the solution. Putting a lid on the container makes the chlorine dioxide much stronger. Some people do this to make a stronger drink. The very best practice is to not allow the drops and acid to go longer than three minutes before adding your juice and drinking it.

To be sure of a strong drink of chlorine dioxide, drink it immediately after adding the juice. (It's not dangerous to allow it to set longer, just not as effective). You can even let it set an hour or no more two. Juices that can be used are apple juice, grape juice, pineapple juice, and cranberry juice.

AGAIN: Do not try to use orange juice. Orange juice prevents the production of chlorine dioxide and thus prevents the MMS from being effective.

Further Technical Stuff: This is just to further clarify some points made earlier. There are two levels of deterioration that take place when we are talking about a dose of MMS solution. (1) The first thing that deteriorates is the Sodium Chlorite. After the vinegar is added, the Sodium Chlorite begins to deteriorate releasing Chlorine Dioxide into the solution. Chlorine Dioxide is an extremely powerful ion containing vast amounts of energy in an extremely small area. (2) It is not a stable condition to hold that much energy and it too begins to deteriorate. The Chlorine Dioxide ion retains its ability to destroy pathogens, diseased cells, poisonous substances, and other harmful items for only about 30 minutes. It really begins to lose its energy within seconds of being released from the Sodium Chlorite, but it usually can do its job for up to 30 minutes. By the end of an hour or so, it has deteriorated to the point that it will no longer destroy pathogens but it can still combine with various other chemicals. Okay, so maybe I was over enthusiastic in saying "vast amounts of energy" as it doesn't sound very scientific. So let's just say, chlorine dioxide begins to deteriorate almost immediately until it is no longer chlorine dioxide. It separates into its constituents of chlorine, oxygen, and energy and nothing else. The chlorine and oxygen under this condition have lost their charge and thus are not active.

As the chlorine dioxide continues to deteriorate, so does the sodium chlorite. The deterioration of the sodium chlorite is at approximately the same speed as the deterioration of the chlorine dioxide. Do you see? More chlorine dioxide is being generated by the sodium chlorite all the time. Thus as the chlorine dioxide is consumed by killing pathogens or by simple deterioration it is replaced by the continued deterioration of the sodium chlorite.

The chlorine in sodium chlorite either combines with helpful chemicals that the immune system can use, or it becomes a chloride which means it becomes a tiny part of a tiny amount of table salt. Not enough to even record. The deterioration of chlorine dioxide in the human body leaves absolutely nothing behind. The action of destroying any pathogen or other harmful item in the body leaves nothing behind but dead pathogens, and again a chloride and oxygen that can only become a part of the water of the body.

Arnold and I founded the Malaria Solution Foundation. He's in charge. I withdrew from that foundation when I realized they were not very committed to treating malaria in Africa. They informed me that they had plenty of money and millions to spend treating malaria in Africa, but they continued with mining and rice distribution programs and nothing was happening with the program to distribute the MMS in Africa. If they really were committed, and they were too busy, they could have sent me.

We have the answer to the disease that has been the biggest killer of mankind for hundreds of years. So while millions of people suffer and die, what is my group doing? We're over in Africa giving out rice bran packets to school children. That's a nice program. It's nice to help children, but our organization was formed to solve the problem of malaria. I may be beating this point to death, but there were a number of people who could not see why I left the foundation and concentrated on writing this book.

After several years I finally realized that I could not leave the data of the MMS information in their hands. The world would probably never know about it. It was then that I finally realized that this information simply cannot be owned or controlled by any one person or group. The Malaria Solution Foundation Web Site (malariasolution.com) will also tell you much about the programs that we conducted in Africa and maybe give you some more confidence in what I have been saying. The MMS really works. (This site, by the way, was just finished in the last part of 2006. It was 5 years since I was first told that they were going to put up a good site). Their last trip to Malawi was last year. It had nothing to do with curing malaria in that country. It had to do with distributing rice bran packets to orphanages. That is a feel good program; but what we founded the Foundation for is not getting done.

You could also check if you want to, with the Malawi government. They conducted their own separate tests with the Malaria Solution (the MMS) and got the same results as we did in the prison, 90% cure for malaria patients in less than 24 hours and 100% cure in 48 hours. Nothing else has ever had even a 10% cure rate in 24 hours or 48 hours.

I have included two pictures of blood on the following pages. These pictures were taken with a dark field microscope that was designed especially for viewing blood. The first picture shows the blood of a person before taking a dose of the MMS. All the cells shown are red blood cells. Notice how the cells are all together touching one another in a clump. This is an unhealthy condition. This person needs more water and minerals.

The second picture shows the blood of the same person 1.5 hours after taking a dose of 10 drops of MMS with the vinegar, with the three minutes wait and with water added. Note that the red blood cells are no longer sticking together, but more importantly, the circles show 3 white blood cells moving towards the larger crystalline blood clot. They will ingest the clot trapping the crystalline particles. Although you cannot see the movement in still pictures, these white blood cells are as much as 10 times more active than normal after taking the MMS. The actual video of this blood shows the movement.

First picture

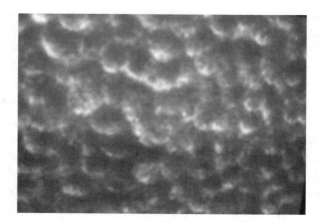

Second Picture

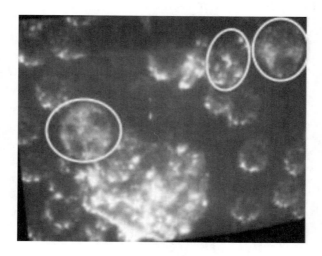

If you are now on the Internet use the following site to obtain these items when you can: www.miraclemineral.org

You may not believe it, but the FDA in the United States has been suppressing all real cancer cures, and information concerning how vitamins prevent heart attacks and all other information or products

that may in any way <u>reduce the income of the large pharmaceutical medical drug companies (Big PHARMA).</u>

Please don't take my word for it; become informed. Read the information available on the Internet. Just go to any search engine and put in "FDA Suppression." There is voluminous documentation, starting back in the 1930's. They often put authors in jail and told them that they will withdraw the accusations if the author would withdraw his claims. Once the author has lost all of his money and is tired of fighting he gives up. There are hundreds of medical facts that are suppressed right now that would save thousands of lives around the world. There are many records of people who have died under very questionable conditions when they have tried to inform the people. Please don't write this off as a bunch of crazy conspiracy nuts. The MMS is one more medical fact that they will try to suppress. Try it and know that it works. Your life and the lives of thousands, even millions, are at stake. Isn't that important enough to at least try it once on someone, or on you? Spend a couple of hours researching this issue. The facts are there.

<u>Treating Symptoms:</u> Modern medicine, by way of doctors, treats symptoms. Drugs that you buy at any pharmacy are 99% directed towards symptoms. In other words, if you have a headache, the doctor gives you something for the pain, but doesn't find out what is causing the headache. If you can't sleep, the drug is something that helps you sleep, but the doctor doesn't find out what is keeping you awake. If you get arthritis in the knee the doctor gives you a drug for the pain, he doesn't find the reason for the arthritis. If you have poor digestion the doctor gives you a tablet that neutralizes the acid and allows the food to go through without digesting. He doesn't find the cause of the poor digestion, or even give you something that will digest the food. There are a thousand different drugs directed at symptoms and the side effect of many of these drugs is death. All drugs have side effects. Not all of them have death as a side effect, but regardless, most of them have caused death at one time or another.

Why do you suppose drugs in this world, especially in America, almost always treat symptoms and not the cause of diseases? It's no secret about drugs only treating symptoms, most people know that already. Ask any person interested in health. Medical drugs treat symptoms and all of the medical research by pharmaceutical companies is directed towards treating symptoms, and not towards finding the cause of the problem. Well, the reason is that if you find the cause of a disease or health problem you can usually cure the problem. In that case you cannot continue to sell the drug over and over until the person dies. Billions of dollars are involved. Treating symptoms does not cure or change the problem. What is the reason that there has been no significant advancement in cancer treatment technology in 100 years? With one or two minor exceptions, the same treatments are still used more than 100 years later. The world has advanced fantastically in almost everything but cancer treatment and many other disease treatments. They refine the treatment, make the drugs more pure, make the needles better, make the X-ray machines better, make the records better, they make the timers better that time the treatment, but the treatment itself does not change.

The pharmaceutical companies spend billions of dollars with two lawyers and often two law offices for each congressman and each senator in the United States. They have tried again and again to suppress vitamins. I don't have time to cover all of the facts here. Please become informed on this subject. The data and the proof are available. The truth cannot be suppressed. Just read the thousands of documents available on the Internet. They spend billions influencing Congress on the pretense of public safety. Do you imagine that we would be much safer if we didn't know about vitamins? The truth affects all countries of the world. At this time the FDA just informed the public that it intends to shut down over 50% of the alternate health type supplement companies. This is because they finally prevailed upon Congress to pass a law stating that all supplements must be under FDA control.

Now, the MMS is such a simple cure that it need not be relegated to doctors. The public at large has the ability to treat themselves. This means that the FDA is going to have a much harder time at suppressing this one. The public, the sick and suffering have this one short window that will be open, we don't know for how long. But this time the FDA cannot suppress a couple of doctors or arrest the author of a book. (They can't find me.) Luckily I am not tied to some expensive lab, and I can move around. But they don't have to find me to stop it. The billions of dollars behind them will definitely try, because ultimately a great part of those billions are lost if the MMS becomes well known. Please, please take the attitude that maybe, just maybe I might just be telling the truth.

This is where you come in. It now rests on your shoulders. I've done what I can do. It's up to you, the readers of this book, to spread the word to the world. It can happen if you will tell your friends. The more people that you get to read this book, the more people you tell before the pharmaceutical companies find out about it, the less likely they will be able to suppress it. Up to this point they are so convinced that I am a charlatan that they have paid me no attention. It's my only safe guard. But when they start getting reports of people getting well and people being cured, it will be a different story. This now is now the second printing of this book. The first printing sold out and thousands of people were cured of many different diseases, but many who used the book did not pass the information on to their friends. Many did, but many did not. If we are going to win, many more are going to have to take a hand, just to distribute the book further.

There is a point, I don't know how many people that is, but a point can be reached which I call the point of no return. If we reach that point, the window can no longer be slammed in our face. That is when enough people have learned about the MMS, have used it, and know it works. Believe me; a few individuals won't do it. It will take millions who know that it works. Please join us. Either use it, or just accept the idea that the public deserves to know. Get as many people to download the free book (The Miracle Mineral Supplement of the 21st Century Part I) as possible (and also Part II). And/or buy this book. When you successfully use the MMS to help someone or yourself, broadcast it widely. We may only have a few months. We probably have less than a year to get it to the public. The elimination and prevention of suffering, misery and death of millions depends upon you. (Sorry to be so dramatic, but that is the fact.)

Again, check Google and use "FDA Suppression" for your search and you will know that I am telling the truth.

Otherwise, you will know that what I say here is true when they begin their campaigns to convince the public that the facts in this book are false. The problem that they will have is that anyone can try it. But that won't stop them, because they know that they can use fear to prevent millions from even considering it. That is why we need millions who have already tried it and know that it works. Join the crusade. Lives are at stake. Of course, if you don't tell your friends there will never be such a campaign from the FDA and pharmaceuticals' Big PHARMA.

If you are short now and don't have the 10 bucks for book II, send me an email according to the instructions given on the copyright page at the beginning of this book and I will email you a free copy. I apologize again for being so dramatic, but I am 74 years old, and in my years I have learned that people would rather hear the facts than someone "beating around the bush."

I also want to say that any excess profit beyond the expenses of distributing this book I will spend in Africa towards eliminating the diseases there. I can now state that I am a part of the Kinnaman Foundation. Money can be donated to the African-America MMS Project at the Kinnaman Foundation and such money is fully deductible for income tax purposes.

 Remember, the MMS does not treat diseases, it aids the immune system.

Look at the copyright page. In the event of my death, this book becomes public domain.

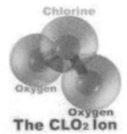

Chlorine

Oxygen

Oxygen

The CLO₂ Ion

Chapter 9.5

A New Look at Disease

Beyond MMS there is another important discovery I would like to tell you about. It is amazing that an inventor should have discovered it instead of one of the world's most prominent scientists. Apparently, it's just too simple for science as the information has been available for 100 years. It was mostly luck that I was in the position to make the discovery. No doubt, 60 years of spiritual seeking made the discovery possible. As with MMS, now discovered, I really have to tell the world. It must be told far and wide or I would forever suffer the consequences, as the sin of omission is just as bad as the sin of commission, as far as karma is concerned

I can't say what it is right up front, because I'd probably lose you. But hang on for a few paragraphs and let me surprise you. I was first introduced to sodium chlorite in about 1985. It was used to purify water and kill the diseases on tropical fish so far as I knew. It was actually being used at that time many places in the world to purify water and as a health drink. I soon discovered that some health food stores carried it and it was called stabilized oxygen. There was always a fair market for it as it seemed to help recovery from many different diseases. There were always many great claims for sodium chlorite (sold as Stabilized Oxygen) but like most medicines it seemed to work only for some people and ten only some of the time.

After my discovery in the jungle that Stabilized Oxygen cured malaria part of the time and then by addition of a food acid it cured malaria all the time, I began to see hundreds of people recover from diseases. When I traveled to Africa I watched thousands of people recover from malaria and other diseases. Then while I lived in my small desert town I watched more people recover from diseases. During that time I sent many bottles of MMS to Africa and hundreds more were cured mostly of malaria, but other things as well. One time I sent enough for one person to treat over 5000 people of malaria in Sierra Leone, another time over

1600. And of course, there were many times where one or two or ten bottles were sent. (I should mention that some of these times Arnold furnished the money for me to send these bottles, and sometimes he didn't.) In addition to that I sold and gave many bottles around town and the neighboring town and other places in the US. I'm not saying all this to brag. I hope that isn't what it sounds like. I'm trying to make a point.

So before I make the point, let me also say that since I came to Mexico one year ago, I have had several thousand emails and hundreds of phone calls. Many were those asking questions, but there were also those who were telling me how they had lost their disease symptoms from Lupus, Diabetes, Hepatitis A, B, and C, AIDS, Cancer, and many other diseases. In Hermosillo my Mexican school teacher partner, Clara Beltrones, has treated about 100 people in her home, many while I was present. To give you an example, last night (this is 12/14/07) a man called and brought his wife by after hearing a local radio talk show. She came in with a standard walker that you push along, but she could not hold on to the walker so he had to hold her hand on the walker. Her right hand and foot was both paralyzed. She had trouble walking on the foot. She complained that her sciatica was giving her much pain. Clara gave her a 6 drops dose one and had her wait one hour while they discussed things. The lady notice the pain going away in her sciatica in the first hour and that feeling was coming back in her hand. After the second 6 drops dose one hour later she noticed feelings coming to her foot. Soon she was moving her fingers and her toes. Before she left she had regained full movement of her hand and her foot. She could move all her toes and the other muscles in her foot. She left, still using the walker, but she did not need help from her husband, and it was obvious that she would soon be walking without the walker as she got a little more used to her new mobility.

I don't mean to say that everyone is instantly healed. Many work with it a lot longer and sometimes there are other things involved with problems other than diseases. Within one year of arriving in Mexico I had sold more than 8,000 books *The Miracle Mineral Supplement of the 21st Century,* and more than 11,000 5.5 ounce bottles of MMS were being sold in the US each month.

It's going to be up to the scientists to prove or disprove what I say here, but I see ample evidence to prove that most disease, I'd say up to 95% of all disease is caused by pathogens that can be killed. That includes 95% of all discomforts not caused by accidents. That includes 95% of all blood diseases, all cancers, and all other so called disorders of mankind. Do you see what I am saying; we are on the edge of solving most disease for mankind forever.

Hundreds of times people come to me and recently to Clara to get a bottle of MMS and they take a dose as we want to show them how to mix the drops. Within minutes their pain of 20 years is gone. Do you see? MMS has no nutritional value what-so-ever. It is a killer, only. It kills pathogens and oxidizes heavy metal poisons. It does nothing else. The only answer is that there was something that was killed as that is only what MMS can do. One might say that some heavy metals were oxidized and that can be the case, sometimes, but there have been times where the subject had first been tested for heavy metals and there were none. It really doesn't matter, does it? If the people are well, who cares?

So far thousands of people have gotten well. I have come to the conclusion that there are thousands of kinds of bacteria, viruses, molds, yeasts, parasites, fungus and other microorganisms that have no name and are not recognized. There are other organisms necessarily micro in nature many of which are pleomorphic in that they can switch back and forth from one kind of microorganism to another. Medical science has no clue about most of them, but when you kill them, the person becomes well and goes back to work or to his life. We can't say they were cured as it upsets almost everyone, including people on our side. Maybe someone can come up with a better answer as to why all these people got well, but for now no one has.

So here is a new look at diseases. People who are sick and in pain are often told that they are imagining it, or that they need it for some reason, or that it is a condition brought on by their genes, or inherited. They often spend thousands of dollars for psychiatric help, and are often even convinced that they are really making it up. Or their mother didn't love them or some such thing. However, in almost every case, pain that was supposed to be made up mentally was often gone in an hour or two or three or several weeks, after they began taking MMS.

So here is a new look at disease. Colonies of virus or bacteria may set right up against a bone and thrive on the bone creating acids that cause much pain. Or mold can gather in areas of low blood flow and grow preventing the flow of nutrients in that area and using the nutrients that do get there. A colony of viruses that live in a muscle can cause muscle pains. Or a colony of virus can from around a nerve and shut off the nerve impulses. Some colonies are worse than others. It is well known that colonies of bacteria can grow on a heart valve, why not other places? Some colonies cause arthritis and others cause diabetes and a hundred other things.

So here is another look at disease. You didn't get sick because you ate too much sugar. You didn't get sick because you ate too much white bread, or too much ice cream, or too much meat or even that you ate too much acid causing foods. All of these things can be contributing factors, and they all can feed microorganisms and thus help them thrive, but the real reason that you got sick was because microorganisms, mostly anaerobic micro-organisms, invaded areas of your body. Your body is really stronger than most people believe. Colonies grow here and there or they invaded your entire body or they invaded various organs of your body. There were and are other factors, such as you breathed too much poisonous smoke, or allowed your body to become too cold, or other such problems, but all those things result in colonies of anaerobic microorganisms starting to grow or getting worse.

Some researchers have reported that when the brains of a person who had Alzheimer's disease is investigated that they find spiroquetes, a form the microorganism that is often considered pleomorphic (they morph into various other viruses or microorganisms). Don't ask me about Alzheimer's. No one has called saying that he has treated a person with Alzheimer's or has treated himself for Alzheimer's. I have had emails asking about it, but none doing it. Just about everything else has been treated and someone has called to mention it, but not Alzheimer's.

As I have stated before, I'm an inventor, not a doctor nor a scientist, however, I have been a research engineer. I set up tests for an A-bomb, worked on intercontinental A-bomb and H-bomb missiles, worked with the first vacuum tube computers, and developed new technology concerning the recovery of gold. Again, this is not to brag but just to mention that I am not totally scientifically illiterate. Thus I can make the statements here and then there will be those who want to either prove me wrong, or those who want to prove me right. I am sure that there will be people who will be checking to prove one way or the other because there are those who have already begun to investigate my suggestions.

It is my suggestion that we have turned the corner into a new age where there is no such thing as an incurable disease. The death knoll for the drug companies has already been rung. Medical doctors will be needed to set bones, improve breasts, do plastic surgery, and various other physical body related things. Alternate medicine practitioners will work mainly with nutrition to improve health, but they will be little concerned with overcoming diseases. Imagine for a minute, if you will, a world populated with healthy people, where there is extremely little disease. It can be a reality in your lifetime if you pitch in and help a little. Hundreds of millions of dollars of research are needed for research with MMS, but we are closing in on it.

Many people are already very successfully with treating their selves. Just see that this book gets out to as many people as you can, and see that as many people get and try a bottle of MMS as possible. If the person next door cannot afford a bottle, well buy him one yourself. Do your part and we will arrive. That is all that the world needs at this point is a bit of help from you, the reader of this book. The world may never meet you, but it won't happen without your help, and the day will come that you will know that you really helped. You will know that you did your part to stop the drug companies and help those less fortunate overcome their diseases.

Now that you have looked at the good part let me tell you about the bad part. In other words, I've got good news and I've got bad news, and I mean really bad news. I wanted to tell you the good part first as I don't like to be a doomsayer. Let me tell you the situation on Earth is worse than 99.999% of the population understands. I have people call me from all over the world. I have thousands of Emails. I have talked to hundreds of people.

So what have I found? Well, you won't like it. And you will think I'm
crazy, but I've got to say it as I could not live with myself if I didn't.
And I'd really rather not mention it as there are enough people who think
I'm nuts already, but I've got to if only to get some people to thinking.
It's this: **Our leaders are trying to kill us.** I talk to medical doctors, to
clinics, to health professionals, and to sick people every day. I doubt that
anyone else talks to more than me from across section of the health
industry from across section of the world. What I have found is this.

There are many new diseases out there. These diseases are not natural
diseases. There are dozens if not hundreds of new diseases. All of the
natural diseases like flu, TB, pneumonia, diabetes, malaria and the
others, MMS handles in a very short time. The recently created diseases
are much harder to handle as they seem to have a certain ability to hide
in the body when antibodies or oxidation chemicals are present. All
these new diseases are traceable back to laboratories of the Government.
None came from monkeys. Our leaders refuse to do anything to stop it
when informed.

There is no way that I can tell you the whole story in a few paragraphs.
There is mercury in vaccinations, chemotherapy simply kills people
nothing more, foods are poisoned with Aspartame, modern medicine has
killed and is killing more people than all the wars put together, and the
America public isn't as dumb as some people think. More than 55% of
the public has quit going to their family medical doctor and has opted for
alternate medical techniques. There must be a reason for that. People
don't just quit going to someone who is keeping them well.

Millions and millions of people are sick from diseases that the
government doesn't even recognize. Morgallens disease is only one of a
series of terrible diseases that millions now have that the government
doesn't recognize. Lyme has been a disease not recognized by medicine
and only now by a few doctors yet millions have the lyme disease in the
world. There are dozens of others. The World Health Organization
(WHO) refuse to go any further than one doctor even after they were told
of 75,000 victims cured of malaria. Their doctor claimed he tested it, but
that makes no sense. He was in Switzerland. No malaria there. People
are well in 4 hours. Testing can be done in one day. Yet it took him a

year and a half to get around to testing it, and then after 3 days he said it wouldn't work.   Once a doctor understands the chemical formula of MMS, he usually will agree that it has merit.   It is so obvious that few doctors have to even test it before agreeing that at least it should work.

For you religious Christian people, be aware, the Bible tells that in the last days the Earth will be deluged with disease and sickness.   I don't believe in the Bible as religious people do, but there are some things there that make one think.   Lyme disease comes from many other places than just ticks.   You can get it from sex, from eating certain meat, even from certain supplies of water.   There are those who want to kill the human race.   They have been working at it for a lot longer than you would believe if I told you.   It's not an easy job, killing the human race, but they have been at it for a god-awful long time. I'm here, right now, watching it every day.

No one is sure where morgallens disease comes from, but hundreds of thousands of people have it, probably millions.   There are those who think that it traces to the chem trails in the sky.   But we don't know. Millions and millions of dollars are being spent on those chem trails.   I know, if you are normal, you are going to tell me those chem trails are just commercial airplanes flying by, and the morgallens disease is nothing more than psychological, and the lyme disease is cured by the family doctor.   And then you will tell me that the reason that we have not improved in the treatment of cancer for over 100 years is because all of the research has found nothing better than surgery and the poison of chemo or radiation.   And if you tell me that then it will never have occurred to you that science should have an answer.

About the chem Trails in the sky: Friends of mine have been in an airplane in the sky right next to a cargo plane that was dumping thousands of pounds of powdered chemicals out the rear.   Don't tell me they don't exist, because they do.   To many people have seen the evidence.

Then, of course, there is AIDS and the millions of people dying from AIDS.   Did you know that in the US, more people died for hepatitis C than AIDS?   And many die from AIDS.   The point is the public trustingly goes on dying like flies with it never occurring to the majority that anything is wrong. There are dozens of diseases that you have never heard of and I only hear of now and then, but thousands are either killed by them or disabled by them. Many call me in terrible pain or suffering asking if MMS will help or if I know a way to use MMS more effectively. It breaks my heart every time. We should have a hundred million dollars to work with this to find the answers. But we have nothing, still we are getting more data each day and I believe we will have the answers to all of these government generated diseases within a reasonable time, hopefully less than a year. You can help, just keep telling people and getting them to buy this book. Thanks for your support.

Chapter 10

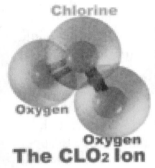

Chlorine

Oxygen

Oxygen

The CLO₂ Ion

Curing Diseases

Now that I have said that to get your attention, it really is the body that cures the disease and that heals any damage to the body. I do not suggest that the MMS cures diseases. It just supplies the immune system with a killer that it can use. When using the MMS the immune system probably becomes more than 100 times more efficient.

(Please note: Some of the basic concepts are repeated a number of times in this book. The reason for this is that people have a tendency to look up the instructions or concepts and then they want to go and use what they have read. They may not have read the whole book. In fact, they usually have not. In that case, hopefully the data has been repeated enough that they will get the essence of the idea. But please read the whole book.)

All MMS used in Africa has been bottled in these 4 ounce green bottles.

PLEASE NOTE: This chapter has been rewritten for the third edition of this book. Mistakes have been corrected and data has been updated as we have learned new things from the thousands of people reporting. Please consider this chapter as the latest data and if there is any conflict between this book and earlier books this book should take preference. Mostly, only minor mistakes have been corrected, however the Standard Protocol, the Cancer Protocol, and the Protocol for flu, colds, pneumonia and other general diseases added at the end of this chapter are important.

About the size of drops: Drops dropped from different size droppers are different in size. The larger the end of the dropper, the larger the drop will be. I refer in all cases to the standard MMS bottle and cap shown in this book (a four ounce green bottle is used). A "standard" eye dropper will create drops 2/3 the size of the drops that drop from the standard MMS bottle. If you are using a standard glass eye dropper that comes down to a point as shown below, you should multiply the number of drops given in all the recipes in this book by 1.5. Again, I stipulate, anywhere the drops are mentioned in this book, multiply the number by 1.5 if you are using the standard eye dropper. (See the pictures below.) When using the bottle dropper cap shown below, use the exact same number of drops that is suggested in the recipes of this book. Avoid using other droppers than these two mentioned here, to prevent getting the wrong amount of solution.

In case the world has stopped using bottle dropper caps as shown below, the dropper end size in this cap is .180" X .180" square. The dropper end size of the Standard Eye Dropper is round and .125" in diameter. All amounts of MMS given in the various receipts are approximate. For those who are more scientifically inclined, 17 drops from the bottle cap equals one milliliter (that's one CC). It takes about 25 drops from the standard eyedropper to equal one milliliter. Water is not the same weight as MMS so don't go astray with various other numbers concerning drops. MMS is 20% heavier than water and that changes the size of drops and the number of the drops for one ml.

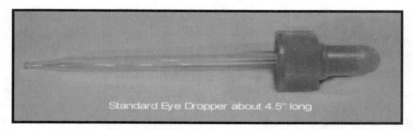

Standard Eye Dropper about 4.5" long

1 Figure 1 when using drops from a standard eye dropper always multiply the number of drops suggested in the book by 1.5.

2 Figure 2 when using drops from this bottle cap use the same number of drops suggested in this book. Buy at   www.sks-bottle.com Stock# 2500-02 Size 20/410 Cap Code C

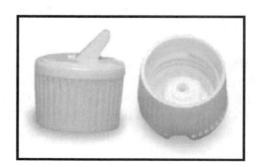

<u>Drops in a Teaspoon</u>: A level teaspoon of lemon juice or 10% citric acid solution is about 80 drops. So a quarter teaspoon is 20 drops. A little too much lemon juice or citric acid makes no difference at all. Just don't get too little or you get poor results. On the other hand, a little too much MMS can make you sick so always count the drops for MMS.

How to Use MMS For Personal Health: *MMS can change the health of your mouth in one week. The health of your mouth is the most important thing to first address with MMS, because the health of your mouth affects the health of your entire body. So when you begin to take MMS also make sure your treat your mouth. After seeing thousands of people getting better after taking MMS, the ones that do the best are the ones that make their mouth healthy. MMS works fast.*

Use 10 drops of MMS in a glass and add 50 drops of lemon, or lime juice, or 10% citric acid solution in the same glass. As usual swirl the mixture, wait 3 minutes and then add about ¼ glass of water. Use this solution to brush the teeth. You can use the same solution the brush your teeth and gums two or three times a day when you are first starting. Be sure to brush your gums. Use a new solution every morning. The MMS will brighten and strengthen the enamel on your teeth. What really happens is that the MMS kills the virus on the enamel that ordinarily does the damage

<u>Abscessed teeth, infected gums, and pyorrhea</u>: Expect the pain of an abscessed tooth to be overcome by the immune system in about four hours. Expect all infection and all pyorrhea to be gone in one week. Expect all loose teeth to be rock solid in two weeks. Expect a completely healthy mouth in less than three weeks. Keep in mind that the MMS solution is the most powerful killer of pathogens known. Once the pyorrhea and infections are killed, the mouth can heal very quickly. Finally you will need to use MMS only two or three times a week and actually you could even get away with brushing only two or three times a week.

There are exceptions, of course. In the case of an abscessed tooth where the abscess is inside the tooth and the MMS cannot reach it through a hole or some other way, the MMS will not then handle the abscess. It will have to be pulled. Also you need to get rid of all the metal in your mouth. With metal in your mouth you are creating voltages and current that can be read on any volt meter. It's ruining your health. I've seen people who regained their sight merely by replacing the metal in their mouth.

As far as treating diseases is concerned, <u>15 drops are a standard dose</u>. That of course means, that you also add one teaspoon of lime juice, or lemon juice and the 15 drops (from the cap in Figure 2 above) in a clean dry glass. (A teaspoon is 80 drops.) Then swirl the glass to mix the juice and drops and then you wait three minutes. After three minutes you add about 1/3 glass of water or fresh apple, grape, cranberry, or pineapple juice and then drink immediately. Without the vinegar, or lime juice, or lemon juice it will not work. Although it is acceptable to add water, juice will also work if it does not have vitamin C added to it. Normally one would then give a second 15 drop dose in one hour. However, as already mentioned, 15 drops is too much to start with, thus one would start with less. But still, two doses one hour apart is often a very good idea. It seems to get better penetration. Please read this entire chapter for more data. Please read the protocols (how to use) at the end of this chapter.

<u>There is a problem with a 15 drop dose</u>. If the person taking such a dose is not fairly healthy, it will have a tendency to cause nausea. The immune system attacks unhealthy conditions using the MMS. There has never been any evidence of an attack on healthy cells. But if one supplies the immune system with excessive MMS, the immune system appears to attack unhealthy conditions vigorously. It's what the body needs, but a nauseous reaction sometimes occurs, occasionally even vomiting. When this does occur, one has simply taken a large dose at first. When you kill a lot of bacteria, virus or parasites that have poison in them, that poison is likely to be dumped into the system. For this reason it is advisable to give a dose of two drops or even one for the first dose just to see what is going to happen.

When giving two drop doses or any dose, one should use 5 drops of vinegar, lime juice or citric acid solution for each drop of MMS. Or read further in this chapter to learn about using citric acid instead of vinegar or lime. Situations vary; the healthier a person is the more drops he or she can start with. When a person is very sick, start with two drops or even one drop and go to the second drop immediately if the first drop didn't make him nauseous. Wait a couple of hours and increase by one drop. Back off for a while if he shows signs of being sicker. A very sick person should receive a dose of some strength every four hours during the day and in some cases every hour, but very small doses. Almost always the sick person will begin to feel better within 24 hours. If the MMS is used by the immune system to break loose some poisons that can then make a person a little nauseous. Just don't give up. Reduce the number of drops per dose to a point where the person is not experiencing nausea. Start increasing the drops at each dose as long as the person does not become nauseous. Keep at it until you have reached 15 drop doses that do not make the person nauseous. Then do two 15 drop doses within two hours. Do that a second time during the day. Keep doing the same each day until the person is well. Normally a person will be well by the time he has increased doses to 15 drops, but if not keep at it.

Larger than 15 drop doses: As already mentioned, if 15 drops is good, so maybe 45 drops is three times as good. Normally don't go that far. In extreme cases maybe try a couple of 25 drop doses within two hours of each other. The fact is I have had reports back from people who, when they did not get the results they wanted, resorted to as much as two 25 drops within 2 hours. In that case they were careful to use 1.5 teaspoons of lemon or lime or 10% citric acid solution. The wait is three minutes or slightly longer. Never, never, never start off with 25 drops. In fact, only in extreme cases go to more than 15 drop doses. The two doses within two hours counts as a very large dose. Be careful. See later in this chapter for how to mix the citric acid solution.

However, I should report also that there have been a few cases that have reported curing prostate cancer by taking as much as 60 drop doses. At least one other person has reported taking 100 drops a day for over a week.

Exception to the rule: One would only start off with a large dose such as 15 drops in the case of parasites. If one had taken a poison or has food poisoning, a good dose of MMS will often help.

My friend next door caught some kind of a walking around flu. His throat was sore and he was continuously coughing and hacking. It went on for three weeks and didn't let up. He then began taking the MMS. He took 15 drop doses for several days with no change. Then out of desperation he squirted in a 30 drop dose. He added a teaspoon of vinegar, waited the three minutes, added the apple juice and downed it. The next day the hacking and coughing was gone. He took a second 30 drop dose and the next day the rest of the symptoms were gone. Later just for research, he tried several doses larger than 30 drops, but he noticed a metallic taste in his mouth the rest of the day, so he decided never to go over 30 drops. I am saying, however, never go over 15 drops unless you absolutely have to.

Normally, lately, I suggest lemon, lime or 10% citric acid solution instead of vinegar. All other factors should remain the same. I have found that many people prefer lime or lemon juice over vinegar. Anyone suspected of having Candida should not use vinegar in any amount. When counting drops, always use 5 drops of lemon or lime juice or 5 drops of the 10% citric acid juice for each drop of MMS. The vinegar has a tendency to feed Candida and there are those who have reported Candida getting worse after a few days using vinegar.

Citric Acid a recent discovery: Dr. Hesselink, the doctor who has written the last chapter of this book made an important discovery concerning citric acid. He was getting his friend ready to go to Africa to use the MMS there. He felt it would be best to give his friend bottles with the dry MMS powder (sodium chlorite) and then in Africa his friend could just add water to the bottles. He then decided to do the same with the lemon juice to be used as the activator. For this purpose he bought citric acid powder since that is the acid in lemons. Well it worked fine. His friend made a big hit and helped many sick people get well.

After the Doctor's friend returned from Africa Dr. Hesselink was sitting talking to one of his other friends who had lyme arthritis, which was an extremely bad case of lyme arthritis. He suggested his friend to mix a dose of MMS and drink the same as the one his friend had used in Africa. That was 12 drops of MMS and 60 drops of citric acid solution. He did so and amazingly the arthritis was gone the next morning but he has reported that it returned in about 6 weeks, since then he requires a dose every few weeks.

Dr. Hesselink has used MMS and citric acid to kill lyme arthritis with several other people. So I have been recommending using the lemon juice at that same strength for some time and it is also working.

Evaluation of the Citric acid incident: Obviously the citric acid works as hundreds of people have used it so far and it worked on Dr. Hesselink's friend's arthritis.

Instructions for using MMS with citric acid as the activator (instead of vinegar or lemon or lime): Obtain citric acid in powder form as citric acid crystals. Some health food stores carry them, or you can order them from a pharmacy (heaven forbid). Make a 10% solution of citric acid. To make a 10% solution put one level tablespoon full of crystals in a clean glass or jar. Then add 9 level tablespoons full of purified water into the same jar. When the crystals have dissolved this is a 10% solution. In all cases when using the citric acid as an activator, use 5 drops for each 1 drop of MMS. Do everything else the same. Wait 3 minutes after mixing, add juice and drink. Since there was some confusion about mixing the citric acid, let me clarify a bit. When you use 9 measures of water to one measure of citric acid crystals that gives you a 10% solution, but that is not a 10 to 1 mixture as some have thought. That is a 9 to 1 mixture. But that gives you 10 parts, that's 9 parts water plus 1 part acid equal's 10 parts total. It is however, a 10% solution of citric acid.

When using the citric acid as an activator be sure to keep in mind all of the other instructions concerning taking the MMS. Start with taking 2 drops of MMS and ten drops of citric acid and then work up to greater amounts, or even start with 1 drop MMS and 5 drops of citric acid.

Lyme disease: For the most part Lyme disease seems to be the worst of all so long as you are talking about diseases that are very hard to cure or that destroy the various organs of the body and is extremely disabling. In the case of Lyme no doubt the immune system needs MMS. The best results so far has been with MMS activated with the citric acid solution as given in this chapter. So far the best result has been to shock the system with a 9 or 10 drop dose on the first dose and then a 12 drop dose on the second dose. This has put the Lyme disease into remission for up to 6 weeks, but then more drops are required. But everyone realizes that remission isn't what they want, they want a cure. So if one continues with MMS I have had some reports of people who are doing very well indeed, by taking smaller doses but 3, 4 and 5 times a day.

In most cases if you are not improving, probably you are not taking enough. However, it might take as long as a year to overcome the Lyme disease. There is no proof of that yet, but the information I have received back is that everyone who has Lyme and who is taking MMS is experiencing improvement.

What time during the day is best to take MMS?
It is best to take MMS just before going to bed. MMS works very fast, and the body likes to start healing very fast. People often become sleepy after taking a dose of MMS. That simply means that the body wants to begin healing. It is well known that most healing is done during sleep. If you get sleepy after a dose of MMS it is a very good sign so take a nap if you can. You will probably feel much better when you awaken. Also, if you take it twice in a day, take one of the doses in the evening before going to bed.

However, if you feel a cold coming on in the morning or in the afternoon do not wait until bedtime to take a dose. Take a dose anytime you feel like something is trying to come on.

Children: It is perfectly safe to have children and babies take the MMS. Of course, children must have fewer drops than adults. The formula for babies is one drop at first and increase up to three drops in the same day. Of course always use the 5 drops of citric acid activator for each drop of MMS. Other than babies, use 3 drops MMS for each 25 pounds (11.4 KG) of body weight for children.

Overweight people: Start with 2 drops only for the first dose and work up to 3 drops per each 25 pounds of body weight. Follow instructions given in this chapter for "working up" to higher doses, but do work up to 3 drops for each 25 pounds of body weight. Overweight people have more trouble overcoming flu and other diseases as the pathogens hide in the fat tissues.

Malaria: The procedure for malaria is to always start with a 15 drop dose, and give a second 15 drops dose in one to two hours. (Remember, if you use a standard eye dropper; multiply these figures by 1.5 which in this case would be rounded off to 23 drops). Expect most of the symptoms to be gone within four hours of the second dose, but don't worry if the symptoms are not gone after four hours beyond the second dose, simply give a third dose. All malaria parasites are dead after the second dose. If the patient is still sick, it will not be from malaria. It will be from some other disease. In that case, continue with at least two 15 drop doses each day until they are feeling well.

Arthritis: There are some things that you should know about arthritis if you have the problem. First, it doesn't matter how bad it is, your body will heal it, but you have to follow the correct procedure. So you need to know what kind of arthritis you have as MMS will help with rheumatoid arthritis and lyme arthritis and some others, but not with normal arthritis.

Normal arthritis is caused by the muscles in the area pulling in the wrong direction. The wrong muscles are trying to take over and move the body in that area. When these muscles begin to pull against one another they create pain and tension in the area and begin to destroy the joint. You can get it back to work again. The book *Pain Free* by Pete Egoscue tells how to get the correct muscles back to work again, and the body then heals the joint no matter how bad the bones are scraping against one another. It just requires some unusual exercises to get the correct muscles back to work correctly. In most cases, even severe ones, the pain is gone in a week. So buy the book at any large book store. Paperback was $15 the last time I looked.

Most other forms of arthritis can be handled with the MMS. Just use the standard protocol at the end of this chapter.

Hepatitis A, B, and C and all other strains of Hepatitis: the patients needs 15 drops twice a day, but will not usually tolerate 15 drops. When using 15 drops immediately, the immune system attacks too hard. Start with two drops and if that does not make them nauseous try three drops on the next dose later that same day. If it does make them nauseous try one drop on the next dose that same day. Always continue with one drop until they can take it without nausea, then go to two. Most people can start out with two drops. Keep increasing the drops until the person can take 15 drops twice a day. Be careful to avoid nausea as that often makes the person afraid of the MMS and they will quit and you won't be able to get them to start again. Remember, the MMS is merely a health drink and you are merely furnishing ammunition to the immune system. A person needs to get used to this mineral drink.

Herpes: The ads on TV can make you sick when you know that herpes can be easily cured when the immune system has the proper ammunition. About a week of 15 drop doses twice a day and no more herpes. Of course, one must start with two drop doses and increase daily until he has reached 15 drop doses and then increase the 15 drop dose to twice a day for about a week. That means the herpes should be gone in about two weeks. However, in very bad cases, it might take up to two months to finally overcome the herpes.

I suggest you to use the citric acid as the activator in the case of herpes. With severe cases take the MMS every two hours for several days. When taking it every two hours one can take smaller doses. This keeps the MMS penetrating deeper and deeper. In worse cases, one may have to use the MMS intravenously. See the chapter one IV.

People like to bash the ideas I give here that these things can be cured by the immune system. So before you send me a bad letter, why don't you just try what I tell you here? It can't cost you much and what you learn might eventually save your life. If it doesn't work, then send me a nasty letter. Let me say though, that for every criticism there have been many hundreds of encouragements.

AIDS: MMS does not attack AIDS. The immune system does. It merely needs the right ammunition. As usual start with two drops but at least three times a day. Increase the drops as quickly as you can until reaching 15 drop doses three times a day. It will take from three days to three months, but usually less than 30 days. Some cases may only clear up with intravenous injections. A doctor should always do this. See the chapter on intravenous injections.

Please note: normally healthy people can take these drops without nausea, especially after a meal. Only people sick with some kind of disease will get nausea when taking the drops. However, nausea is a good indication that the drops are doing some good.

Just so you know when we first learned about the use of citric acid I measured the strength of the solution. The chlorine dioxide present measured much higher than when the vinegar or the lime or lemon juices were used. But the body seemed to tolerate it more easily and thus I decided to see what a reasonably healthy body could tolerate. I started low and built up slowly to 30 drops twice a day. I never felt any nausea or other negative reactions. Thus we know (because of the reaction from hundreds of people other than myself) that as long as there is nothing there to be killed, destroyed or neutralized one can expect no reaction from the dose.

Sometimes even sick people do not experience nausea when taking MMS, but do not be surprised when people get sick or have nausea, or diarrhea, or even vomit after taking a few drops of MMS. Try to take it or give it immediately after a meal. The MMS allows the immune system to correct various conditions in the body and this creates solutions that the body must expel during the process. This is normal however; if you always start with only two drops it is unlikely that you will make anyone nauseous.

Chlorine dioxide is more powerful than any drug by far and more powerful than any other nutrient, at least that is the case in the immune system. The immune system selects out and attacks many things that are not natural to the body and it does it immediately. On top of that, it also destroys poisons that have been generated by the disease. That's why thousands of malaria patients just got up out of their beds and went home in four hours. That's why many AIDS patients in Uganda went home in three days. The fact is a single dose has at times given the immune system enough ammunition to totally overcome hepatitis C. That's probably why it is the only thing known to overcome an abscessed tooth (when the abscess is on the outside of the tooth).

On vary rare occasions someone may have a little nausea from two drops, but that seldom will be the case. I mean rare as in one in 500 cases. But in the case of malaria and some other diseases caused by parasites, one does not start with only two drops. The malaria victim is very sick and needs relief. It takes 15 drops to do any good. So give them 15 drops and wait a little over an hour and then give them another 15 drops. They will have tremendous relief and the malaria parasite will be dead. This is also true of many other diseases caused by parasites. On the other hand, some diseases have the ability to dig in deep and it may take weeks or even months of taking the MMS for the immune system to completely destroy them. The fact is that MMS is usually extremely fast acting. The malaria in each area is different. A friend just back from Uganda used 6 drops and then another 6 drops in an hour and that cured all of the malaria he treated (70) cases.

Diarrhea and vomiting may not always be avoided. In other words, if you take MMS in any amount you may get diarrhea. Everyone does not get diarrhea, but some people need to be cleaned out. If that is true in your case, you will probably not be able to avoid diarrhea. It seems that your body knows what is needed when MMS is taken. As the immune system becomes more activated, the more things begin to take place in the body. There are things that the body does not want to allow to be processed through the digestive system, so it will cause vomiting. It hasn't hurt a single person so far and everyone has felt better after vomiting. In every case when diarrhea hits or vomiting takes place assume it is what is needed and it is a good indicator that healing is taking place.

In rare cases when the body's bowel system is not working, and one needs to eliminate he may get sick, or develop rashes on the outside of his body as the poisons are attempting to get out through the skin. In this case use a laxative. The best one that I know of that thousands use is the herb senna. Sennosides are extracted from the senna herb. They exercise the bowel muscles expelling more waste than any other way. Sold by Wal Mart.

<u>Using MMS in the eyes:</u> Follow these directions WITH EXTREME CARE, as you can cause problems to your eyes. Use one drop of MMS, 2 drops of citric acid, wait 3 minutes and add about a tablespoon of distilled water or eye drops that you buy from a drugstore. Wash your eye with the liquid from the tablespoon making sure it gets directly into your eye. Allow it to stay in for a couple of minutes. Do not try to guess 2 minutes. Use a watch with a second hand. Then use distilled water or eye drops to wash the eye until you are certain that you have washed every bit of liquid out of your eye. Do this every two hours until the infection in your eye is gone. <u>Begin taking MMS by mouth using 3 to 4 drop doses every hour until you notice a big improvement in your eyes. If you cannot put drops in your eyes, you can depend upon the doses by mouth if you do it every hour. REMEMBER: You MUST NOT allow the liquid with a drop of MMS to remain in your eye beyond 2 minutes. If you do it can be uncomfortable for a while.</u>

(I burned my eyes once. I used inactivated MMS (I didn't add any citric acid to it). I left it in my eye thinking that since I didn't feel anything it didn't have enough strength to do damage. But MMS that is not activated is very alkaline and it burned. It didn't do any noticeable damage to the eye ball, but the skin around my eyes dropped and stretched downward about an inch. I looked terrible like my eyeball might fall out and I was worried, but it cleared up in a few days.)

<u>Cancer, including leukemia:</u>   The theory here is the same. Chlorine dioxide gives the immune system almost perfect ammunition to attack cancer cells. We believe the theory has proven true as many people with cancer have told us that the cancer went away or reduced greatly after taking the MMS. However, there is not yet enough research in this area. Still, it's a lot better than standard medical treatment. People have often told us, and we have noticed that skin cancer usually dries up and drops off within one week of taking 15 drops of MMS twice a day. We do not claim that the MMS cause the effect, but we did observe the effect. Some cancers are harder to treat than others and in the case where the cancer does not start to disappear within about two weeks of starting to take 15 drops twice a day one should also get some Indian Herb from a lady in Oklahoma.

An update for this 3rd edition is that when one is working with cancer and it is not getting better and over ruling concept is that you are not taking enough MMS. Start as always with 2 drops in the morning and go to 3 drops in the afternoon. Then 4 drops the next morning then begin taking it every 4 hours, then every 2 hours. Keep increasing the dosage and frequency of taking the doses. Anytime you begin to notice nausea, decrease the number of drops in the doses. Then begin increasing the number of drops right away again. You could get up to 10 drops every 2 hours while awake. Also remember, you must always activate with vinegar, or lemon, or citric acid solution, and of course, use the 3 minute wait before adding juice or water to drink it. I favor the citric acid, using 5X the number of MMS drops. The secret is more drops and keep at it until the cancer is gone. Find some way of checking to see if it is getting better.

There are a lot of people who say that after taking the Indian Herb that their cancer went away, but again we do not claim that. She has many letters that indicate that. We merely report what people have said. The information on where to get the Indian Herb is at the end of this chapter.

Do not hesitate to go to at least 30 drops twice a day of the MMS, or 15 drops four times a day when necessary, or more. Just keep taking less if you notice nausea, but then continue to increase when the nausea go away.

As I write these lines, my friend next door has just overcome a small melanoma cancer on his arm. I mentioned that he was taking larger doses at 25 drops per dose. (I do not necessarily recommend doses that high, but do what works). In any case he had already checked with his doctor to confirm it was actually a melanoma. After only a week of taking the MMS the melanoma begin to have a white ring around it and it then it became smaller and smaller until after about two weeks it was gone. That is, at least we could not see it anymore and there was no longer any sore feeling.

On a small cancerous sore on the back of my hand that would not go away for over a year, I put one drop of MMS mixed with 3 drops of lemon juice, and as usual waited 3 minutes and then added 2 drops of

DMSO. It immediately felt like someone had put a blow torch on my hand. But the pain was gone in 3 minutes. A large brown spot appeared much larger than the small sore. I put Vaseline and a bandage on it and in 2 days the entire brown spot fell off leaving a large gaping hole. I put more Vaseline on it and another bandage and in 4 days it healed completely up and did not even leave a scar. (Note: I have removed the warning about DMSO from this book as there seems to be no problem with it.) I would say, in this case, that the DMSO carried the MMS deep into the cancerous sore, killing it in three minutes and when the pain stopped it was dead. It is not my suggestion that anyone try this. (Let me know if you do.)

Note: There are three protocols at the end of this chapter, one for cancer, one is a standard protocol, and one is for flu, colds, pneumonia, and other normal home sicknesses.

Asthma: MMS has often stopped an asthma attack in 10 minutes or less, but it doesn't work every time. MMS works best with asthma over a longer period of time. It depends upon the condition of the asthma whether or not it stops an attack instantly or how long it takes to cure a condition of asthma. MMS will always help, but if a person is "beyond repair," then MMS will not do the job. However, over a period of time it will often cure the asthma.

One lady called up and asked if MMS would help asthma. I said that I thought it would. She began taking MMS and her asthma got worse. She called me and I said, "Sometimes it can get worse before it gets better, but don't stop." Well, believe it or not, she continued taking the MMS for 1.5 months with it remaining in a worse condition, but she kept the faith. She continued and refused to stop. And then it began to get better. It continued to get better until it was completely gone. The entire time only took 2 months. I don't know what to say about that kind of faith, but it worked.

Start with two drops twice a day for the first day, taking the drops after a meal. If the person gets nauseous he will often stop taking the solution and refuse to take more so be careful to avoid making someone nauseous. In any case, work up to 15 drops twice a day. It may take months before one can do this without being nauseous. This is because the MMS is slowly destroying something and is bringing about detoxification of the body. (That's what I think, but the fact is I have watched many people get well from various diseases and they usually are well and feeling energetic when the drops are no longer causing nausea.) Asthma is not easy to clear up, but it has cleared up in those who kept with it.

Arteriosclerosis: I guess there are many causes for hardening and clogging the arteries of the body, but cholesterol seems to be one of the best known reasons. Several people have reported to date that taking the MMS reduced the clogging of the arteries due to cholesterol. One lady called to say that she was in very bad shape. They had told her that her veins were 80% clogged. They couldn't say how much worse because they couldn't measure any more than that. She took large doses of 15 drops, three times a day, for 30 days and when they measured again; the clogging was less than 50%. That is a tremendous change in 30 days. That's not much to go on, but it gives you an idea. Remember, we are just talking about a supplement. Also remember that 975,000 people die each year from medical drug causes. No one is dead from MMS.

There is a great deal of evidence to indicate that cholesterol deposits in the arteries veins around the heart are not the cause of heart attacks. The evidence points out that the walls of these vessels, about 10 inches on the heart, are collapsed 70 to 80 times every minute with each beat of the heart for our entire lives. The walls of these vessels are strengthened by vitamin C and with a deficiency in vitamin C they lose their strength. When the vessel walls crack they remain collapsed and this is when the heart attack happens. The cholesterol that medical people say is clogging the veins has really been deposited there to compensate for the deficiency in vitamin C. It is the body's secondary defense to prevent collapsed walls of the arteries and veins. Take 6 to 10 grams of vitamin C daily. Reduce the amount if you get diarrhea. Dr. Matthias Rath researched this data. Get his book, *Why Animals do not have Heart Attacks*. Check the Internet. The proof has been established as well as it can be, certainly a hundred times better than the idea that cholesterol drugs will make you less likely to have a heart attack.

A number of people have reported lowering their clogged arteries. No reports of bad results from this. The body may be able to heal the arteries as fast as the cholesterol is removed.

My opinion in this case would be to take a lot of vitamin C for a few weeks before using the MMS to clean out the cholesterol. Make sure the walls of the blood vessels are strong before removing the cholesterol. Read Dr. Matthias Rath's books. A rare few people (2) have called to say that after starting MMS they notice heavy heart palpitations. Later they called back to say that the palpitations were gone. Who knows what caused that, but in my opinion if the bacteria that sometimes grows on the heart valve were to be killed it would probably cause palpitations for a while.

All known diseases and negative medical conditions: I have not listed a great number of diseases which can be handled by the immune system in hours, days, or only a week or two, as there are so many. The MMS will probably help the immune system do its job no matter what the disease. Diseases that are not caused by viruses, bacteria, and other various germs may not be attacked directly by the MMS, but the benefit may come indirectly. Almost any disease generates various poisons which in turn cause the body to be sick. When the immune system has chlorine dioxide which, of course, is furnished by the MMS it can often neutralize such poisons. Never assume that MMS will not improve the immune system no matter how weak of a condition the immune system might be in or no matter what disease may be present in the body.

Take MMS daily or twice a week to keep the body clean of most poisons and disease causing organisms.

Diseases that the immune system cannot help directly: The immune system can use the MMS to attack diseases caused by bacteria, viruses, parasites, fungus, yeast and molds, but many diseases are caused by other medical conditions. Maybe this is the case, but since the first edition hundreds of people have reported almost every medical condition known as having been improved. Examples of diseases that do not respond to MMS are, well, maybe NONE. Some diseases need to be handled by the proper diet. The immune system, when supplied with

MMS, almost always produces some improvement in these diseases and their associated conditions.

Everyone who has reported having lupus and also reported taking the MMS has also reported feeling back to normal. Much diabetes that has reported taking the MMS has also reported doing better, and most have reported all symptoms gone. Even those with depression have reported feeling better. One child with ADD has reported all symptoms were gone in two weeks.

There is much benefit from improving the immune system as these diseases often cause weakened conditions and weaken the immune system as well. Bacteria and virus have a tendency to attack in weakened areas of the body. Pneumonia, for example, is more likely to attack when the body is weakened. With MMS the immune system can fight back and often overcome the infections or other conditions that have been caused by the weakened condition. This can in turn help other diseases to clear up.

For those people who would like to overcome any bad condition not caused by bacteria or viruses, the book *Eat to Live* by Joel Fuhrman, M. D. can give you many important insights into the causes of such conditions and how to overcome them.

Remember, chlorine dioxide is the most powerful killer of pathogens known to man. When used by the immune system, it is still the most powerful killer of pathogens and the most powerful detoxifier known. Two days of supplying the immune system with 22 drops a day of MMS can be as effective as 35 intravenous chelating drip treatments and more. (MMS can also be used intravenously either with drip or direct injection, see Chapter 13. I would suggest that chelating clinics use MMS with IV's as they can then be of real benefit.) MMS is not a chelating solution. MMS is or to be more correct, the chlorine dioxide generated by MMS is an oxidizer. It oxidizes the heavy metals and poisons instead of chelating them.

I say all this with only the best intention. I have plenty of axes to grind, but I do not do this for any other reason than mankind must have this amazing Miracle Mineral Supplement. I am not selling anything. (Well maybe this book, but any profit will go towards helping the people of Africa overcome the diseases there.) I tell everyone exactly how to make MMS in their own kitchen. I even suggest places that you can buy the chemical and I give complete details for you to make it. My only intention is to see that mankind gets the discovery. It is too important for me to have any other agenda. You can even make it and sell it on the Internet or to your neighbors. But more important, you can make it and save lives. Just follow the directions here and give it to anyone who has some terrible disease. You can be of help to many, many people. Look around you, there are always those who need it. You can help old people with their health problems and young people, too. If you sell it on the Internet, just don't make any claims. If you give it to someone and they get well, you can tell that story on the Internet.

I have from time to time been accused of treating diseases without a license. Some doctors have climbed on their high horse and said that I was putting lives at risk. I have always answered that they have one hell of a nerve being critical of simply giving a mineral solution that is not a drug. Any medical doctor is to some extent a part of the medical system. They either approve of Big PHARMA or they go along with them. Each year in the United States more than 975,000 people die of medical drug causes. More people die from that than any other cause of death. That's 975,000 deaths that should not have occurred.

When I mention medical drug causes I am talking about those who died because they were given the wrong drug in the hospital or a clinic. Others were given an overdose or those who had an ADR (adverse drug reaction). There were also others who had a drug taken away too quickly, or who died from drug side effects (many). Why do you think that when they advertise a drug on TV that they required to mention the drug's side effects. One of the things that they say is, "Serious or fatal reactions have occurred."

The fact is that the majority of drug deaths could have been prevented. Yet it continues year after year while the government agency (the FDA) will spend millions stopping a health food item that might have caused one death. Drugs make money for the drug companies and for doctors.

They (Medical people) feel that they must attack any item that might take the place of a drug and reduce their income.

The government statistics agency has provided the causes of death in their statistics, giving 699,697 for heart disease and 553,251 a year for cancer. They do not mention one single death caused by medical prescription drugs and their statistical research shows none. When a person with cancer dies from being given the wrong drug, the government simply reports it as a cancer death. The drug death is included in the report, but not in the government statistics. Gary Null PhD who researched much of the report "Death by Medicine" was able to dig out the true statistics because the data is available and it cannot be suppressed. Refer to the references given at the end of this chapter.

The people in the USA are spending billions of dollars on medical treatments and we could have the best medical treatment on the planet, but it has not even come close. And then there are those doctors who are so scared they will lose revenue that they feel that they must attack the MMS.

So let me say this. Since we are not talking about a drug, why attack it or me? Why not take a day or two and check it out? Try it. See if it works. It's simple. Does it work or doesn't it? Don't take my word, or someone else's word, try it yourself. As I mentioned previously, the entire country of Haiti would now be malaria free if medical doctors had not put a stop to our work there.

Warnings: (1) Do not allow children to use MMS unsupervised. (2) Do not allow MMS to set in direct sunlight even if it is in a colored bottle as it will create pressure in the container which could rupture and cause severe burns. MMS that has set in direct sunlight can cause very painful burns. (3) Never allow full strength MMS to remain on your skin for more than 20 seconds as it can cause mild burns.

In the case of a brown recluse spider bite, use only diaper rash ointment (Desitin) or other diaper rash ointment containing at least 40% zinc oxide. I mention this as some people have tried to use MMS for brown recluse spider bites and it had very little effect on the poison. Desitin contains 40% zinc oxide. It will kill most of the poison and reduce the pain and itching of a brown recluse spider bite in less than one day. I say this after seeing dozens of people treat their bite with this diaper rash ointment.

Black Widow bites: As long as we are talking about spider bites let me mention a remedy for Black Widow bites. Slice open a stem of freshly cut Aloe Vera leaf and put the open slice part against the bite. Use a piece about two inches by two inches. Then tape the Aloe Vera leaf over the bite with tape holding it tight against the bite and excluding most of the air. Leave it for at least 12 hours before putting a fresh piece on the bite. Most or all of the bite poison will be gone in 12 hours.

Insect bites, mosquitoes and other bugs not particularly poisonous but irritating. A really heavy mosquito bite can be very uncomfortable for several hours. Use MMS as if you were going to drink it. Put 10 drops in a glass and add a full teaspoon of citric acid. Wait three minutes; then put the solution full strength (just the drops and vinegar) directly on the bite. Rub it in with the tips of your fingers. The itching from the bite will be gone in about 5 minutes and the bump will begin to diminish immediately.

You do not need to wash this solution off. Once you have added the vinegar to the MMS you have negated its ability to burn your skin. Once vinegar has been added the alkalinity of the solution has been destroyed. However, when using the solution in larger areas of the body than a small insect bite always add about 1/2 cup of water to the 10-drop solution that you make mix.

Using MMS on the Outside of the Body: Please read this carefully. It is possible to cause problems on the outside of the body when using MMS in too strong of a solution. When adding six to ten drops in a glass with ½ teaspoon of citric acid solution with the exception of insect bites in a small area of the body, always add over ½ glass of water before putting on the outside of the body or in the hair. Never add the 10 drops mixture to any kind of body lotion. When the MMS solution is too strong on the outside of the body, it can weaken the cells and make them more susceptible to bacteria and infection. On the other hand, when used in a weak enough solution, like adding the ½ glass of water, it can help a great deal. For jock itch and that sort of thing, after applying some body lotion then spread the solution of MMS from the ½ glass of water with your finger tips.

Sores on the head: Follow the instructions for the insect bites above, but be sure to add ½ glass of water to the 10-drop solution of MMS citric acid or lemon juice. When combed into the hair with enough solution to penetrate to the scalp it will cure most head sores in a few hours. If you use it daily it will make a healthy scalp, but it also makes you a blond. In other words once or twice a month is okay, but when used daily you begin to notice that your hair is bleaching blond after a few days. (It is a very nice blond.) However if you rinse it out in 2 to 5 minutes it will not bleach at all and it will keep your scalp very healthy.

Prevention: Information has already been presented that MMS improves the immune system. The fact is that the MMS is a super preventative for almost any disease known. It's my opinion, after observing hundreds of people taking MMS; it will prevent most cancer, including breast cancer. But not just cancer, any disease that the immune system can attack can be prevented or aided in prevention by supercharging the immune system with MMS.

I would appreciate email letters from anyone noticing information concerning all aspect of the MMS, either pro or con. Note: If you cannot afford health insurance, you definitely should be taking MMS every day.

When your problem doesn't clear up right away: Many people call and say, "I've been taking 12 drops twice a day for weeks, but when I go to 14 drops I have diarrhea badly." I always reply that chlorine dioxide is the strongest oxidizer known. And that is all it is. It only oxidizes and nothing else. So if your body has a lot of unhealthy gunk deposited in critical areas that is making you sick, or if it has poisons such as heavy metals deposited, or if there is a heavy load of bacteria growing somewhere, or any other unhealthy condition it will continue to work on that stuff day after day. After all, you are only using a few drops each day, and those few drops only contain a couple of milligrams of chlorine dioxide. You may have thousands of times more stuff that needs to be oxidized than a few drops can handle, but it is working on it. And the fact that you get sick or have diarrhea when you take a heavier dose proves that it is oxidizing the stuff and your body can only throw off a certain amount each day. If you give it more to throw off than it can do without getting violent, then it will get violent. Just keep the dose up just under the nausea level. You will finally get there, but know that it is working as long as it makes you sick when you take too much. When it quits making you sick, you will be well. Some diseases allow much heavier loads of bacteria and virus. It can take a while. Don't get discouraged, keep at it.

Bird Flu, Pandemic and other Mass Hysteria: For over 100 years chlorine dioxide has been used to sterilize hospital floors, benches, and equipment, and to purify water, and for sterilizing meat. During that time no pathogen has ever developed any kind of a successful resistance to chlorine dioxide. Due to the nature of chlorine dioxide it is doubtful that any pathogen ever will. Several doctors have mentioned that the very nature of microorganisms' structure eliminates the possibility of ever developing a resistance to the oxidizing powers of chlorine dioxide. It's like trying to develop a resistance to hand grenades or dynamite. The explosion is too violent to resist. It is doubtful that any of these new mass hysteria or germ warfare diseases will be able to resist chlorine dioxide, that is to say, MMS. Chlorine dioxide was used to kill Anthrax during the 2001 Anthrax attack. Now anyone can use it in the body as well. Be sure to keep some present in your medicine cabinet.

One other point, you can bet that the pharmaceutical companies will soon find an inoculation for bird flu. They will then want to inoculate everyone in the world, especially in the U.S. They will say they want to save us, but all they really want is to make billions of dollars.

Diabetes, ALS, and many other diseases of which they claim they don't know the cause: There are a number of viruses that might be considered exotic. They really aren't, but unless you are a doctor you won't hear much about them, but you should, because they are abundantly present. The Coxsackie B virus, according to much of the present medical literature, causes up to 1/3 of the heart attacks. It causes the heart to become inflamed. The heart doesn't work very well when inflamed. It is also reported that this virus causes the pancreas to become inflamed thus causing type 1 and type 2 diabetes. When MMS is taken it has a tendency to lend the immune system some ammunition. Killing the Coxsackie B could cause the heart to palpitate for a short while. Go slow and take small doses.

Then for ALS (Lou Gehrig disease) there is medical literature indicating the echo virus – 6 and – 7 is most likely the cause. If that is so, then there is a chance that MMS can help cases of ALS. In which cases I would start at one or two drops every two hours and increase the number of drops up to 6 to 8 drops every two hours for as long as one is awake and up out of bed using, of course, the citric acid activator and three minute wait before adding the juice or water and drinking the solution. The idea is to keep the body as saturated as possible with the chlorine dioxide. Of course there is no guarantee, but up to this time there has never been even a slight glimmer of hope. If you are diagnosed with ALS you have 2 to 5 years and that's all. They had stuff that they claimed slowed it down a bit, and of course, they got a lot of money for it, but there never was any real data indicating the ALS was slowed down. Trying MMS just may work. Nothing else does. So it's worth a try.

Curing diseases with drugs. Can it be done? No. The only thing that ever heals the body is the various mechanisms of the body. Healing is controlled by the body. NO drug or no nutrient can heal the body. NOT ONE! There are things that the body can use to aid in the healing, but in the final analysis, the body always does the healing. Drugs occasionally help the process, but normally the body needs nutrients instead of poisons, which all drugs are to a greater or lesser extent. MMS is the same. It cannot heal or cure the body of anything. It may or may not kill pathogens in the body without the body's control. However, once the germs or pathogens or poisons are destroyed, healing can take place at a much faster rate. This is why healing in so many parts of the body seems to happen so much quicker. It is not that the MMS has healed anything. It cannot. But it can clear the way for healing to take place.

<u>Overcoming cancer and many other terrible diseases.</u> <u>Be sure to read</u> <u>this paragraph</u>. MMS seems to be effective against most diseases, but some diseases require much more MMS than others. Normally the answer is if you are not getting improvement, take more MMS. This means that you should start off with 2 drops, using the lime or vinegar or citric acid and the 3 minute wait as always then add juice or water and drink. Continue to increase the number of drops twice a day, if you can. Go to 3 drops, then 4 drops, then 6 drops and so on until you reach 15. Stay at 15 drops a day for several days, and then do it twice a day. Then, if you do not notice improvements increase the number of drops. Always reduce the number of drops if you feel nausea, but continue to increase the number of drops, keeping below the nausea level as much as you can. Increase up to 20, or 25, or even as much as 30 drops twice a day, for a serious condition.

Be very careful. If you feel nausea, reduce the number of drops. Do not remain at high, 20-30 drop levels unless you really see an improvement in the condition you are trying to handle. When the condition is overcome, be sure to drop back to only 6 drops a day for maintenance.

However, if you do get nausea, vomiting or diarrhea do not be worried. Many times the body needs to get rid of something. Many times a health expert or doctor may advise you that you need to get yourself cleaned out. Well, if you need it, the MMS is going to do it. It's not a bad sign.

<u>Antidote for too much MMS:</u> For someone who has taken a large dose of MMS and is then nauseous, it is possible to drink a glass of cold water which may handle the nausea. If not handled add 1000 to even 5000 MG of vitamin C. Bicarbonate of soda also acts as an antidote. Use a level teaspoon full of bicarbonate or take an Alka-Seltzer tablet in a glass of water. If you us the vitamin C do not use the bicarbonate of soda or Alka-Seltzer. Use either one but not both.

<u>Overdose of sodium chlorite:</u> Anyone who has consumed more than ½ teaspoon of the miracle mineral should immediately begin drinking water, as much as possible. It is possible to drink as much as several tablespoons of MMS right straight from the bottle, but this would make one very sick. If this occurs begin to drink as much water as possible. It

is best to add ½ teaspoon full of bicarbonate of soda to each glass of water. Be sure to see a doctor or emergency poison clinic and explain you have taken sodium chlorite solution.

Training: You have read this book and hopefully you now know how to use the MMS. BUT if you make up some MMS for others, YOU must train people to use it properly. Do not expect that you can rely only on the directions on the bottle. No, no, no and no! People must be trained to use the MMS. If you give someone a bottle, sit down with them and actually do a training session. Have them drop two to six drops of MMS in an empty glass, add 5 drops of lemon, lime or citric acid solution for each drop of MMS that they use. Wait three minutes, add ½ glass of apple juice, then you drink a dose and have them drink a dose.

Please, believe me, this is the only way it works. People must be shown. In the past eight years every mistake in the world has been made, and many of the mistakes simply keep it from working.

I already told you about the lady that took 30 drops the first time. She was sick for three days. I told one other lady that she must put six drops in an empty glass and add ½ teaspoon of vinegar, wait three minutes and add ½ grass of apple juice. She promptly went home and added six drops of MMS to ½ cup of full strength vinegar. She later told me that before she finished drinking that ½ cup of vinegar sweat was running off her forehead and down her neck. The vinegar got in her eyes and she could barely see.

Everything that could go wrong has gone wrong. Some prepared it the night before (never allow more than ½ hour between mixing it and drinking it), and some tried it in their coffee (never do this). Almost no one gets it right without at least one session of training. It's too simple. Everyone expects it to be more complex. So please, please, train each person to whom you sell or give a bottle to. Not to do so means you are asking for failure and it is unfair to them. Also, don't think that most people will be able to do it right and only a few will fail. Not so! Most will fail, in one way or another, if not trained. Just be sure to do the demo with each sale or gift.

I plan to have training classes in Mexico for those who want a real education in using MMS.

Follow the instructions and you can save lives and watch people get better.

<u>Benefits that happen within the body when someone takes MMS.</u> These are the things that I have observed over the past 10 years. Some of it is my opinion; however, I have discussed all of the following information with medical doctors who have agreed with me. But then, some of that was their opinion as well.

So this is what appears to be happening in the body when MMS is ingested after using the various activators listed in this chapter. <u>The first thing</u> that the MMS does is destroy anaerobic microorganisms including viruses, bacteria, fungus, molds, yeast, and parasites. These are the disease causing organisms. There are many reasons to believe that this is what happens. This generally happens between 4 hours and 4 weeks, but in less than one week in most cases. This includes all forms of infection and other microorganisms. Also blood diseases such as leukemia.

<u>Secondly,</u> the MMS oxidizes the heavy metals within the body. I believe this because there have been a number of tests where the hair roots were checked before and after taking MMS. Afterwards, the heavy metals were gone. That includes mercury, lead, and several other metals. Unfortunately, hair root testing is not totally accurate, but it is a good indication. Oxidation of the heavy metals is not the same process as chelating, but the results are the same. When a heavy metal is oxidized it is neutralized and is simply washed out of the body.

<u>Thirdly,</u> the MMS is carried throughout the body and where it neutralizes foreign matter that is generally poisonous to the body. When oxidized, these poisons are neutralized and merely wash out of the body. Almost all poisonous material will be acidic in nature, thus it allows the MMS to recognize it. These poisons will all be attached at various locations and they will be hindering the function of the body. As they are oxidized they will no longer stay attached and will be washed out of the body.

Fourth, most forms of poisons from snakes and other venomous animals are oxidized when adequate amounts of MMS are taken. Most food poisons found in restaurants or in your refrigerator are oxidized, which is why one should take a number of doses when feeling the effects of food poisoning.

Fifth, the poison generated in burns, particularly type 3 burns when covered immediately with MMS, or even within hours, is neutralized by the MMS. The MMS should not be left on more than 1 minute. It must be rinsed off with water.

I am collecting Stories of Success of people who have used the MMS. If you have a Story of Success please email me at jim@jimhumble.com just put "Story of Success" in the subject. These stories will save lives. Please send in yours. If you don't put "Story of Success" in the subject area of the email or the spam filter will kick it out. Please use real names of people who are willing to be named. Someone will call you to verify your story. We need, the world needs, stories that can be verified.

References and sources
The Indian Herb Anti Cancer Herb is sold by a very nice lady by the name of Kathleen. She lives in Texas in the USA. Her phone number is 806 647-1741 the cost is $60.00 for a vial.

Death by Medicine by Gary Null, PhD, Carolyn Dean MD, ND, and others. A free copy can be downloaded from the Internet at www.newmediaexplorer.org/sepp/Death%20by%20Medicine%20Nov%2027.doc

Available MMS for you to purchase immediately. If you don't want the hassle and you would like to try my exact formula, you can order it from Subtle Energy Therapy in Canada at www.health4allinfo.ca and there are a number of companies and people listed on my site, www.miraclemineral.org , that now sell MMS and that have been verified by me. For empty bottles if you make your own see that last part of chapter 17.

For emergency use today, you could buy a bottle of Stabilized Oxygen from a local health food store. Make sure it is made from sodium chlorite. Normally Stabilized Oxygen is 1/8 strength of MMS. So when the instructions in this book call for starting with 2 drops of MMS, you will need 16 drops of the Stabilized Oxygen. For treating any kind of a condition you will need to reach 120 drops a day. Don't forget the lemon or citric acid, or vinegar activator. The bottle isn't going to last very long. For just maintenance to keep your immune system up and in good shape you will need at least 48 drops a day. It still isn't going to last long as most such bottles are one ounce or less. Buy MMS from Canada or one of the other suppliers listed on the MMS Web Page for $20 a bottle. It will last you two years if you use a 6 drop maintenance dose twice a week. Or better still, buy the sodium chlorite and make your own.

Other places to go for answers.

I have answered thousands of e-mails concerning almost everything and any thing imaginable concerning MMS. These questions and answers are being prepared so that you can use them. They are listed on an internet site with the URL of www.jimhumbleQandA.com A search engine is provided and you should be able to find almost any answer imaginable. If worse comes to worse, you will be able to e-mail me.

MMS Cancer Protocol and extreme diseases

Telling if MMS will help the cancer – and MMS cancer protocol and other extreme diseases.

The health of you mouth is extremely important. Please see the first part of this chapter under the heading "How to use MMS for personal Health" if you are serious about getting well you must follow the data given there.

Here is something your doctor will never tell you, there has been a medical test for cancer that is 99% effective for more than 25 years. It is more effective, less dangerous and cheaper than all other medical cancer tests. It's called AMAS cancer test. You don't have to go to a doctor; the test is available on the Internet. The cost is $165. The kit is free, you take a smear of your own blood and send it in and pay when the results are ready. The test is for specific cancer antibodies that will be present. Go to www.oncolabinc.com. I have no financial interest what so ever.

You can get an idea if the MMS will handle the problem by evaluating the nausea. That is, if you start out at say one drop or even 1/2 drop and it does not make you nauseous and then you begin to increase the drops twice a day once in the morning and once in the evening. That is if 1/2 drop doesn't make you nauseous in the morning, then in the evening or late afternoon try one full drop. Then the next morning take two drops and in the evening 3 drops. Sooner or later the number of drops is going to make you nauseous. You then take a drop or two less the next dose for a time or two and continue to increase the drops. You are always looking for the nauseous point, taking less for a time or two and attempting to take more.

You will be able to know if it is going to help you if you can continue to pass the nausea point and increase the drops. What is happening is that when nausea hits, some of the cancer has been destroyed and it is now a poison that the body can clear out. Being able to clear out this poison is a part of it. The body can clear this poison out but it might generate some nausea in the process, or diarrhea or even vomiting. That's not bad. The idea is that as the cancer is destroyed the body must clean out the poisons. As the cancer is destroyed the body can tolerate more and more drops. That's the indicator, is the body being able to tolerate more and more drops? If you find that you finally can increase the drops without getting nauseous it is an indicator that the body is doing its job. In the case of cancer, you have got to work at it. You start out slowly but increase quickly. At first you might just take the drops twice a day, but as you find you can do it twice a day without nausea, then increase to three times a day, and then four, and even as much as five times a day.

Also, if say, 5 drops are making you nauseous try 4 or 3 drops and, if say, 3 drops does not make you nauseous go to 3 drops but take 3 drops as many times a day as possible. As soon as you can tolerate 4 drops then go to 4 drops several times a day. Keep increasing the drops as fast as you can tolerate them.

What would indicate that you are not getting well is if the body got nauseous every time you take a dose no matter what amount of dose it is, and the body never seems to be able to increase the doses without nausea. If you can take say two drops at a time without nausea and you get nausea when you go to three drops, you may have to tolerate the nausea for a short time, but if the nausea always occurs when you take three drops, it shows that you are not gaining on the cancer. That can happen if the cancer is growing faster than the MMS is killing it. There is, however, always hope. One way would be instead of increasing the number of drops, increase the number of times that you take drops during the day. Read below. There are other items that can help. Never, however, in any case stop taking the MMS.

So if there is an indication that one is not improving, then I suggest the following direction. Purchase some Indian Herb from Kathleen in Texas. It costs $60 a vial and that is plenty. Phone 806 647-1741 she has a thousand letters from people who have been helped. She and her father have been selling the Indian herb for over 60 years. When you get this herb use it with the MMS to get the best results.

The AMAS cancer test listed above gives anyone a fantastic advantage. One can do a test, use the MMS for several weeks or a month and then do a second test to see how much improvement has taken place or to see if any improvement has happened at all.

When I mention drops of MMS I always mean add 5 times that many drops of lemon, lime, or citric acid solution, wait three minutes and then add 1/3 to 2/3 glasses of water or juice and drink. Never use MMS without the addition of lemon, lime, or citric acid or in an emergency if you have no citric acids, use vinegar. Use only apple, grape, cranberry or pineapple juice without added vitamin C or ascorbic acid or see #6 below for overcoming the taste. **End Cancer Protocol.**

2. The Standard MMS Protocol also for children

<u>The health of you mouth is extremely important. Please see the first part of this chapter under the heading "How to use MMS for personal Health" if you are serious about getting well you must follow the data give there.</u>

Note: When following the instructions below, keep this paragraph in mind. Always activate the MMS drops with one of the food acids, either lemon juice drops, or lime juice drops, or citric acid solution drops (to make citric acid solution add 1 level tablespoon of citric acid and 9 tablespoons of water. Store it in a bottle with a lid.) Always use 5 drops of one of these food acids to each one drop of MMS, mix in an empty dry glass and wait at least 3 minutes, then add 1/3 to 2/3 glasses of water or juice and drink. (You can expand the 3 minutes out to 10 minutes, and after adding the juice or water you can wait up to an hour before drinking.)

1. All protocol for taking MMS in the Americas starts with one or two drops. Never start with more than one or two drops. People who are very sick and/or sensitive should start with ½ drop. Activate the drops as given above.

2. If you do OK and do not notice nausea on the first dose, increase by one drop for the second dose. If you notice nausea reduces the amount of MMS for the next dose. Do two doses a day, one in the morning and one in the evening. Continue to increase by one drop each time you take a new dose. When you notice nausea, reduce the dose by one drop, or bad diarrhea reduce by 2 or 3 drops. Usually reduce for one or two times before going back the amount that it took to make you nauseous.

Note: If you notice diarrhea or even vomiting that is not a bad sign. The body is simply throwing off poisons and cleaning itself out. Everyone says that they feel much better after the diarrhea. You do not have to take any medicine for the diarrhea. It will go away as fast as it came. It will not last. It is not real diarrhea as the body is just cleaning out, and it is not caused by bacteria or virus. When the poison is gone, the diarrhea is gone.

3. Continue to follow the procedure given in 2 above. Until you reach 15 drops twice a day without nausea. At that point increase to 3 times a day. Stay at 3 times a day for at least one week and then reduce the drops to 4 or to 6 drops a day for older people and 4 to 6 drops twice a week for younger people.   .

Note: Once you have completed step 3 above most of the viral, bacteria, mold, and yeast load will be gone from your body. Your body will be clean. You no longer have to worry about feeding the microorganism load. You can base you diet on nutrition, rather than not feeding the load. The diabetes will be gone, thus you no longer need to worry about sugar. You won't have to worry about the pancreas over reacting thus giving you a shock of insulin. Instead it will give you just enough insulin to knock the blood sugar lever to the right level (You won't feel sleepy after eating a candy bar). Your body will then be able to easily adsorb vitamins and minerals and many other nutrients it might have been missing up to this time. You should feel better as time goes by. Do not quit taking the MMS.

For Children: The protocol for children is essentially the same. One should usually start at 1/2 drop. Just make a one drop drink and pour out 1/2 of the drink before giving it to the child. Then increase from 1 to 2 to 3 drops as given above, but do not go beyond 3 drops for each 25 pounds (11.4 kg) of body weight. With a baby start with 1/2 drop and increase to one drop up to 2 drops, but no more. So if you give 1/2 drop in the morning wait until the afternoon before giving 1 drop and then the next morning for 2 drops. If the baby or child becomes nauseous wait an extra hour or two before giving another dose and also give a smaller dose. Give smaller doses until the baby or child can tolerate more, but do not stop giving doses. **End Standard Protocol.**

3. Clara's 6 and 6 Protocol

The health of your mouth is extremely important. Please see the first part of this chapter under the heading "How to use MMS for personal Health" if you are serious about getting well you must follow the data given there.

For people who have pain, flu, colds, pneumonia, or other diseases that are <u>not</u> generally considered incurable and physical pains that have been present for some time. When people are very sick and in bed they should use the standard protocol #2 above and start out with a tiny dose.

I've named this new protocol Clara's because she was the first to really apply it consistently. You may have read the last chapter in the second edition of this book. You will recall that there were a number of success stories about Clara treating people in her home. Since then I have rented an office from Clara and her mother, I have seen quite a few more people come in. Last night 12/14/07 a lady about 65 years old and her husband arrived to buy some MMS and Clara always gives them a 6 drop dose, has them wait one hour, and then she has them mix the next dose to make sure that they have it right. Then she has them wait a few minutes up to an hour before they leave.

Both the right hand and the right foot of the lady that came in last night were completely paralyzed. She came in with a walker but she could not hold on to the walker so her husband had to hold her to the walker. It was a chore getting in the door. Clara gave her a 6 drop dose with 30 drops of citric acid as the activator, she waited the 3 minutes as always and then added 1/2 glass of water and handed it to the lady. The lady lifted the glass with some difficultly to her mouth with her left hand as her sciatica (lower back pain) was also paining her. Within 40 minutes she was starting to feel a reduction of pain in her back and some tingling in her hand. At 60 minutes she could slightly move several fingers. Clara handed her another 6 drop identical drink. As we waited for the second hour to pass, Clara called me in from the office. The lady was exercising her hand. She had complete mobility in her hand and she had her shoe off and was exercising her toes. In fact she was exercising her entire foot and she could move her toes and other muscles better than most people I know. When she left, she was still using the walker, but her husband didn't have to help her and her lower back pain was gone. I could see that she would be walking without that walker in a few days. This is not unusual. It happens around here all the time.

So this is "Clara's 6 and 6 protocol" using MMS. It is simple. It's for most conditions such as flu, colds, pneumonia, physical pains either immediate or chronic, and most other home sicknesses.

Step No. 1. Put 6 drops of MMS in a glass and add 30 drops of 10% solution of citric acid, or 30 drops of lemon juice, or 30 drops of lime juice. Shake the glass so that the acid and MMS are mixed and wait at least 3 minutes. A little longer is OK in case you walked away and forgot. 10 or 15 minutes would be OK as the solution remains at about the same strength. Then add about 1/2 glass of water to the solution and drink. You can also use a juice that does not have added vitamin C. Use apple juice, grape juice, pineapple juice, or cranberry juice.

Step No. 2. Wait one hour and do exactly the same thing as in step No. 1. Normally the person will experience some relief within two hours of taking the first dose especially if he goes ahead and takes the second dose. Of course, here is no guarantee. If the person does or does not experience relief he should go to 7 and 7 that is a 7 drop dose and in one hour a second 7 drop dose, but he should do this only if he did not get sick. By getting sick I'd mean that he was nauseous for more than 10 minutes or he vomited, or he had diarrhea. In the case he did get sick you should not increase to 7 and 7, but rather again do 6 and 6. If he was very sick it would be best to drop back more, such as 3 and 3, but that seldom happens. Normally do 6 and 6 until one can tolerate it without being nauseous, and then begin increasing to 7 and 7, etc.

For flu and pneumonia and bad colds and other diseases that can be life threatening do this same process two or even three times a day until you are feeling well. <u>Do not give the flu a chance to get a foot hold</u>.

Once the flu is gone, one should begin increasing drops towards 15 and 15 or you could revert to the Standard protocol as given above and increase as quickly as reasonable to 15 drops and then increase to 15 drops twice a day or 3 times a day for one week as explained below.

The general goal of the number of drops that anyone should take is 15 drops 2 or 3 times a day and of course, less for children. For children normally it would be 3 drops for each 25 pounds (11.4 KG) of body weight. This number of drops, 15, would be OK **twice** a day for a grown up that weighed 150 pounds (68.1 KG) or less and 15 drops **three** times a day for a grown up weighing over 150 pounds. This is not an exact number. One should evaluate his own case and how he feels to decide the number of drops. **This number of drops pretty well ensures that one's body is completely free of pathogenic microorganisms and heavy metals.** Once one has reached this goal for a week, he should drop back to a maintenance level of one 6 drop dose twice a week. (In all cases when drops of MMS are mentioned we also mean that 5 drops of lemon, or lime, or citric solution is added for each 1 drop of MMS and one then waits 3 minutes before adding water or juice and consuming it.)   .

Of course, the goal of it all is not being sick. So take 6 drops twice a week. If you feel the flu coming on, then do the Clara 6 and 6 protocols as described above. You will have the flu for no more that 12 to 24 hours and usually less than 6 hours after taking your 2nd dose. However, never give the flu a chance. The best way to kill the flu is to take 2 or three drops every hour all day long until you know the flu is gone. The 6 drops twice a week keeps your immune system strong and the pathogens weak. You probably remember from school that there are always pathogens in your body. The 6 drops keeps them at bay. **End Clara's Protocol.**

Special Note by the Author: It's been mention elsewhere in this book; I did not invent this technology. If you will go to chapter 22 you will see that Chlorine Dioxide has been used in the body by many others for a period of 20 years or more. I merely brought it to the public when it would never have been brought otherwise. Over a period of 12 years, I have had a more widely and diverse experience with it than any other person. I admit that I thought at first that I was the inventor. I did invent it, but I was the second or third inventor, or maybe even tenth inventor. Others were already using it on a very limited basis, and for many years. I carried it on over a much wider area to the public.

So anybody who wants to say that I was not the first inventor, I will have to agree with them. I don't know who invented the use of chlorine dioxide in the human body. The area is clouded as it has been used for many years by many different researchers. And sodium chlorite has been used by hundreds of researchers in the body without ever realizing that they were actually using chlorine dioxide. It may be that none of them realized it was chlorine dioxide the one causing the results that they were getting. In each case their research was limited to only several diseases or several types of diseases. So as far as patents are concerned I could not claim first use and thus could not obtain a patent. (Of course, I did not want and do not want a patent). All I ever wanted was to see this Miracle Mineral used throughout the world and that is indeed happening.

Chapter 11

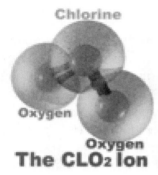

Treating burns

The MMS solution has an amazing ability to treat burns. There is some kind of a chemical created in a burn that is neutralized by MMS. A burn is best treated by MMS immediately after the burn, but it can still help even hours later.

The CLO₂ Ion

When a burn happens, no matter how bad, one should squirt the MMS full strength straight out of the bottle all over the burn. Do not use the vinegar in this case. Using the tips of your fingers, very lightly with a feather touch make sure it is spread completely on the burn. LET IT REMAIN THERE **for only 30 seconds to a minute.** Do not allow your fingers to press on the burn in any way. If you had a paint brush handy, that would be best. But don't spend any time looking for a paint brush. The sooner you get the MMS on the burn the better. The acidic chemical in the burn is neutralized by the alkaline solution of the MMS. The pain stops immediately, within seconds. <u>Wash the MMS off with water</u>.

When treating a burn, make sure you leave it on for at least 30 seconds. Count slowly to 30 before washing it off. **You absolutely must wash it off or the burn will become worse**. If you do this correctly, the burn will heal in about ¼ the ordinary time for a similar untreated burn. You may need to treat the burn two or three times or more.

The MMS must be washed off with water within 30 to 60 seconds. If water is not available do not use the MMS until you are sure that something is available to wash the burn off. Any drinkable liquid will do for washing the MMS off of the burn if there is no water available.

Sunburns can also be treated. Use a cloth very lightly or with the tips of your fingers very lightly spread the MMS full strength on the sunburned area. Use plenty of the MMS so that it spreads quickly and easily. Leave the MMS on for 30 to 60 seconds and then rinse off with water. It must be rinsed off completely. Do not leave it on. Waiting more than about 5 minutes will make it worse. If you rinse it off, the pain vanishes immediately.

If you have a hard time following directions or if you cannot understand **"Wash it off"** please do not attempt this action. It must be rinsed off of the burn within 5 minutes. MMS is a miracle with burns when used right. It will stop the pain and save lives, and make the burn heal much faster, but if you do it wrong, (in other words if you don't wash it off) it only makes it worse.

Just two days ago, a visiting doctor went out to the beach and sat for several hours under a beach umbrella. Well those umbrellas don't keep the reflected sun from burning you, and he was burned very badly. Unfortunately, he did not come back from the beach that day, so I was not able to treat him until the next day. I put full strength MMS into a two ounce spray bottle and sprayed his body everywhere there was red areas. The red covered most of his body. We left it on for one minute and then he showered. When he came out of the shower he said, "I can't tell you how much better that feels. He was flexing his shoulders and other muscles where he could not flex before without much pain.

After several hours he complained that much of the pain was back. I sprayed his complete body again, but this time we made sure that there was complete contact by very lightly rubbing the solution on with finger tips and then he waited <u>5 minutes</u> before taking the shower. This time when he came out of the shower he said that all the pain was gone and this <u>time the pain did not return</u>.

As you can see, it may take more than one treatment and it might take a little longer than the one minute. You may even need to try a third treatment or more for third degree burns, but in any case never leave it on. Always rinse it off.

Please tell your friends about the free Part 1 download.

Chapter 12

MMS and Longevity

Chlorine

Oxygen

Oxygen

The CLO₂ Ion

As I already mentioned, I wish I could absolutely say that the MMS will give you 25 years more of life. I can't prove that at this time, but I believe it. The thing that kills older people is a poor immune system. As you get older, your immune system goes bad. MMS changes that. When one is taking the MMS on a regular basis his immune system becomes supercharged. There is little to nothing that can get by the immune system in that case.

Our dark field microscope has shown that the longer one continues to use the MMS the more supercharged the immune system becomes as far as white blood cells are concerned.

After treating hundreds of people for six years, it is my opinion that no disease known to man that is caused by pathogens (viruses, bacteria, parasites or other micro organisms) can withstand an immune system being treated daily with MMS. One might need to increase dosing on occasions when the flu season is extremely bad or other diseases are around.

The body seems to recognize flu bugs. For a person taking the MMS it then tends to react as it always has when flu hits, except for one thing: The reaction usually lasts less than 24 hours, and on rare occasions as much as 48 hours. The flu is 1/10 as severe as when one is not taking the MMS. Most diseases will never occur, but some do show up as a mini disease that is gone in hours. Colds come and are fully active, but they are usually gone in an hour or two.

When taking the MMS as a maintenance dose the diseases that usually kill older people simply won't get to you. However, it will be your job to keep yourself in good condition otherwise. If you remain a couch potato, you will probably still last a little longer, but nature's old rule, "If you don't use it, you lose it" will probably always be in play.

The MMS gives you the tools to live a great deal longer, but it will be up to you to make that happen. That includes taking other nutrients. When the MMS kills off the pathogens your body is still going to need the proper nutrition to remain healthy. That means the proper balance of vitamins, minerals, proteins, and oils. Old age is normally a mass of deficiencies of various nutrients. The MMS kills off the diseases and neutralizes the poisons, but the deficiencies can kill you all by themselves. Staying young or just remaining alive, you got to work at it.

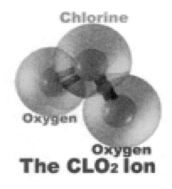

Chapter 13

MMS Intravenously

There is more data to report this time concerning using MMS intravenously (IV). You may or may not be aware that up to several months ago no one had ever used MMS by IV after being activated by citric acid or vinegar or any other acid. Although a hundred thousand infusions of sodium chlorite had been done in hospitals and clinics throughout the world only raw inactivated sodium chlorite solution had ever been used. Of course that was because no one has ever thought to activate it during those times.

After talking to many lyme disease victims who were not getting well by simply taking MMS by mouth and after talking to a few who had not notice much help even by IV I began to feel really worried. Also I talked to several people who were not getting very much results with morgellans disease and that worried me even more. If these two diseases cannot be cured, then curing all the other diseases is not going to be enough. There are literally millions of people who have these two diseases and the number is rapidly approaching epidemic proportions.

The public doesn't hear about this because it is simply being either ignored or suppressed. Thousands of people have either emailed me or talked to me on the phone. I get reports from a cross section of the US and the world. We can't ignore these diseases and the dozens of similar diseases that are all traceable back to government laboratories in the world. If we do, they will kill us. Most people are not worried at this time except for those who get the diseases or when a loved one gets a disease. Some people think that they must be bitten by a tick, but not so. There are many ways to get these diseases. Most people report no tick bite.

So based on the fact that something has got to be done I started thinking about using MMS IV after activating it with one of the food acids. As you have already learned this creates up to 1000 times more chlorine dioxide than inactivated MMS. Of course we know the tremendous advantage this gives us when taking MMS by mouth but the diseases that don't seem to clear up by mouth are lyme and morgellans disease and other "created" diseases. I reasoned that normally the activated MMS had to travel into the digestive system and thus get into the blood in the stomach walls. The chlorine dioxide there is picked up by the red blood cells in the stomach lining and carried thought the body. The question that kept coming to me was, "That's good for the red blood cells, but what about the blood plasma?" The plasma is the liquid that carries the red blood cells around. Does the chlorine dioxide also somehow get into the blood plasma from the stomach, because if it doesn't, that could be one reason why the MMS doesn't seem to be doing the job with lyme and morgellans diseases.

Well, I had to find the answer to that question, or at least to the question: "Will MMS be more effective by IV if it is activated?" I couldn't afford to have tests does with lab rats thus I decided to go ahead and be the lab rat. I talked it over with Dr. Romero and he was dubious about me doing the tests but when I said that I would do it anyway, at home if necessary, he agreed to watch over the tests, because he knew I wasn't kidding. I hired a nurse who could do IV work and we started tests a few days before Christmas 2007.

The question was, would I get the same reactions by activated IV as we get by mouth, or would it be something different. I hoped it would be different, because if it was the same, then doing activated IV might be the same also and thus not much improvement. Making a long story short as I can, I finally tried 1 drop of MMS activated with 2.5 drops of 10% citric acid solution in 150 ml of saline IV solution.

Well the first thing that happened was nothing, and that was strange as several doctors had said that the citric acid would burn like the devil in my veins. But there was no burning or other feeling except for the needle prick going in. There was nothing! I began to be disappointed, but who could expect something from one drop, not even fully activated (I used 2.5 drops of acid instead of the normal 5 drops. That's actually equivalent to ½ drop of MMS). An hour passed and I decided to go home.

Then on the way home, at about 1.5 hours after the infusion, it hit me. I began to get colder and colder and then began to shiver. I was freezing and also experiencing nausea. I was sick, but quite elated. Something different was happening and this had never happened before. I called my friend Dr. Hesselink, who wrote Chapter 22 in this book and who has been doing oxygen therapy for many years and he assured me that it had to be a Herxheimer reaction. (That's a reaction as the result of destroying something in the body that releases a poison.) That could only be because the chlorine dioxide is going deeper into the body tissues. I had been taking 30 drops of MMS with absolutely no results, so the activated IV had to be going deeper to destroy further microorganisms in order to make the Herxheimer reaction.

So I continued. The same amount of activated MMS didn't create any reaction the next day. So I tried activation with 5 drops food acid and 1 drop MMS. I again got the Herxheimer reaction and when I did it again, the reaction did not occur. I continued this way until I got to 4 drops. Each time getting the reaction on the first increase and then not getting it the second increase. I was amazed that there never was the slightest bit of pain in my veins, but I did have a pain in the back of my hand when the needle was not put in correctly. Then Christmas came and there was too much activity. I had to stop.

Then at the first of February I began to do the tests again. I started and went to 4 drops much quicker this time and then a standard thing that often happens, a body survival mechanism kicked in and my veins started knotting up and refusing the solution. There are standard ways of overcoming this mechanism, but we did not have any of the drugs required. So I again stopped until the drug can be obtained. I later found that the drugs that prevent the veins from knotting up are Heparin and Procaine. Don't use them until you know exactly how much to use.

And that leaves us at this point. I may have to publish this book before we have the answer, but my opinion at this time is that it will probably have a very good effect on lyme and morgellans and might even kill them. If the chlorine dioxide is getting to where they are hiding, it is going to kill them. It is already proven that chlorine dioxide kills the diseases, it's just that these laboratory generated diseases seem to be able to hide in places that antibiotics and MMS by mouth cannot reach.

There is one other thing you should know. One lady that has had lyme extremely bad and terrible sick decided without my knowledge to use MMS activated by IV. She mixed up 16 drops with 75 drops of food acid. She waited the three minutes and put it in 200 ml of saline solution. Then a nurse friend did the infusion for her in an hour's period of time. She became very sick the next day. The skin on her face, which had become very old and wrinkled looking, completely peeled off, leaving her face looking very young again. The lyme had apparently infiltrated her skin and when killed it also killed the skin as well. So she took 4 times as much activated MMS as I did and she lived through it. In fact she felt much better, but the lyme was not gone. However that was only one treatment, who knows how much good continued treatments would have done. By the way, even that much food acid did not cause pain in her veins.

This lady then went back and did two more infusions of 16 drops with the added 75 drops of citric acid solution in the 200 ml bag of IV solution. This time she became quite sick again. She had diarrhea, nausea, and vomiting. Then most of the rest of the skin pealed from her body. It was extremely painful, but she felt much better when the ordeal was over. <u>I would never suggest this course of action. It's dangerous and not necessary in my opinion. One should start at low levels of MMS and increase slowly to 16 drops or more.</u>

So you see, my evaluation that MMS activated and intravenous will probably kill the diseases is based on this lady's results as well as what I learned about myself.

So I'm just reporting the continued research at zero money. It needs to be done. It's not the way things should be done, but then we wouldn't even have MMS if things were done the way that they are supposed to be done. Please understand, I'm not bragging or complaining or anything else. I just feel that the public should know what our great government and other great rich and wealthy philanthropists are not doing nor helping with. I have often asked them for help.

I hope you understand. The lyme and the morgellans disease are increasing throughout the world. There are many diseases with names I can't pronounce and many diseases not yet named. It started in the US and has spread throughout Europe, Asia, and most of the other countries. It is far worse than most people realize. Something has to be able to control it. I'm not the only person out here saying this, there are many others. I don't want to say it. I don't want to be considered a kook. I don't want to be a hero. I'd rather go prospecting in the jungle as that gives me the most pleasure. But as the saying goes, somebody's got to do it.

Well, we will soon see. In the mean time read the rest of this chapter. It tells what has already been done by IV.

Twenty ml push method. MMS has been used intravenously with faster results than by mouth. Six to 18 drops of MMS in 20 milliliters of sterile injection solution bought from a pharmacy in a foreign country for injection purposes was used. It was a glucose solution. The injections were done in the veins of the arms. The injections must be fast at about 20 seconds for the 20 ml solution. The reason is if you do it too slow it burns the vein, so get it in fast. The injections were done one or two per day for up to three days. More days might be okay, but that is all we did. All injections were done under a doctor's supervision by nurses. Do not try this yourself or without a doctor.

Using the push described here 25 people were treated who claimed to have AIDS. Five people called back and said that they checked negative for AIDS.

250 ml drip method. Seven drops of MMS in a bottle of 250 ml of glucose drip solution was used for the first treatment and 22 drops of MMS was used in a bottle of 250 ml of glucose drip solution the second treatment the same day and continued at 22 drops for up to 30 days in a row. The drip speed was adjusted for about two hours for the full 250 ML. The results were spectacular. All drip solutions were done by nurses familiar with the process under doctors' advice. Do not try this.

Keep a blood pressure machine handy with many tests at the very beginning. If the blood pressure drops more than 20% stop the action. Give fruit juice to bring up the pressure. If you are using saline solution change to glucose solution to keep the blood pressure up.

The blood in the veins and drip solution itself acts as a neutral solution which adjusts the alkalinity of the MMS downwards, thus causing it to begin releasing chlorine dioxide. It is carried throughout the body getting to places that it would not otherwise get. After adding the MMS we always waited 1 hour before beginning the process. The reason for this was to allow some chlorine dioxide to be generated.

When using IV the drops should always be adjusted to the maximum amount of drops without causing the patient to be sick. A normal person does not become sick with 22 drops of MMS in a glucose 250 ML IV solution. Normally, an AIDS patient will become very sick at this level of drops. Thus one should start with 2 to 5 drops and increase by a couple drops each treatment. Should the patient become nauseous during the treatment or immediately after, on the next treatment one should use 2 drops less. Then begin increasing the drops until the patient can take 22 drops without becoming nauseous. Continue at 22 drops increasing to 22 drops twice a day until the patient tests negative for AIDS. At any time the patient becomes nauseous the treatment should be stopped immediately for that treatment. But do not stop the treatments. Just use a couple drops less the next treatment. A couple of doctors have suggested that one never use more than 250 ml of solution at a time. It may cause the lungs to take only water if using more ml in an infusion.

Thousands of infusions have been done with sodium chlorite at the same strength as given here without problems. Remember, no food acids were use in any of these infusions. You must know what you are doing. Be very careful to not get any air into the injection tubing as air in the veins can kill a person.

Nausea is not a bad sign. It indicates the MMS is working. But if the patient feels really bad, he can drink a glass of water to which 1000 MG of vitamin C has been added.

For further information concerning IV sodium chlorite check with the various research papers listed by Dr. Hesselink in chapter 22 of this book or the paper listed on the miraclemineral.org web site under important information.　This paper tells of IV infusions done with Dioxychlor which is the same, made for sodium chlorite and used in the same proportions as MMS.

Chapter 14

Chlorine Dioxide and Blood Chemistry

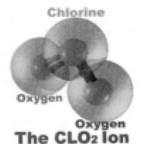

Chlorine

Oxygen

Oxygen

The CLO₂ Ion

To understand why the Miracle Mineral Supplement works one must understand some of the chemistry of chlorine Dioxide and some of the chemistry of blood. Chlorine dioxide is a gas that is dissolved in water when in the body. Chlorine and chlorine dioxide have been used as disinfectants for more than a hundred years and there is little doubt that they simply destroy pathogens of all kinds. Both have been used in water purification systems for more than 50 years. In recent years, in water purification systems chlorine has been used less and chlorine dioxide a great deal more as it has many benefits over chlorine. Chlorine dioxide is used extensively in water purification systems throughout Europe. Although chlorine dioxide is somewhat more expensive than chlorine, its many benefits over chlorine has resulted in it being more extensively used in water purification systems than chlorine. In 1998 The American Chemical Society, Analytical Chemistry Division said chlorine dioxide is the most powerful antimicrobial agent known to man.

Chlorine dioxide kills pathogens by oxidation, a completely different chemical reaction than that of chlorine (chlorination) and oxidation results in no harmful chemicals. A 10-ppm drink of chlorine in juice will cause a healthy person several hours of nausea, while a 10-ppm drink of chlorine dioxide causes no nausea at all for a healthy person, and yet it is more efficient in killing pathogens than chlorine.

None of the functions or elements of the human body including friendly aerobic bacteria are affected by chlorine dioxide in diluted solutions of 50-ppm or less. On the other hand, solutions of 0.1 to 1-ppm seem to induce a spectacular immune response reaction attacking anaerobic bacterium, viruses, parasites, fungus, harmful molds, yeasts and other pathogens. Without realizing it, hundreds of thousands of Americans have been drinking diluted solutions of chlorine dioxide for more than 100 years in various health waters sold to the public. Diluted solutions of salt treated with electricity have been sold as "health water" under various names such as "Willard Water" which is still being sold. Most of these waters contain low levels of chlorine dioxide as a result of the electrolytic treatment. The chlorine dioxide concentration in such water was very low and thus was never strong enough to do a thorough job of killing pathogens in the body, however the benefits claimed for these health waters were more than likely caused by the chlorine dioxide as there is no other element in the water that would seem beneficial. Other health drinks have been sold that contain various chlorine derivatives. Stabilized Oxygen which is a diluted solution of sodium chlorite when diluted further with water very slowly gives off chlorine dioxide. The MMS is just a stronger solution to which a food grade acid has been added. The acid such as vinegar or citric acid often used in soft drinks reduces the solution to an acid condition but still within a food range which releases up to 1 ppm chlorine dioxide, a level of concentration that is sometimes found in processed food but is 100's of times that which is produced in Stabilized Oxygen.

Because of the acetic acid in the vinegar, or citric acid, when added to a sodium chlorite solution, the solution begins to release chlorine dioxide on a linear timed basis for up to 12 hours. Stomach acid does not tend to significantly change this timed release. The amount of salts and vinegar or citric acid is calculated to release one milligram of chlorine dioxide per hour. An hour is the amount of time that it takes one milligram of chlorine dioxide to deteriorate into table salt and other harmless chemicals plus one very useful chemical. The production of chlorine dioxide and its constant deterioration into table salt and chemicals brings about a lessening level of chlorine dioxide in the body for approximately 12 hours at which time all chlorine dioxides deteriorate leaving no trace and nothing that is deleterious to the body. Thus the poison index after that period of time is zero.

Hospitals and laboratories have used chlorine and chlorine dioxide for more than a hundred years as a disinfectant for cleaning floors, benches, and tools. No pathogen can resist them and no disease, either bacterial or virus has ever developed a resistance to chlorine dioxide. The human body has very few mechanisms that can differentiate between oxygen and chlorine dioxide. Since red blood cells cannot tell the difference, strong evidence indicates as the MMS enters the stomach, absorption mechanisms in the stomach walls allow the red blood cells to absorb the chlorine dioxide and carry it to various areas of the body where oxygen ions are normally taken.

The natural pH of the human body is approximately 7. At pH 7 chlorine dioxide, in the absence of light, is fairly stable for a few minutes. However, disease pathogens are essentially all anaerobic and have a different fingerprint than that of friendly aerobic bacteria as do malaria parasites. As mentioned above, the red blood cells readily absorb the chlorine dioxide and once in the cell they attack the malaria parasite because the surface of the parasite has a lower pH than the blood.

Chlorine dioxide is an extremely high explosive and it is so volatile that it cannot be transported. The only way that chlorine dioxide can be utilized is for it to be generated on site and used as it is generated, or generated in situ (in place). It is the volatile nature of chlorine dioxide when it contacts pathogen that makes it so effective both in water systems and within the human body. As doctor Hesselink has pointed out in chapter 22 of this book, the very nature of the malaria parasite prevents it from ever developing a resistance to chlorine dioxide. However, we also believe that the volatility of chlorine dioxide also helps prevents pathogens from developing a resistance to it. It's sort of like trying to develop a resistance to hand grenades. You just can't do it.

Normal levels of oxygen in the blood cannot destroy all of the pathogens present under disease conditions, however, when chlorine dioxide is adsorbed with the oxygen it is a different story. When a chlorine dioxide ion contacts a harmful pathogen it instantly accepts five electrons from the pathogen, or it might be more descriptive to say that it instantly tears off five electrons. An extremely fast chemical reaction is in essence an explosion, and this is exactly what happens on a microscopic level. The damage to the pathogen is a result of losing electrons to the chlorine dioxide ion and the release of energy. The pathogen, basically, is oxidized by chlorine ions and as a part of the action the chlorine becomes a harmless chloride (table salt). Two atoms of oxygen are released as ions from the chlorine dioxide ion but the oxygen has little effect other than to attach to hydrogen ions making water or attach to a carbon ion to make carbon dioxide.

It is the process of the chlorine dioxide ion oxidizing pathogens or other harmful chemicals that is beneficial to the body. Although the two oxygen ions of the chlorine dioxide ion are released, their charge level does not result in oxidation. The same process continues throughout the body where chlorine dioxide ions contact pathogens. It does not attack beneficial bacteria or healthy body parts, as their pH is not below 7. It will also oxidize diseased cells, such as infections or cancer. In the event that the chlorine dioxide does not contact a pathogen or other poison, it deteriorates into table salt and hypochlorous acid that is useable by the body.

A scientific paper published on the Web by Lenntech Company (see the end of this chapter) explains the oxidation reaction strength of chlorine dioxide as opposed to many other oxidizers. Chlorine dioxide is the weakest oxidizer of them all. However it has the greatest oxidation capacity of all the oxidizers with the ability to accept 5 electrons. Ozone as a comparison is the strongest oxidizer of them all and oxidizes everything in its path that is capable of being oxidized, but it can accept only 3 electrons. Chlorine dioxide being a very weak oxidizer oxidizes only microorganisms, heavy metals, and diseased body cells that are easily oxidized. It does not have the oxidation strength (electron potential) strong enough to oxidize healthy body cells, or aerobic beneficial bacteria. However, when contacting items within its oxidation potential range, it has the ability to accept more electrons that any of the other oxidizers, and thus it is extremely effective.

The lymph nodes, for example, are one of the areas where the blood normally releases oxygen to oxidize various poisons in the node and then it carries the oxidized poisons away to the liver. The red blood cells carry the chlorine dioxide ions the same as oxygen and thus chlorine dioxide ions are also released in the lymph nodes. The chlorine dioxide ions are inert to normal cells but they will destroy disease pathogens found there.

A minute amount of naturally produced chlorine dioxide is found in the human body and one of the chemicals that chlorine dioxide helps to create as it deteriorates is myeloperoxidase a chemical that the immune system needs. The immune system uses this chemical, myeloperoxidase, to generate hypochlorous acid. The body uses hypochlorous acid extensively to kill parasites, bacteria, fungi, viruses, tumor cells, natural killer cells, and to destroy some waste products under normal conditions. However, diseases and body conditions can result in a deficiency in the hypochlorous acid needed to destroy the pathogens that are present. This is due to a medical condition known as myeloperoxidase deficiency. In the case of many other diseases there are other immune system reactions that can overcome the diseases, however in the cases of malaria and other extreme diseases, there is not enough hypochlorous acid to kill the parasites or pathogens, nor are there any other immune system reactions that can destroy them. Thus the hypochlorous acid created by chlorine dioxide as it deteriorates in the body is probably another mechanism by which malaria and other diseases are destroyed.

In the case of the MMS, when taken by mouth by a malaria victim after adding vinegar and juice, all malaria symptoms including chills, fever, aching muscles and joints, headache, nausea, and other symptoms are gone within four hours in 98% of all cases. The other 2% are symptom free within 12 hours. Although some malaria victims are sick from other diseases, we have never found a case in which the malaria parasite was not destroyed. To this date, July 1, 2006, more than 75,000 malaria victims have been treated with no serious side effects reported. Since normally two deaths per each 250-malaria victims is expected, and zero deaths were reported in the 75,000 cases treated, we must assume that 300 lives have been saved and that the MMS is doing its job.

In February of 2006 clinical trials were conducted in a prison in the country of Malawi East Africa. The results were a 100% cure rate of all malaria victims treated in the prison. Several months later, in the same year, the Malawi government made its own separate clinical trials. They reported with the same results. All malaria victims treated recovered and there were no failures.

In the case of AIDS, when the MMS is injected as an IV solution into the blood, it is carried in the blood plasma throughout the body while generating chlorine dioxide that is no doubt absorbed into the red blood cells. In a series of 390 AIDS cases treated by IV in a small clinic in Kampala Uganda over an eight-month period beginning March 2004,

60% of the cases were considered free of AIDS in three days. The remaining 40% were judged free of AIDS in four to 30 days. Most of the AIDS victims treated were those that were sent home from the local hospital to die as the hospital could do nothing for them. Unfortunately, AIDS blood tests could not be made as the money and facilities were not available, however, all victims were known AIDS victims and the majority went back to work or to their lives with no AIDS symptoms left. Only two cases out of 390 were considered to have failed. Those few that were reviewed later, from one week to a couple of months were still symptom free.

References: Wikipedia Free Encyclopedia on the Internet.   Search chlorine dioxide.

References: Web sites that provide many additional references.

Myeloperoxidase   Deficiency   Article   by   Javed   Sheikh,   MD
www.emedicine.com/ped/topic1530.htm

Dictionary Definition: Myeloperoxidase deficiency: Deficiency of the enzyme myeloperoxidase which may predispose to severe fungal infections. The enzyme is critical to the oxygen-dependent killing of bacteria by leukocytes (white blood cells). MedicineNet.com

A Focus on chlorine dioxide: The "Ideal" Biocide   G. D. Simpson, R. F.   Miller,   G.   D.   Laxton,   and   W.   R.   Clements
www.do2.com/reading/waste/corrosion.html
Advantages of chlorine dioxide   www.purate.com

Advantages of chlorine dioxide
http://www.newton.dep.anl.gov/askasci/chem00/chem00472.htm

http://www.aet.org/science_of_ecf/eco_risk/chlorine.html

www.epa.gov/safewater/mdbp/pdf/alter/chapt_4.pdf

Chlorine dioxide research paper at http://www.lenntech.com/water-

disinfection/disinfectants-Chlorine-dioxide   this is one of the better papers.

Please tell your friends about the free Part 1 download.   Go to the following address www.miraclemineral.org/friends.htm

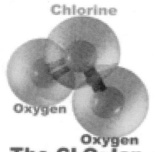

Chlorine

Oxygen

Oxygen

The CLO₂ Ion

Chapter 15

Overview of the Use of MMS and Main Points

The specifications of MMS are as follows:

1. MMS consists of 28% sodium chlorite powder dissolved in distilled water. (Since Sodium chlorite powder is only 80% sodium chlorite and cannot be manufactured any more pure than that, the actual percentage of sodium chlorite in MMS is 22.4 %.) (When mixing use 28% sodium chlorite powder by weight and 72% distilled water). Sodium chlorite powder is 80% sodium chlorite and 19% is table salt (sodium chloride) and less than 1% of several other sodium chemicals that are considered nontoxic. Be careful here. Do you see why a 28% sodium chlorite powder mixture is only 22.4% actual sodium chlorite? If you don't, read it again. The powder is only 80% sodium chlorite. The characteristics of sodium chlorite are important. It is a hazardous material for the purpose of shipping. It comes in white or slightly yellow flakes. A hundred pounds is shipped in a metal drum 14 inches in diameter, and 27 inches high. Smaller amounts usually come in plastic jars. It can cause fires if it contacts organic materials and a spark.

2. A maintenance dose of MMS is six drops from the green bottle with the white bottle cap as given in Chapter 10. All drops mentioned in this book and on this page are drops as given in Chapter 10.

3. A full dose to overcome diseases is 15 to 18 drops from the green bottle with the white bottle cap, also shown in chapter 10. For disease normally a full dose is given twice within two hours each day until the disease is gone. See protocols at the end of chapter 10.

4. When using Stabilized Oxygen at the standard 3.5% to make MMS (using vinegar), use eight times the number of drops as is

specified in the various recipes listed in this book. If you are using a standard eye dropper as shown in Chapter 10 use 12 times the number of drops as is specified in the various recipes listed in this book.

5.   One drop of MMS contains nine milligrams of sodium chlorite

6.   When 6 drops are mixed with ½ teaspoon of vinegar in a dry clean glass, one milligram of chlorine dioxide will be generated in three minutes. The solution will not become much stronger than one milligram as the chlorine dioxide near the surface of the liquid goes into the air. You can make it stronger by putting a lid on the solution preventing much of the chlorine from escaping.

7.   When ½ glass of apple juice, grape juice, or pineapple juice is added to the mixture given in number 6 above, and the drink is consumed, one milligram of chlorine dioxide will be generated each hour for approximately 12 hours within the human body.

8.   Chlorine dioxide, generated by MMS, is the most powerful killer known to man of microorganisms, such as, viruses, bacteria, parasite, molds and yeasts. Chlorine dioxide has been known and used for over 100 years as a sterilizer for hundreds of uses in hospitals and the food industry. No other chemical or drug has an equal effect. Adding vinegar to sodium chlorite creates the same power to kill microorganisms in the body.

9.   Do not allow MMS to set in direct sunlight. It creates high pressure and has been known to blow the lid off. The liquid after contacting sunlight becomes very strong and will create burns if not washed off immediately. In the case of contact with eyes, flush with water for several minutes.

10.   Any dose of MMS requires ¼ to ½ teaspoon of vinegar or citric acid with the exception of intravenous use. Without vinegar or citric there is very little benefit. Normally, do not use vinegar or citric when used intravenously. The blood will accomplish what the vinegar would do otherwise, but it does it more slowly.

11. Any vinegar is okay to use, but must be 5 - 6% acetic acid.

12. Any sodium chlorite for use in laboratory or for use in water treatment for humans is acceptable for making MMS. (When using 15 drops and then adding juice to drink, the amount of impurities in 15 drops is insignificant when considering the maximum allowable daily impurities that might be allowed for a human being to consume.)

13. Sodium chlorite is used throughout the world to generate chlorine dioxide for water purification, for bleaching of paper pulp, for bleaching of cotton, and hundreds of other uses in industry.

14. Sodium chlorite was first used for treatment of humans in 1926 at Germany by Dr. William F. Koch, MD, Ph.D. It has been use in the U. S. since 1930.

15. Since 1926 it has been considered by those who use sodium chlorite that it is Stabilized Oxygen and that it furnishes oxygen to various parts of the body. That is a mistaken idea. No useable oxygen is available from sodium chlorite. But Chlorine dioxide is also an oxidizer. It is a weaker oxidizer than oxygen and cannot oxidize health body cells, but equal quantities as oxygen can oxidize a much greater amount of material that can be oxidized.

16. Vitamin C that is used in juices as a preservative will completely prevent the MMS from working. Do not use juices from off the shelf unless you are sure no vitamin C has been added. Some pure apple juices do not have added vitamin C. The natural vitamin C in juices is not a problem.

17. Orange juice will prevent MMS from working. It prevents the chlorine dioxide from being generated.

18. Apple juice, cranberry juice, grape juice, and pineapple juice are okay to add to the MMS drink after the three minute wait if the juices have not had vitamin C added. The best idea is to use fresh juices

that you know do not have vitamin C added. Most other juices
prevent the MMS action that is necessary. Very few manufacturers
do not use vitamin C as a preservative. Read the label very carefully.
If vitamin C has been added do not use the juice.

19. Shelf life, if the bottle has not set in the direct sunlight, is two to
four years if the bottle is dark glass or plastic. Clear glass or plastic
is okay for a short period of one or two days. If the bottle sets in the
direct sunlight it will last only about an hour even when if it is in
dark glass or plastic.

20. Full strength MMS is alkaline at a pH of 13. It can cause a slight
burn if not washed off of the skin in less than a minute. Flush with
water. When vinegar is added to the drops of MMS the pH is then
4.5. When apple juice is added after three minutes the pH matches
the apple juice exactly, which is approximately 4.8. The other juices
mentioned in this book are similar. Use only apple juice, grape juice,
pineapple juice, or cranberry juice that has not had extra vitamin C
added.

21. MMS can be used to purify water. Use 4 drops per gallon when
in the jungle or in the woods. Wait 8 hours after adding the drops.
The water is then safe. Or use 3 drops and the activate with 15 drops
of citric acid or vinegar, wait 3 minutes and then add it to a gallon of
water in a foreign country to make the water safe. The gallon of
water with activated MMS is safe in less than an hour.

22. Sodium chlorite powder is hazardous. It cannot be allowed to
come into contact with heat and organic materials at the same time.
It can causes fires. The liquid made from the powder is not
hazardous, but if it is allowed to dry out and become a powder again
it will be hazardous.

See chapter 17 for information on buying sodium chlorite.

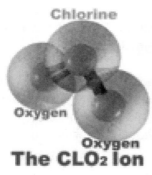

Chlorine

Oxygen

Oxygen

The CLO₂ Ion

Chapter 16

How to Make MMS in Your Kitchen

MAKING 12.6 OUNCES OF MMS: There are more than 1,412 doses of MMS in 12 ounces. That should last you and your family for a couple of years. MMS is light sensitive so you must bottle it in a very dark glass or plastic bottle, or in dark opaque plastic. Dark green, blue, or brown transparent plastic is okay. The light that goes through these dark colors will not harm the MMS. Don't worry about the MMS being out in the daylight for a couple of days. However, never allow it to set in the direct sunlight. Sunlight will ruin it in an hour even when it's in a dark plastic bottle.

The reason that we use 12.6 ounces is because that's how many ounces of MMS 100 grams of sodium chlorite will make. The reason for that is 100 grams of sodium chlorite is the easiest amount that you can purchase. Many chemical supply houses sell 100 grams for about $30. Five or six pounds can be purchased at laboratory chemical supply shops for $300, but if you are serious bulk quantities of 100 pound barrels sell for about $275 to $700 at different industrial chemical companies. (See Chapter 15 for data on buying sodium chlorite.) An update from a reader tells me that a 110 pound barrel sells for $224.40 at the Los Angeles Chemical company. But they have a $300 minimum thus he bought two barrels.

However, if worse comes to worse, and you really need to do something immediately to cure some problem or you just want to prove it works there will certainly be at least one health food store near you that carries Stabilized Oxygen. Buy some of that and use eight times as many drops as is given in this book as a dose. The dose that they suggest on the bottle isn't enough to cure a mouse. (Or if you just want some MMS exactly to my formula and don't want to fool around, buy a bottle from my friend in Canada, it's just $20 for a bottle that will last you for 2

years.   See the end of Chapter 8).   Or see my Web Site
miraclemineral.org for a number of suppliers in the US. If you are using
a regular eye dropper then the drops are much smaller than from the
bottle mentioned in this book so you should use at least 16 times the
drops given in the instructions in this book. (That is if you are using the
standard 3.5%, Stabilized Oxygen from the health food store). I hope
you understand that MMS at 28% plus is 8 times stronger than the
Stabilized Oxygen however, they also provide a standard dropper with
small drops so use 12 drops of Stabilized Oxygen for each single drop of
MMS that you would use. Do everything else told here, that is add the
vinegar or citric acid or Lemon or lime wait 3 minutes, add apple juice
and drink. The bottle is gone in a week or two. On the other hand,
expect most diseases to be cured in that amount of time. Also keep in
mind that there are a few groups that sell Stabilized Oxygen that isn't
really Stabilized Oxygen, but rather some other chemical that they think
is better than sodium chlorite. Do not expect other chemicals to work,
because they will not.

In the last several years different companies have offered various
strengths of sodium chlorite solution thus making different strengths of
Stabilized Oxygen. One group sells it at 25% which is close to the MMS
which is 28%. If you did get the 25% strength it would be okay to just
use all of the recipes and drops as given in this book.

See the end chapter 17 for directions on how to find and buy sodium
chlorite and also see chapter 17. It's harder to get now-a-days because of
the terrorist problem.

What you will need to make 12.6 ounces of MMS:

1. You will need at least a 15 ounce bottle. It can be clear plastic if
    you do not intend to keep the liquid in the bottle for more than a
    couple of days. This is OK if you are waiting to transfer the
    liquid to dark bottles or containers. Just be sure that you do not
    leave the liquid MMS in the clear bottle. You could actually get
    away with leaving it in a clear bottle if you kept the clear bottle in

a closed tight cabinet. Don't leave it in a refrigerator as refrigerators are opened to the light too often.

2. <u>At least one quart of distilled water.</u> Do not use any other kind of water. It's okay to used purified water if it says, "For all distilled water purposes." Do not use spring water of mineral water unless it is an emergency and you can't wait.

3. <u>A plastic pitcher that has a good pouring spout.</u>

4. <u>A one quart pan or larger that can be heated.</u> Do not use metal including stainless steel. Use glass or Corning Ware or a new Teflon coated pot that does not have any scratches through to the metal.

5. <u>Some kind of fairly accurate gram scales.</u> Should be accurate to 1/10 gram. An electronic postal scale will do. Postal spring scales would be okay if you had some accurate weights to adjust the scale with just before you use it.

6. <u>A black marking pen.</u> Be sure you have one on hand.

7. <u>Some small bottles to put the MMS solution in after you make it</u>. Many pharmacies have small brown bottles with droppers. It's okay to use these bottles so long as you never allow the MMS solution to get up into the rubber bulb. If you tip the bottle over, remove the dropper and wash it out with water making sure the bulb is washed thoroughly.

8. <u>You will need at least 100 grams of sodium chlorite.</u> When buying this chemical make sure it is chlor<u>ite</u> that you are buying and <u>not</u> chlor<u>ide.</u> Chloride will not work. You will notice that the sodium chlorite comes in flakes, either white or slightly yellow.

When buying sodium chlorite don't tell them what you are using it for. Tell them it is for water purification tests. The first thing that they will tell you is that their chemicals are not for internal use. That is not something to worry about. That is what all the sources of sodium chlorite specify, even those that sell their chemicals for public water systems. Remember, when you add distilled water you are diluting the chemical. Then when you use only 12 drops and you dilute that with ½ glass of water or juice, any impurities are also diluted. By the time you have done that much dilution, the impurities are always way below the maximum allowable impurities per day that you can afford to put in your body. The sales people are always worried about being sued, so they will always try to talk you out of buying the chemical, or even refuse to sell it to you if you tell them what you are going to use it for. (See chapter 17, second half of chapter, for information on buying sodium chlorite.)

Checking the sodium chlorite powder to make sure it is real.
I worry that someone might try to fool you into thinking some other powder is sodium chlorite in order to make you fail at curing someone, or just some clerk might be too dumb to sell you the correct powder. So here is how you check to make sure that you absolutely have the correct powder. First you must buy the strips that test for chlorine from any swimming pool store. Cost is $6.00 to $12.00 for 50 test strips.

(1) When you open your package the sodium chlorite must be flaky. Several companies have sold sodium chlorite that is not flaky in the last couple of years. If there is no flakes assume that you do not have sodium chlorite, but go ahead and do the other steps given here. If the chemical passes the following tests it is indeed sodium chlorite and they, for some reason, ground the flakes before you got it.

(2) Crush up a few of the flakes into powder. (Do this by putting the flakes into a tablespoon and crushing with a second spoon).

(3) Put ½ teaspoon of the crushed powder into an empty glass and add three level teaspoons of distilled water. Swirl gently until the powder is completely dissolved in the water. You could warm slightly to aid in dissolving or you could heat the three teaspoons of water before adding to the powder.

(4) Now drop 10 drops of this solution into an empty glass. Add ½ teaspoon of vinegar. Any vinegar will do as long as it says "5% acetic acid" or "5% acidity." Wait three minutes.

(5) Wet a pool chlorine strip with this solution. It should read at least 1 ppm chlorine present. It is actually reading chlorine dioxide (pool chlorine strips can't tell the difference).
(6) Now wet a second pool chlorine indicator strip with the original solution from which you took the 10 drops. This solution should read no chlorine present (because you haven't added the vinegar to that solution) or less strength than the above (5) test.

If your powder fails either step 5 or step 6 you do not have sodium chlorite powder. Someone is fooling you or they have made a mistake. Run the test one more time to make sure. If it doesn't pass the test, don't use it. Don't accuse anyone. Don't upset anyone. Just ask for some real stuff.

<u>If your powder is okay, follow the steps given below</u>.

<u>Making the MMS solution</u>: The MMS solution is 28% sodium chlorite powder. The 100 grams is 28% of 357 grams. That is 12.6 ounces. If you buy a bottle of 100 grams, you should just check that it indeed has 100 grams in it before adding it to the solution. One hundred grams is 3.54 ounces.

<u>Step 1</u>: Verify that 100 grams or 3.54 ounces is contained in your bottle of sodium chlorite.

<u>Step 2</u>: Measure out nine ounces of distilled water and add it to your heating pot. Be very careful to get nine ounces exactly.

<u>Step 3</u>: Now dump the 3.54 ounces (the 100 grams) of sodium chlorite into the 9 ounces of water in the heating pot. The heating pot should not be on the fire yet. Put the heating pot on the hot plate and stir until dissolved. Once the white flakes or powder is dissolved immediately remove it from the fire. It should never be heated to the boiling point. It should only be warm when the sodium chlorite is finally dissolved.

Never go away and leave it heating. It dissolves fast. Stay and stir until dissolved.

Step 4: The liquid should be yellow and clear. Pour into the pitcher and then use the pitcher to pour into your plastic container with a lid. Put the lid on and set aside to cool.

Warning: when the MMS is spilled on a table or on the floor it must be cleaned up with plenty of water. Never allow it to dry. The white powder is very flammable when dry.

Step 5: Purchase a dark colored bottle or a number of small colored bottles and transfer from your original bottle if it is not a dark bottle.

Make up labels with the data for use on them taken from the label at the end of chapter 17, and glue the labels on the bottles. You can use your computer for making the labels. The MMS lasts for several years. It should have maximum data on the label for someone a couple of years from now who might want to use it. For example, if a hurricane damaged much of your home and help was days away, if the bottle had proper information it could be used to help you or save your life. If it was just a dark bottle with no label, no one would know to use it.

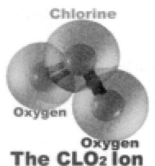

Chlorine

Oxygen

Oxygen

The CLO₂ Ion

Chapter 17

Making 13 or 1300 bottles of MMS in Your Kitchen

Bottling the MMS

The MMS is bottled from powdered <u>sodium chlorite</u> referred to in this chapter as Salts. Be careful because we still get people who mistake sodium chlo<u>ride</u> for sodium chlo<u>rite.</u> They sound similar, but they are quite different, so use only sodium chlorite.   Use this same process duplicated exactly to produce 13 bottles or 1300 bottles.

<u>Bottling 13 plastic bottles that contain 5.5 oz Each of MMS</u>

Note: The MMS in a <u>four ounce</u> bottle actually weighs 5.5 ounces, because it is much heavier than water.

Please do everything exactly as I say. Once you have bottled 300 - 500, bottles then, if you must, change to what you consider a better way. But at first, do it my way. You are not playing. People's lives can depend upon you doing it right. Read these instructions several times, and then read each step as you do it. There is data on plastic bottles at the end of this chapter. We ask, if you do your own bottles that you label them so that people can know what they are and how to use them. Someday there will be a bottle sitting on a shelf for several years and a sick person will look at it. If he knows how to use it, it may save his life.

<u>What you will need</u>. Please get all the items that I mention here for the first 13 bottles which will contain 6,059 doses of MMS at six drops per dose.

1.   One plastic temporary holding bottle is need for each group of 13 bottles you intend to make. Use 64 ounce juice bottles. Go to the store and buy at least two 64 ounce juice bottles. Dump the juice into some other containers and rinse the juice bottles out. Save these juice bottles

to use over and over. Buy juice bottles that have easy hand holds. Do not try to use extra larger bottles, they are too hard to handle.

2. Enough distilled water for all the MMS that you are going to make. You can use purified water if it says, "For all distilled water purposes." Do not use any other kind of water. Do not use spring water or mineral water unless it is an extreme emergency.

3. A plastic pitcher that has a small pouring spout. Use the tall pitchers. Check the spout to see that it will pour into the MMS bottle easily. Or use a coffee maker glass pitcher for pouring the MMS into the bottles.

If you intend to do more than 13 bottles then invest in a larger container such as one of the containers used to place a 5 gallon plastic jug upside down in to dispense drinking water. These containers have a valve at the bottom that works very well for filling the bottles.

Do not use a funnel for pouring into the MMS bottle. It uses up too much time. Fill each bottle to the top. Do not leave any air room in the top of the bottle. This is so it won't splash during shipping and worry the postal workers, or even worse the airline workers.

4. A four quart pan that can be heated to be used for dissolving the salts. Use only glass or Teflon coated steel. The Teflon coat must not be scratched through to metal. Do not use stainless steel or aluminum. You could make a poisonous MMS if you use metal for dissolving the Salts. That would be a disaster. If you use stainless steel you will notice that the MMS discolors the metal. That's because it is dissolving the steel out of the other metals. Do not bottle such a solution. Corning Ware is also okay to use.

5. Fifteen four ounce colored empty bottles. Remember, it takes 5.5 ounces of MMS to fill a four ounce bottle. Use the flip spout caps. Tighten these caps hand tight only, but very hand tight. See further data. See the label at the end of this article and see data for ordering bottles at the end of this article.

6. Fifteen flip spout caps that fit the bottles. See data for ordering bottles.

7. Several super glue tubes. For gluing the lids on the MMS bottles.

8. A can of 3M Super 77 Multipurpose Adhesive bought from the hardware store for about 10 bucks. Do not buy any other adhesive. Do not buy any other 3M adhesive. If you do you will just make a mess and waste some bottles.

9. A can of Shellac. This is for spraying the labels to prevent problems in damp environments. This is necessary, otherwise in a few weeks or days the bottles become a mess. Spray the labels before they are cut out.

Notice the freezer bags filled with sodium chlorite and the flip spout lids in the bowl.

10. A cardboard box approximately two feet high. Cut a slot into the top of the box so that the MMS bottle will lie in the slot, but not fall through. Put a mark on the box near the top of the label where it will stick onto the bottle. This is so that when you are putting labels on the bottles that you get most of them in approximately the same area of the bottle.

11. Thirteen labels. Make the labels on a computer, eight at a time on letter size paper (8-1/2 X 11) and cut them out with a razor knife and a straight edge. After you cut them out spray six labels at a time and stick them on. It takes less time than it takes to remove labels from their backing. Also it is very hard to find the right labels that your computer will print each label exactly in the center of the label. It's much easier to just print 8 labels on a page and cut them out with a razor knife. Buy special paper for the labels. Get glossy paper from an office supply store, or order special labels, but ordering labels can be expensive.

12. A box of one quart freezer bags should be Zip Lock.

13. You will need one fairly accurate grams scale. Don't use a cheap spring postal scale. Use a more expensive electronic postal scale or other accurate scale. It should be accurate to 1/10 gram.

14. You will need 632.8 grams (that's 22.4 ounces or 1.4 pounds) of the sodium chlorite to make your 13 bottles of MMS.

15. A black marking pen. Be sure to have one on hand.

The procedure:

The MMS is 28% Salts by weight. The Salts are a powder that is dissolved in distilled water. So keep in mind that the MMS will be 28% Salts. This is what makes it so much heavier than water. Do not make a mistake here. People's lives depend upon it. Just follow the instructions below and you will get it right.

Step 1. Fill one freezer bag with 632.8grams of salts. (This is the point where you fill one bag for 13 four ounce bottles, or you fill more freezer bags for more bottles.) Zip the bag or bags closed and store in a clean dry place at room temperature. Mark on the bag(s) "632.8 Grams of Sodium Chlorite" and put the date. This is a temporary step, but who knows what might happen to make you forget what is in the bag.

Step 2. Measure out 1,627.2 grams of distilled water (that's 57.6 ounces) and put it in an empty juice bottle and mark the level with a black marking pen. (When this amount of water is added to 632.8 grams of standard 80% sodium chlorite salt you will have 80 ounces of MMS). If you are making more than 13 initial four ounce bottles you will be using this same amount of distilled water for each group of 13 four ounce bottles. So once you have marked on the juice bottle, then use that juice bottle to fill your other juice bottles.

Step 3. Put the four quart nonmetal heating pan on the burner and pour the distilled water from one of the bottles in which you have 57.6 ounces of water into the pan. Do not let it boil. Keep the temperature well under boiling. One hundred fifty degrees is plenty hot.

Step 4. Once the water is warm, dump the contents of one freezer bag made in Step 1 into the heating pan with the water. Stir it constantly until all of the salts are dissolved. The solution will be slightly yellow and foggy. This is normal. The pan will be less than ½ full. Remove the heating pan with the solution from the burner. This solution now weighs 80 ounces. The solution will turn clear but yellow within several minutes, but so long as all of the salts have been dissolved you can proceed to step 5.

Step 5. Set the 64 ounce juice bottle into a plastic container or another non metallic pan. Use the large funnel. Pour the contents of the heated pan into the 64 ounce juice bottle. Although the solution at this time weighs 80 ounces it will fit into one of the 64 ounce juice bottles. The additional pan is to prevent you from spilling the MMS. Keep in mind that if the MMS gets spilled it makes a mess. If it dries, it makes a white powder that will burn or explode. There is not enough to cause damage from explosion, but if it starts a fire there could be a lot of damage. Do not spill the MMS. If you spill it, wipe it up and then wash the spot with plenty of water.

Step 6. Write on the bottle "MMS" and the date created with the black marker pen.   Leave room for the next time you use the bottle. Remember, you cannot leave the MMS in the clear bottles for very long. Generally not longer than one week.   The light, even just room light begins to deteriorate the solution in the bottles.   This step is just a temporary step in the process of making MMS.

The bottle is being filled from a coffee maker pitcher. Notice the clear but slightly yellow MMS liquid.

Note: Do not put labels on empty bottles. Wait until the bottles are full and closed before adding labels, because any spilled solution ruins the label.

Step 1. Take the 64 ounce MMS juice bottle and open it. Using the plastic pitcher with the small pour spout, or the coffee maker pitcher pour in enough MMS to fill about five MMS bottles. Don't measure this; just pour it 1/4 full or so.

Step 1A. Alternately, pour the entire contents of four or five 64 ounce MMS juice bottles that now have 80 ounce contents into the water cooler unit described in 16 above. Use the spigot to fill 12 to 20 green bottles. It's best not to have more than that number of bottles without lids at one time.

Step 3. Install tops on each of the green four ounce MMS bottles. Do
this by holding each cap on its side and dropping 2 drops of super glue
on the threads of the cap and then turn the cap onto the bottle. Tighten
the cap as tight as you can by hand using something like a towel on the
cap to help you tighten it. A towel works best, do not use pliers. After
an hour, the caps should be impossible to remove by hand. Caps closed
by using pliers usually are too tight and they begin to leak.

Step 4. After the top is tightened on each bottle, grasp the bottle in your
hand and squeeze it as hard as you can. Look for leaks. Drops of liquid
will drop off the bottle normally if there is a leak. In rare cases a fine
spray or stream might come off the bottom of the bottle. You need
plenty of light to see the fine spray. Normally there will only be one or
two leaking bottles per 100 bottles, but it is important that you find any
leaks as one bottle can foul up an entire shipment.

Step 5. Keep the bottles in a clean dry place. It is ok to keep bottles at
normal room light but do not allow them to set in the sun.

Step 6. Adding the Labels: (See "Making the Labels" below) Take six
labels and lay them face down on a sheet of newspaper. Spray the labels
with 3M Super 77 adhesive. Don't attempt to do more than six at a time
as the adhesive tends to dry and if you use more than six the last labels
will be too dry to stick. If they do dry, re-spray those that have dried
before attempting to stick them on the bottles.

Step 7. Place one of the filled bottles in the slot on the cardboard box that
you have already prepared. (See item #9 under "What you will need" at
the beginning of these instructions) Pick up a single label that has been
sprayed with adhesive, hold it over the bottle near the mark that you have
made, adjust it by eye to be straight, and press it down on the bottle.
Smooth the label on the bottle with your hand. Be sure to smooth it
down tight.

Step 8. Do steps 7 and 8 on all of the bottles, doing six at a time.

Step 9. Preparing the bottles to be shipped: Using a one quart plastic
freezer storage bag, place two green MMS bottles in the bag laying them

down in the bottom of the bag. Wrap the top of the bag around the two bottles, close the zip lock making sure it is tight, and place a rubber band around the bag and bottles to hold them in place. Now put the bottles in the bag into another bag and close it. If they leak in shipment the liquid will hopefully remain in one of the bags.

Step 10. Do Step 9 until all bottles to be shipped are ready. This prevents problems of leaking bottles when shipping. A single leaking bottle can stop an entire shipment preventing the treatment of hundreds of people. It could even result in the post office stopping future shipments. Be very careful.

Step 11. Have them boxed for shipping. Unless you are very good at doing shipping, do not try to box them yourself. Keep in mind this shipment is of utmost importance. Don't take chances. When at the shipping store don't take chances to save money on the packaging. Have it done as best as possible. From the shipping store take the box to FedEx or DHL for shipping.

Making the Labels:

1. Most draw programs have provisions for making labels. Otherwise you can buy a cheap label program. Normally you would use the program to set up a single label as shown with this literature and then the label program will automatically make a number of labels depending upon the labels that you select. In this case select a label that has eight per page. That will give you approximately the correct size of label when cut out. Or duplicate the label given below.

2. Buy good paper. Pay $8 to $10 a ream. Don't use photo paper. Photo paper is very expensive and not suitable as it is too thick. Buy a special paper at any office supply store that has a glossy surface, but is standard paper thickness. Print the labels on the computer. After the computer ink has dried, before you cut them out, spray them with shellac so that they are soaked, but spray them only once.

3. Cut them out with a razor knife using a ruler as a straight edge. Do not spray on the adhesive until after you cut out the labels.

4. An alternate method would be to have labels printed professionally.

Buying the Bottles and Caps:

When searching for plastic bottles the key words anywhere in the world are **pet plastic** bottles. Pet really stands for polyethylene terephthalate, but no one ever uses the actual words. Everyone uses the words pet plastic bottles. So use pet plastic bottles for your search word and that will show you hundreds of companies sell plastic bottles. Be sure to always buy dark plastic as light will cause the solution to deteriorate. The plastic can be "seen through" so long as it is very dark.

Dr. Ron Neer a (dentist) decided he wanted to do something to help spread MMS around the world so he found that the New York SKS Bottle Company was charging unreasonable prices to ship the bottles out of the country and then he found that he could get the bottles cheaper than SKS was selling them for and cheaper than any other place I could find. So below is his phone number and web site.

Check him out. Remember one thing he sells both the bottle and the cap and his prices reflect bottle and cap. Any other bottle company will always list the price without the cap. These caps are important as they are an approved type for shipment by the Department of Transportation. The DOT states that the caps must have a seal so that the bottle won't leak even if the cap comes loose. They are not more expensive; they are just built differently. So if you want to make some MMS no matter how many bottles you buy, you will find Dr. Ron has the best prices, but go ahead and check that out; just remember, the prices include both bottle and DOT approved cap. This is a dispensing cap from which you can count the drops. (The 4 ounce bottle holds 5.5 ounces of MMS because the MMS is heavier than water.)

I have listed him here in my book because I want you to make MMS. I want you to have the experience. I want thousands of people to know how to do it and to be doing it. Ron sells both 2 and 4 ounce bottles. So here is his data:

Dr. Ron Neer Phone (816) 682-6425
www.h2oairwateramerica.com

Bottle and Cap combinations:
4 oz. green or blue pet bottles with
dispensing cap snap top 3 mm orifice.

Qty	Price	per unit	Height	Diameter	weight
1	1.50	1.50	5.25 inches	1.5 inches	15.42 grams
24	$24.00	$1.00			
675	$202.00	$0.30			

2 oz. green pet bottle with dispensing cap
snap top 3 mm orifice.

Qty	Price	Per Unite	Height	Diameter	weight
1	$1.25	$1.25	4.0 inches	1.25 inches	9.2 grams
48	$46.56	$0.97			
1296	$324.00	$0.25			

Miracle Mineral Solution
and water purification drops

Notes: For absolutely purified water or juice always wait 3 minutes after adding the lemon, or lime or citric acid to the drops in this bottle before adding them to the water or juice to be purified. When treating animals, use the same proportions as given for children. Use 1 tblspn citric acid powder and 9 tblspns water to make a 10% solution of citric acid.
Warnings: Do not use full strength.
Dangerous – Keep out of the reach of children. Keep out of direct sunlight.
Antidote= In cases of accidental ingestion drink several glasses of water.

Sold by
Net Weight:5.5 Oz. (163 Gm) Contents: Distilled Water & 28% sodium chlorite

Directions for Use: Always begin with 2 drops or less and increase one drop a day up to 15. Always add 5X as much lemon, or lime, or 10% citric acid solution as the number of drops from this bottle, wait 3 minutes after adding the acid before adding this solution to the water or juice to be purified. Then drink the purified water or juice. If nausea should occur use less drops and acid before adding to the water or juice. For children start with 1 drop, increase daily up to 3 drops for each 25 lbs (11.4 KG) of body weight and for babies 1 drop up to 2 drops. Be sure to add the acid solution and wait as explained above.
Use pineapple, grape, apple, or cranberry juice without added vit C. Do not use orange juice. For maximum effect a second glass of purified water or juice should be taken after one hour.

The label printed above is just a suggested label that you could use. Notice how it is worded. Most of the sellers of MMS are now using this label.

Buying larger amounts of sodium chlorite. It comes in 100 pound and 110 pound steel barrels.

If you want to do a little more, like make up 100 four ounce bottles to sell and give to your family and neighbors, you will need at least 10 pounds. As you can see from the prices, buying a 100 pound barrel will cost you less than trying to get 10 pounds. The problem is you need a company to buy 100 pound barrels as a general rule. Some of these companies listed on the Internet will sell to individuals.

Of course, you can make up your own company and that will work in many cases, but there are those companies that require your company state or city resale number. You might be able to find a local business that will receive the sodium chlorite for you and let you use their name for this purpose or just order it for you. Alternately, you could just buy a resale number from your city.

Finding industrial sources for 100 pound drums is a little harder than buying lab supplies. Go to Google and put in "Drinking water chemicals," or "drinking water treatment chemicals." Of course, use Google for the country you are in. Most countries will have sodium chlorite for water purification. Or look up NSF on the Internet or NSF/ANSI Standard 60. This is an association which many companies sell sodium chlorite. Just start calling the various companies that sell sodium chlorite for water purification. You will eventually find one that will sell you the 100 pound barrel between $250 and $400. Then it will cost you about $150 shipping because it is a hazardous chemical. But remember, with that barrel of 100 pounds you can make 186,000 doses. That is approximately 1/10 cent per dose depending on the amount you paid.

At a last minute decision, on my way south to the first edition of this book, I managed to buy a 100 pound barrel of sodium chlorite from the Los Angeles Chemical Company of Los Angeles, California for the price of $278.00. The lowest price so far. I picked this barrel up at their Las Vegas division. Since I picked it up myself there was no shipping cost. They will not sell to an individual. You must be registered with them as a company. I formed a small company in a Nevada town and then called them to order a barrel. They put my company in their data base when I called them up. They then ordered the barrel for me and told me it would be available at their location in Las Vegas the next week. There was no problem. I paid for it with my personal credit card at the time I picked it up as I had not established credit with them.

Buying Sodium Chlorite Further Data

My suggestion is that you get an extra supply of sodium chlorite if it is at all possible. The government will be acting at the request of the drug companies to limit the sales of sodium chlorite. Once sodium chlorite swings into use as MMS it will eat into the profits of the drug companies. They will fight. They can't win, but you can believe that they will try. You can help this program simply by buying 100 pounds and storing it.

Buying small amounts of sodium chlorite (100 grams up to 5 pounds).

There are a few chemical supply companies that supply chemicals to chemistry students. These along with other chemical supply companies for laboratories are the easiest to do business with. Normally you can order over the Internet. Just use Google and put in "sodium chlorite". Or if you just want Stabilized Oxygen put in Stabilized Oxygen. Or put in "laboratory chemicals" and "sodium chlorite." The companies listed below are in the USA. I have included them just to give you an idea of what kind of chemical supply places will have sodium chlorite.

Here are several lab supply houses that sell sodium chlorite:

www.advanced-scientific.net

At this date, 9/1/06, they charge $36.45 for 100 gm, $117.00 for 500 gm, $361 for 2,500 gm (5.5 pounds).

www.labdepotinc.com

Same prices as Advanced-scientific above.

https://secure5.nexternal.com   same prices as above.

Buying larger amounts of sodium chlorite. It comes in 100 pound steel barrels and in 110 pound steel barrels.

If you want to do a little more, like make up 100 four ounce bottles to sell and give to your family and neighbors, you will need at least 10 pounds. As you can see from the prices above, buying a 100 pound barrel will cost you less than trying to get 10 pounds. The problem is, you need a company to buy 100 pound barrels as a general rule. Some of these companies, listed on the Internet, will sell to individuals.

Of course, you can make up your own company and that will work in many cases, but there are those companies that require your company state or city resale number. You might be able to find a local business that will receive the sodium chlorite for you and let you use their name for this purpose or just order it for you. Alternately, you could just buy a resale number from your city. In any case, good fortune and good luck.

Chapter 18

The Humanitarian Project

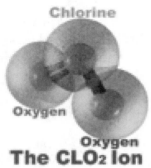

Chlorine

Oxygen

Oxygen

The CLO₂ Ion

I will work with any humanitarian project anywhere that needs my help to bring about the goals listed below. If you have the where-with-all, please get in touch with me. The profit from this book will be spent as needed for distribution and any leftover will be spent for distribution of the MMS in Africa.

A certain amount of humanitarian work has already been done, but it is not enough. It isn't even a drop in the bucket. Much more has got to be done to change Africa and thus changes the world.

Why change Africa? The facts are the industrial nations spend untold billions of humanitarian dollars in Africa each year. It's untold because no one knows how much, but it is tremendous. Go to any city in Africa and you will see numerous nonprofit NGO's (Non Governmental Organizations) there spending money doing humanitarian work. The Red Cross is there, the World Health Organization, World Vision, USAID, Doctors Without Borders, Global Fund, City of Hope, and dozens of others exist in almost every city in Africa.

Why all the money spent? Why are they so far behind us? Africa is right on the equator. It is mostly warm and a very good environment for disease. Just malaria alone sickens 500,000,000 people each year. When people are sick, they can't work. They can't plant the crops, or harvest them when the time comes. They can't build houses or produce wheel barrows. In other words, with sickness, nothing much gets done. It isn't that they are lazy, nor is it because they are uncivilized. It's simple, when 500,000,000 people get sick, you have that many who can't work, and it then requires almost that many to take care of them. It takes much of the resources to just take care of those who are sick.

When I was young I always heard that Africa was so far behind us because they weren't civilized or because they are always fighting, or because they are lazy. But the fact is, as I stated in the above paragraph, when you are sick you simply can't work. The situation is that their country has problems that the rest of the world has never had. As part of the human race it is our job to help them solve those problems. If you don't feel sorry for them, that's okay, and if you don't feel responsible for them, that's okay. But the fact is, we, as part of the human race cannot afford to ignore them. The disease that will kill the entire human race may be fermenting there now. Or the man that saves the human race may be being born there now. One thing is certain; the human race cannot afford to not confront either of these possibilities. If the human race is to survive on this planet for any reasonable time, we cannot let any problem go unchecked.

When you hear someone talking about any country or continent taking responsibility for their own situation, you should stop and think. We are the people of Planet Earth. It's up to us to take responsibility for our own situation and that includes the fact that we must solve the African problem if we expect to feel safe at all.

It's amazing, but we can cure the majority of the poverty in the world merely by furnishing a cure for malaria. That won't cure all of the poverty, but a whole lot of it. Then if we can cure AIDS, we will also cure a lot more poverty. This money that would then ordinarily would go to Africa could stay here to build a space program, or greater roads, or more training for our poor.

And one more thing, if we treat all of Africa the human race will be taking one giant step towards survival. If we don't work to help one another in this way, the human race will eventually cease to exist on this planet. Since this planet came into existence there has been more than 50 catastrophes that would have destroyed all of mankind had we been here when they happened. We are here now, and such a catastrophe is over due to happen again. One of the places that the money that we will save when we don't have to spend billions on Africa can go towards preparing for the next catastrophe. If we don't, the human race is condemned to extinction. The next catastrophe will happen; there is no doubt of that. It's impossible to think that it will not happen; it's just when will it happen? It could easily be tomorrow, or it could be 25,000 years from now, but it will happen. If we are not ready, that's the end of the human race.

There are a lot of reasons to help those who really need it in the world, but probably the greatest reason is the benefit that the helper receives. When an individual has no reason for helping or aiding others, he is that way because he is solely interested in himself and his immediate family and goals. Do you see that not only narrows his play field and his interests, but it narrows his thinking. When hard times come, his thinking will still be narrowed. He won't have the broad prospectus that might be required for survival. And that's only a small part of it. When one begins to think about others the mental area in his mind broadens. His interests broaden his enjoyment of life changes. He understands others better, and thus his life is easier because of it. A person who remains interested in only his family and his goals only knows his small area of the world. His world is very small. When he becomes interested in others and their problems his thinking broadens greatly. The world that exists within his mind expands. He has more data that he can include in his thinking and his problem solving. Life for him is better and life for humanity is a bit better because of his broadened outlook.

This is a reason for helping mankind, and anything you do for others is helping mankind. Your life will be better because of anything you do in that arena.

There is now little doubt that the MMS can cure most of African diseases. Once the diseases have been mostly cured, Africa will need to be put to work including those in the small villages. I have talked to a number of chiefs and other leaders and they have agreed that the work plan I have and one that I used in Orange County California back in 1956 will mostly work in Africa. Implementation will cost, but the program will eventually pay for itself and make money and it will put Africa to work. Anyone wanting to know more about this program please contact me.

If you still don't believe in the MMS, give it a try. Buy some Stabilized Oxygen sold at thousands of places and follow the instructions in this book. If it scares you to take it, try giving it to your dog first. It won't hurt him and you will have more confidence in taking it or giving it. Just remember, his body is smaller than yours, so give him a smaller proportion. If he weighs 1/10th as much as you, give him 1/10th the amount you would take. But regardless of how you test it out, please do it. You just might be the one that makes the difference, and the life you save may be your own.

I suggest that you buy at least one bottle from one of the suppliers listed on the MMS Web Site miraclemineral.org it's only $20 and it will last you a year. My friend in Canada at www.health4allinfo.ca has agreed to furnish enough MMS to treat a whole country in Africa. He will furnish it as needed in any Africa country that will accept it. The only problem is, he cannot also furnish the money to distribute it to the African country. We need someone to step up to the plate and furnish the money. The first country will cost about three million dollars. The next country will be a small fraction of that, but there will be numerous expenses including training people to use the MMS. Many people will want to come and be trained. We will need to accommodate them as it will be the best and cheapest way to get people trained to treat the rest of Africa.

There may be other humanitarian organizations that will come along and help, but we cannot depend upon them. So far they have refused to even admit that we exist or that the MMS exists. I have written to Bill Gates foundation many times and always receive polite letters of refusal. That's better than most. Usually I don't even get a polite letter of refusal.

To begin to cure malaria and AIDS in any country, one program would go as follows: To this point I have found large amounts of Africans who cannot contribute money toward their own health. Furthermore, many of them do not trust the drugs that are supposed to cure them enough to spend the little money that they have on them. Thus, in the beginning our treatment must be free or it simply won't happen.

Once we have picked a country that will accept us we will need to buy a compound from which the operation can be conducted. Several clinics would be set up in the local area where anyone could come for a dose of

MMS. Then a number of vehicles would be purchased. There would be one MMS trained member for each vehicle. Local individuals would be hired, two for each vehicle. In the beginning they would be trained by the MMS members. The vehicles would travel out to the villages delivering the MMS solution and training the village chief and other members how to dispense the MMS solution.

Local people work in Africa for $30 to $40 a month. They would be trained quickly to deliver the MMS solution and to train the villagers. Then probably in each country a manufacturing plant would be set up in the MMS compound. This would save a great deal of cost as the main cost so far has been shipping of the solution. The actual cost is less than one cent per dose, but the shipping increases the cost considerably.

As more people were trained more delivery cars would be purchased. Each car would have a route to follow. There would be trained people in each car to continue to make sure that the villagers know how to use the Solution. With the proper money, the expansion of cars and trained people would go fast as it takes only about three weeks to train an individual in the dispensing of the MMS solution. The average country of Africa should take a little more than a full year to get the MMS solution delivered to the people and responsible individuals properly trained.   It is hoped that after the first two months working with the locals, that extra individuals can be accepted from other countries for training.   Thus, other countries can begin programs to get the MMS solution to their people.

A great deal of money is needed, but it will be billions less than Bill Gates has in mind to give to research organizations that Africa will never see. Of course many other organizations and countries will read this book and begin their own programs; at least I hope they will.   The human race certainly needs them to. We can't fail if you, the reader, take some interest. Come to Africa, or set up a discussion group as to how you can help, or make some MMS and see that the old people and sick people in your neighborhood are treated. That alone could make the difference. Or just see that plenty of people get this book. Send me a letter or email and let me know how you are doing.

There is a point, I don't know how many people need to know, but a point can be reached which I call the point of no return. If we reach that point, the window can no longer be slammed in our face. That is when enough public individuals have learned the data, have used it, and know it works. Believe me; a few individuals won't do it. It will take millions who know that it works. Please join us. Either use it, or just accept the idea that the public deserves to know. Get as many people to download the free e-book *The Miracle Mineral Supplement of the 21st Century* Part I and then purchase part II if possible. And when you successfully use the MMS to help someone or yourself, broadcast it widely. We MAY only have a few months. You probably have less than 12 months to get it to the public. The elimination and prevention of suffering, misery and death of millions depends upon you. (Sorry to be so dramatic, but that is the fact.) Have your friends download the free book at the www.miraclemineral.org Site or better still have them purchase the hard copy for $19.95 at the same site.

One more thing, this is now the end of July, August 1, 2007. A fair number of organizations and people were expecting great changes to take place in July. They were expecting our government to change and for freedom to return. They were expecting help from above. Some were expecting help from God and others were expecting help from higher beings who were on their way here. I had a number of phone calls and several emails telling me not to worry. I could soon publish my book and everything would be alright. One group said a space ship was being set in orbit right now.

I'm 75 years old. The message in the above paragraph has been given to me many times during the past 68 years. So let me give you, the reader, a message. I've had this message for more years than most of you would believe. It's this: Mankind is going to have to save mankind. No wonderful help from above is ever coming. No wonderful beings of light or any other great being is going to arrive and save us. If we get saved, we are going to have to do it. God is not going to save us. Remember the old saying, "God helps those who help themselves." Well look at it. In the 20th century more people were murdered and killed than all the centuries before. God didn't save those hundreds of millions of people who were shot, or burned, or blown to bits. We are just going to have to save ourselves.

Well, do as you wish, but promise me that every time you pray, you will go out and either give this book to someone, or better still, sell it to someone, because if they buy it, they will read it. In that case you really will be doing something to help mankind.

One more thing I wanted to mention. Please learn to make the MMS and save some of the sodium chlorite powder somewhere, at least for your family. It won't always be available. On the other hand, make lots of it and sell it when you can. Make some money, because there will be a big demand for it eventually, and if you have it you will be able to sell it. Few people realize at this time that when most of the people in the US can either make it or get their hands on it, most of the power of the FDA will be broken. The FDA bases most of their power on their ability to stop things that will decrease the income of the major pharmaceuticals. But with the MMS available to the people eventually most of the drugs will not be needed. That may take a while, but it could happen. See Chapter 23 if you have doubts

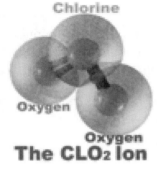

Chlorine

Oxygen

Oxygen

The CLO₂ Ion

Chapter 19

Research Needed

Of course research is need, billions of dollars worth of research. This is the most effective medicine that has ever been invented up to this time. We must know what is the maximum dose for every kind of disease that exists. We must know when to use it intravenously and when not to. We must know when it will cure cancer and when it will not. We must know if there are any bacterial diseases or virus diseases that it is not effective against and why. We only know, at this point, that it cures many things. The amount of knowledge is a tiny bit of what we should know.

Anyone interested in research should contact me. Up to this point I have the most experience with the MMS, however, there is no doubt that many medical men will know more about it than me after I describe what I know to them. Medical men and alternate medicine people need to begin working with it, as many lives can be saved and much suffering can be alleviated. I am definitely willing to tell all I can to anyone doing research.

The drug companies have a great deal of technology that could be used with the MMS. One important research would be to develop carriers that can carry the chlorine dioxide deeper into the body before it is released. Thus possibly getting to some of those incurable diseases that have not been touched so far (as far as we know). However, the chances of getting the drug companies to do such a thing are very slim. Their thinking has always been to make the patient feel more comfortable by eliminate some or most of the symptoms, because that will never cure the patient and thus you can continue to sell the drug for a long time. I suppose we couldn't keep them from improving the formula if they decided to do so. But they don't deserve to do so because they will sell the results as some sort of drugs for hundreds or thousands of dollars. We'll see how that works out.

I know that there are those who are doing a certain amount of research at this time. I hope they will keep it up and maybe help inform the public. If you have read Chapter 13 you do know that there is some research going on or maybe by the time this book is published that phase of the research will be completed.

Chapter 20

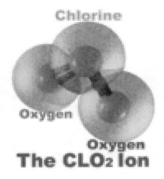

The Basic Details for use of the MMS

The solution does not become the Miracle Mineral Supplement until you add 5 drops of one of the food acids for each drop of MMS from the bottle. The food acids consist of lemon juice, or lime juice, or 10% citric acid solution or in emergency vinegar, and until you have waited three minutes, and until after adding the fruit juice or water for drinking. Then drink immediately. (A longer than three minute wait, up to 10 minutes is OK.) After adding the fruit juice one can wait up to 1 hour before consuming.

Lemon Juice and lime: Lemon juice or lime juice can be used. Generally use 5 drops to each one drops of MMS.

Citric Acid: I believe at this time that citric acid is the most effective, but we need more data. Mix the citric acid 1 to 10 with water. That's a 10% citric acid solution. One way to make it is to use a level tablespoon full of citric acid in a glass and then add 9 tablespoonfuls of water. When using this 10% citric acid solution, use 5 drops for each one drop of MMS.

Vinegar: Any kind of vinegar is okay as long as it says at least 5% acetic acid. Use 5 drops for each drop of MMS, but Lime or lemon or citric acid is preferred.

Juice: Use Apple juice, grape juice, pineapple juice, or cranberry juice. The juice must not have Vitamin C added, it prevents the activation. Read the label carefully, or make fresh juice.

Orange juice: Do not use orange juice or other citrus juices. They prevent the activation.

Please read Chapter 10 carefully.

How much to use:

(1) For maintenance use six drops MMS with one of the food acids mentioned above.   Young people can use it twice a week, but older people (over 60) should use 6 drops every day.

(2) For most diseases especially liver diseases, and including other problems: Start with two drops or less if one is very sick. Give the first dose, wait one hour and give a second dose. If you don't notice an increase in nausea, go to three drops four hours later. The next day start with three drops in the morning and give a second dose in one or two hours. Then go to four drops in the after noon or evening before bed. Continue increasing the drops each morning doing a second dose in about one hour and a single dose in the afternoon or evening until you are taking 15 drops three times a day. See the protocols at the end of chapter 10 and follow them.

Vomiting and diarrhea are a part of getting well in many cases. If your body needs either one of them, it will do it. However it is always very short lived. Your body knows. Do not allow yourself to continue with

Number of drops that might be required: Don't go over 15 drops twice a day for at least 2 weeks, but if nothing seems to be getting better after two weeks increase the drops. When nothing is happening and you are not well, increase the drops of MMS and always use the appropriate amount of acid drops and the 3 minute wait.

(3) For malaria and other parasite diseases use 15 drops the very first dose. Wait one to two hours and give another 15 drops. Do the same the next day. Continue for 3 days. Check for parasites. If parasites are present, continue up to three months. All parasites will be dead long before three months. Remember; always use the vinegar, wait, and juice. In most cases parasites including worms will be dead in three days. Malaria normally clears up in 4 hours or less.

(4) <u>Snake bite;</u> take at least 15 drop doses every ½ hour for two hours, and then every hour for two hours, and then every two hours. Continue every four hours until you are out of danger. As usual, use the vinegar, wait, and juice. Do not cut a snake bite in any case. Be sure to see a doctor, but do not allow him to cut the snake bite. It's okay to use a suction device on the bite. Cutting spreads the poison too fast.

(5) <u>Burns, 1st, 2nd, or 3rd degree burns:</u> Do not use vinegar. Squirt the MMS directly on the burn full strength from the bottle. Make sure it covers the burn. <u>Wait no longer than 60 seconds and then wash the MMS off with water.</u> It's very good to use to stop pain and burning for sunburns, but WARNING, do not leave on more than 60 seconds. It must be washed off. Most any drinkable liquid is okay to use to wash off in extreme emergencies. (The MMS neutralizes the acid created by the burn, but if left on the burn it will create a different kind of burn).

(6) <u>Food poisoning:</u> Take 12 drops for the first dose and 6 drops every ½ hour. Be sure to use the vinegar, wait, and use about 1/4 glass of juice or water.

(7) <u>Children:</u> For a baby use 2 drops. For older children use three drops per 25 pounds of body weight. Start out with less for a baby like two drops or even one, then work up to three drops in a few hours if needed. Same with children except with malaria and parasitic diseases. In that case use the full amount to start with which is 3 drops for each 25 pounds of body weight. If the parasitic disease is not handled in several days use as much as twice the figures given here.

(8) <u>Animals, use with any sick animal:</u> For smaller animals use three drops per 25 pounds of body weight. For horses and other larger animals, use one drop for each 25 pounds of body weight. Use an appropriate amount of vinegar, wait, and normally use water added instead of juice. Most animals will go ahead and drink, but you may have to force feed the animal. In that case a turkey baser with a large squeeze bulb bought at most grocery stores works fine. If there is a question use smaller doses at first.

<u>The Miracle Mineral Supplement Contents </u>is bottled at 28% sodium chlorite powder and distilled water. It is a clear slightly yellow solution.

Small amounts appear totally clear with no yellow showing.

Sodium Chlorite Powder is only 80% sodium chlorite. The balance is mostly table salt with less than 1% other nontoxic sodium chemicals. The amount of sodium in any dose is not enough to consider harmful to any diet. Because sodium chlorite powder is always only 80% pure sodium chlorite the actual amount of pure sodium chlorite in the MMS solution is 22.4%.

Sodium chlorite in a six drop dose: There are 54 mg of sodium chlorite in a six drop dose of MMS and about 10 mg of salt. Not enough to count during any one day. Sodium dioxide is also generated. There is one to two milligrams generated initially by the vinegar, and then one to two mg per hour is generated as the chlorine dioxide degenerates into table salt and water.

Chlorine dioxide: 12 drops of MMS with the added vinegar generates from 1 to 2 mg of chlorine dioxide. When it is diluted with ½ glass of juice there is less than 1 ppm in the solution. (There are still 1 to 2 milligrams that goes into the body, but 1 ppm is less than what is acceptable in some foods by FDA guidelines). The MMS solution then continues to generate 1 to 2 milligrams per hour of chlorine dioxide for up to 12 hours in the human body.

Chlorine Dioxide: The American Chemical Society, Analytical Chemistry Division stated in 1999 that chlorine dioxide is the most powerful killer of pathogens known to man. Chlorine dioxide is used in many industrial processes. It has been used to sterilize food products such as red meat and poultry for over 50 years. It is used in hospitals and clinics as a sterilizing agent.

Buying Sodium Chlorite: See 2nd part of chapter 16.

Formula for Sodium Chlorite: $NaClO_2$. Na=Sodium Cl=chlorine and O_2=Oxygen (The O_2 in all cases here merely indicates that two atoms of oxygen exist. It is not an indication of the charge.) The actual charge on the oxygen is -2 (minus two) which leave the oxygen in the neutral condition. It's the same charge as the oxygen in carbon dioxide. It can't be used for oxidation.

Formula for Chlorine Dioxide: ClO_2. You can observe that just the Na (sodium) has been removed to make the chlorine dioxide. The O_2 is two oxygen ions with a charge of two electrons each. That is considered minus two (-2) because electrons have a negative charge. Oxygen ions at this charge cannot oxidize anything and thus are not available to the body for oxidization. The Cl stands for chlorine which is a chlorine ion in this case with a positive charge until it oxidizes and destroys something in which case it winds up with a negative charge as well. It then is a chloride which is the same as chloride in table salt. It cannot do further reactions.

Formula for Oxygen: O_2 that means that an oxygen molecule consists of two oxygen atoms that are bound together. The oxygen enters the body for the purpose of oxidation in the elemental state. When it oxidizes various items in the body it releases energy creating the warmth of the body. During the oxidization process the oxygen atoms are charged to -2 (minus two) electrons. They are then oxygen ions. They have reached their neutral state. In the neutral state (minus 2 electron charge) they cannot be used by the body. In this state they form carbon dioxide and are expelled from the body as one breathes out. They are then recharged by green trees and other green plants.

The oxygen ions that are attached to chlorine dioxide, like carbon dioxide, have a minus two electron charge and thus are neutral. The body cannot use them. They either form carbon dioxide or they become part of the water of the body.

Oxidation: In the old days of chemistry, it was thought that oxygen was the only thing that oxidized metal, other chemicals and things. But as a better understanding of chemistry came about it was soon learned that any element or ion or molecule that brought about an exchange of electrons was basically the same oxidization process that oxygen created. Oxygen accepts electrons from other elements or molecules and at the same time causing the release of some energy in the form of heat. That's oxidization. Well so do many other elements, molecules and ions accept electrons or create an exchange of electrons and release energy. Oxygen can accept 2 electrons at which time it becomes neutral and can accept no more electrons. However, a chlorine dioxide molecule can accept 5 electrons. Thus it also oxidizes, but with much more whamo.

 Oxygen when neutralized by a minus two charge normally leaves the body as carbon dioxide. That means that carbon dioxide has two ions of oxygen, but neutralized oxygen. The two oxygen ions are then charged back to their elemental state by green plants and the sun, again making them available to create oxidization in the body.

Chlorine, itself, is also an oxidizer, but it oxidizes by chlorination, that is, it not only exchanges electrons, but it combines with whatever it is oxidizing making many new compounds. Some of these compounds are cancer causing.

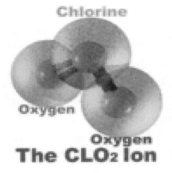

Chlorine

Oxygen

Oxygen

The CLO₂ Ion

Chapter 21

Heart Attacks, What Causes Them and the FDA

<u>Read this chapter and you will know why heart attacks are not related to cholesterol and clogged arteries and how you can prevent heart attacks.</u>

I almost didn't write this chapter because this book is about MMS, but this information is something that everyone who is interested in health should know. It also gives a little more data about the FDA.

Let me first make a few statements that are undisputable facts, provable in court of law and by a hundred different sources including the Internet. The data I am going to tell you is absolutely undisputable, yet most people ignore it.

The first thing you should know is that most of the FDA experts are also on the payroll of the pharmaceutical companies. You would think that would be against public policy. But no, it seems that they have the right to moonlight just like anyone else, even if it is counterproductive. Should you want the facts on this, read the book **Deadly Medicine** by Thomas Moore.

Secondly, in 1992 the FDA started a public campaign to deny the America people the right to purchase vitamins without going to a doctor and obtaining a prescription. They spent millions of dollars of taxpayers' money pushing this cause, but it didn't work. Worse than that, it backfired against them. Not just thousands but millions of American people arose up against this attack on our liberty and wrote their congressmen. In August of 1994 congresses fixed their wagon on this score attempting to do it permanently, but that evidently wasn't possible. A law was passed unanimously by both houses and signed into law by the president. Did you see that? <u>Unanimously.</u> That's what the America people can do if they really try. (All of this is now a matter of public records).

The law was called DSHEA (The Dietary Supplement Health and Education Act of 1994). This law attempts to guarantee the American people free access to vitamins and other essential nutrients and to the educational data concerning these nutrients. The reason why the educational data was included is that the pharmaceutical companies had been campaigning to prevent any and all claims of health benefits concerning vitamins from being published. Do you see? They would have even prevented books from being printed telling us about vitamins. They spent not just millions but billions on this idea. Now we have a law to protect us. The Constitution should have been enough, but we need all the help we can get.

But that still wasn't enough. The pharmaceutical companies banded together to form a cartel at the international level. They started a worldwide campaign to ban all data concerning the health benefits of vitamins and minerals and other natural substances from being distributed anywhere in the world. They approached the world through the United Nations Food Standards Commission. They thought that they could force the industrial nations and the world to accept vitamins as prescription medicine. Disguised as a consumer protection initiative, this concept was to be recommended to the UN General Assembly. There were to be trade sanctions on any countries that refused to accept vitamins as prescription medicine.

That was the year of 1997. The main actor in this pharmaceutical vitamin cartel was the German government. Germany exports more pharmaceutical products than any other nation. They might have succeeded except for one doctor, Matthias Rath, M. D. On June 22, 1997, he gave a speech to an audience in Chemnitz, Germany. He exposed the cartel and their intentions in that speech and connected them to the pharmaceutical companies who were profiteers of World War II and even the Holocaust. As a result of this speech and several other speeches and hundreds of thousands of protest letters, the idea was so controversial by the time it was to be presented to the UN General Assembly that they did not succeed.

Even bigger than that, May 20, 1999 these multinational pharmaceutical companies admitted to forming a "Vitamin-Cartel" to fix the prices of raw vitamins and materials. They defrauded hundreds of millions of people worldwide of more than 100 billion dollars. They were fined about one billion dollars. The U.S. Justice Department declared that they were the largest illegal cartel ever uncovered. This tiny fine in reference to the total amount they bilked from the people of the world was inconsequential.

Are you starting to see? The pharmaceutical companies have no conscience. They will do anything to prevent a loss of money or to make money. They care not how many deaths that they cause. The pharmaceutical companies through the FDA have suppressed dozens of discoveries concerning cures for cancer, heart disease and many other diseases for more than 50 years. I know that you probably think that is crazy, but so would you think that about the above information if it were not so much a part of the record. There is nothing that I have said above that can be disputed. It's all a matter of record. It all happened just as stated above and can be investigated by any high school student and proven to be facts. The proof of the suppression of the discoveries of cures for cancer and other diseases are slightly more covered up at this time, but still quite provable. The FDA has depended upon the incredibility of what they have done and the indifference of the public to maintain their farce.

One other story of facts. The amino acid Tryptophan was sold in health food stores throughout the US as an aid for sleep. It really worked and thousands of people bought it as opposed to several drug sleep aids. Tryptophan replaced several millions of dollars that the drug companies were no longer able to sell. Then guess what, Tryptophan evidently caused the death of one person in the US and several in Japan. The FDA immediately took it off the shelf of every health food store in the US. This amino acid is manufactured in Japan and it was found that somehow an impurity had gotten into the amino acid jar. Although the problem was fixed and acceptable purity rules were put in place in the Japanese manufacturing plant, it was never allow back in the US.

It was later found that American FDA agents had visited the Japanese Tryptophan plant before the impure jars of Tryptophan were shipped. So now drug companies that sell sleep drugs make millions of dollars selling the drugs that replace the Tryptophan. Do you see? One person dead from amino acid impurities and America can no longer have

Tryptophan, but hundreds of thousands of people are dead from drugs and that is completely acceptable. Am I the only one that sees something wrong with that?

It can now be shown to any researcher that every person in America is in some way personally touched by suffering and death as a result of the FDA's betrayal of the American people. But worse than that every person in the world is to some extent affected by the suppression of data for the cure of many different diseases. The indifference results mostly from realizing that one can really do nothing to change the status quo. But now that can be changed simply by everyone informing his relatives, friends and neighbors of this book.

You may think that law I mention earlier in this chapter the DSHEA of 1994 has protected us. Well, not so. As soon as it was out of the public eye the FDA has been at it again to get congress to pass a law saying that all supplements must be approved by the FDA before sales in the US. Now the FDA has publicly stated that they intend to shut down 50% of the supplement business in the US using this new law. Now with 970,000 drugs related deaths each year and not even one single supplement related death per year in the entire health food field the FDA is going to limit our right to have supplements unless they approve of them. They are not fooling around. They have stated their intention to enforce this new law with vengeance. Congress has betrayed the America public once again. The DSHEA law will be useless with this new law. They were informed of the damage this law would cause. There is only one reason why they will agree to this law in both the house and senate. They are bought and paid for. These laws are in the works in both the house and the senate and are scheduled to be law in 2010. So far all congressmen and senators have been in favor.

About the FDA suppression of cures: I am going describe two of the more important suppression incidents below and then tell you where you can check my data for accuracy. Be advised, however, I am only hitting the top of the iceberg. There are many more cases that I do not have time and space to cover. You can also see why I moved out of the country to publish this book. Now you are going to say, "But the constitution of the U.S. allows you to publish anything." Well, the FDA doesn't care about that. They arrest such authors and scientist inventors and charge them with almost anything. But they don't care. They can keep an author in jail for a long time on trumped up charges. The judges in that area of the law are FDA judges. They keep saying that if the author will withdraw his book or say his cure doesn't work they will withdraw the charges. By the time the author has spent all his money on lawyers he often gives in. Dozens of cures have been lost because the inventor or author just was too tired of fighting to go on, and he died of a heart attack, or he did spend years in jail.

Actually, it's a lot worse than just that. They seize property and destroy businesses. They often take everything that is in a business including the car and bank account. Many times they do it without a search warrant. They destroy a person's life. During the trial they have their own judges who will not allow any reasonable defense. A hero who has spent his life helping people and searching for a cure to one disease or another can find himself in prison for years. These incidents are a crime of the worst kind against humanity. They destroy the business and a person's whole life to suppress a cure. They do it in the name of public safety and no one can stop them.

You ask why they do it. They do it for the billions of dollars that the pharmaceutical companies will make if the cure is not given to the public throughout the world. It often scares clerks about their jobs. If a cure is found for cancer, thousands of jobs will be lost. Radiation therapy jobs will be lost and chemotherapy drugs will no longer be manufactured. Hospitals will go out of business. But millions of lives will be saved and untold suffering will be stopped. Would you rather save the jobs, or stop the suffering and then have those people retrained for other jobs?

I do not have nearly enough money to publish this book widely, but I am depending upon the American people, the Mexican people, and the People of South America to get this data out. If everyone will send this book to at least two people, or at lease see that at least two people download the free e-book Part 1 from www.miraclemineral.org, the America people will have a cure that will eliminate more than 50% and as much as 80% of the drugs consumed by mankind at this time. In the long-run millions of lives will be saved and the suffering that will be stopped is incalculable. If you have read this book you know that this is true, and if you don't know that it is true then give MMS a try. It cures cancer when used properly or used with other know cancer cures such as the Indian Herb mixture. And as I have said all profits from the book will be used by me to distribute this book in the world or in Africa to bring this cure to the African people. I have got to be careful with what I say, or they will prosecute me on something like this. So let me say that is my intension at this time and I will do my best to carry it out, but I cannot guarantee that all profit will go that way for absolute certain at this time. And of course, I use this money for living expenses.

Billions and billions of dollars have been spent on the search for a cure for cancer by using the present theory of cancer. For more than a hundred years there have been two basic theories of cancer. The other theory has been suppressed. Lives have been destroyed, people have been jailed and sent to prison, and books have been burned. Every conceivable **disgusting** thing that can be done has been done to prevent the second theory of cancer from ever coming to scientific light or becoming known to the public. Funny things, all of the demonstrated cures of cancer have been based on the second theory, or similar concepts. More than two dozen or more of those cures have each had more than one thousand documented cases of complete cures from cancer, some of them more than 10,000 documented cures and several more than 100,000 cases recorded.

So let me tell you in a few nontechnical sentences the difference between the two different theories of cancer. The present theory of cancer is that healthy body cells for some unknown reason mutate into cancerous cells. The general idea is that the unknown reason is aging, poor diet, heredity, a bad condition that slowly mutates into cancer, or something along those lines. Using this theory, billions of dollars have been spent on research and millions of men, women and children have suffered and died for more than 100 years while no significant improvement in cancer treatment has happened. That's 100 years without an answer or even a real improvement. Of course there are a lot of scientists that would like to argue against that. There was what they call a great improvement in the chemotherapy chemicals in about 1948 but there is still more people dying of cancer than ever. There is no indication that chemotherapy increases one's chances of living.

Does that seem like a poor picture to you? The same treatment for over a 100 years and no real change in the treatment for more than 100 years and they still use it and research it, and still a higher percentage are dying of cancer than ever before.

The second theory which is the unaccepted theory of cancer is that cancer is caused by a very unusual virus that changes its size and shape from a virus to a bacterium and back to a virus again. There are a lot of technical terms I am missing, but that's the basic concept. This second theory is called pleomorphism. Research into this theory is not allowed. You may say, "I thought America was a free country." Well, that's so, but not to those who want to do research into this particular theory of cancer. No money is available for such research, and those who try hit a blank wall. Nobody cooperates with them. Their colleagues won't talk to them anymore. The FDA, FTC and the AMA put every possible stop in their way that they can find. Let me say again, all the suppressed cures that have worked have been based on this very unusual virus theory or similar concepts.

Please, please, please, don't believe me. Go to the Internet and dig deep enough to find the facts. The facts are there, and when you have facts you can prove them. There is always proof somewhere there, often hidden but recoverable. We need millions of more people who know the facts. They don't have to be technical; they just need to know what is really going on. So let me tell you one book to read to get you started. It's *The Cancer Cure that Worked* by Barry Lynes and John Crane. They give references and tell where you can go to get the actual records.

In this book we are talking about MMS. So far many people have stated that after taking the MMS that their cancer went away. MMS kills viruses and bacteria. It has been established for 100 years that chlorine dioxide kills viruses and bacteria. We have not proven that MMS will attack mutated cancerous cells. But what has happened is that skin cancer including melanoma dries up and flakes off like the scab of a sore. It doesn't look like the cancer was attacked; it looks more like the cancer just quit growing and the body simply healed the area. That's what would have happened if the virus were killed. Well, we don't know do we? Yet.

Here is one more thing that the FDA really doesn't want you to know.
Heart attacks have nothing to do with cholesterol levels in your blood.
The AMA and other medical research oriented groups have not produced
a single study that proves that people with high levels of cholesterol have
more heart attacks than those with low levels.   They have proved,
however, that they can sell billions of dollars of cholesterol lowering
drugs. Dr. Matthias Rath has shown that the basis of heart attacks is
vitamin deficiency, mainly vitamin C. Get his books. Believe me. He
has proven it. Vitamins prevent heart attacks, not cholesterol lowering
drugs.

Dr. Matthias Rath points out that there are several thousand miles of
blood veins in your body. Those don't clog up and cause problems. If
cholesterol in the blood was causing problems, it would cause problems
throughout the body. Only the ten inches of veins right at the heart are
affected by cholesterol. Now why would that be? It's because those
veins at the heart are smashed flat at every heart pump, like 70 or 80
times a minute, millions of times a year. They fail not because they are
clogged, but because the walls of the veins cannot take being flattened so
many times, and they crack. Vitamin C is what causes the walls of blood
vessels to be strong. Scurvy is a vitamin C deficiency, and heart attack is
part of the same problem. The deposit on the walls of those particular
veins is only to increase the strength and prevent the veins from being
totally flattened and not for the purpose of clogging the veins. When the
vein cracks it stays flat instead of opening again and that is what is
causing heart attacks. Vitamin C is what prevents heart attacks. Read
Dr. Rath's books, and be sure to buy some vitamin C.   The
pharmaceutical companies definitely don't want you to read his books,
because you won't buy their cholesterol drugs.

Cholesterol is the body's response to a deficiency of vitamin C. The
body seeks to strengthen the walls of the blood vessels and prevent them
from cracking by depositing the cholesterol.

I should mention that Dr. Rath worked with Dr. Linus Pauling for many
years.   Dr. Linus Pauling agreed with Dr. Rath's findings and they
worked together to further verify and understand the use of vitamins in
the body. Dr. Linus Pauling was the only man in history to receive two
unshared Nobel prizes in the medical field. His agreement and help with

these findings adds a great deal of credence to them.

Modern medicine insists on treating the symptoms and refuses to find the cause, because if they find the cause they will cure the problem. If they cure the problem, they will not be able to continue selling drugs. It's sorry, but the fact is that it is all based on money.

Let's first talk about Dr. William Frederic Koch. Dr. Koch developed a medicine from herbs which he called glyoxylide. He cured his first cancer patient in 1917 and thousands thereafter when you count what he did and what the other doctors did using his medicine. What do you think the conventional treatment for cancer was at that time? The treatment that had at that time already been in use for many years began more than 100 years ago. I'll bet you couldn't guess what it was in a hundred years. Well amazing as it may seem, it was x-ray and radium radiation, the same as it is now. One hundred years and they are still using the same treatment and guess what, more and more people are dying from cancer. Does anyone see anything wrong with the picture here? Don't you think at some point or the other those responsible would say, "Maybe we ought to do a little research into an alternate idea?" No, they just go blithely on researching the same basic theory. It is the result of the pharmaceutical companies only making money available for certain kinds of research that they know will get nowhere.

Dr. Koch said that you don't want to kill the cancer cells; you want to remove the virus that is causing the cell to be sick and thus allow the cancer cell to return to normal.

The FDA and FTC attacked Dr. Koch for years. He was driven from the U.S. and traveled to Brazil where he had phenomenal success treating advanced rheumatoid arthritis, insanity, diabetes, cases of advanced cancer, and even leprosy. The FDA was extremely alarmed and demanded that he return to the U.S. Later when he did return he was arrested on trumped-up charges. Two trials were held and both times the jury acquitted Dr. Koch despite the fact that the judge would not allow a single cured patient to testify. The trials went on from 1942 to 1946 and cost the government more than $10,000,000 which is the equivalent to $100,000,000 in present day money. They could not prove that Dr. Koch's technology did not cure cancer, but by this time none of his herbs for his cure were available in the U.S.

Colonel Charles March took over as head of the FTC and attempted to stop the attacks against Dr. Koch, but he met with a sudden and questionable death. Deaths of that nature in those times seem to happen to a number of people involved with alternate medical treatment. That is not to say that such deaths do not happen now, because they do. A very good friend of mine, who discovered several cures for several important diseases went home about 5 years ago and a bomb in his apartment, blew both of his legs off. He lived, but the idea that they don't stop people now days is a lie.

Although the FTC could not legally stop Dr. Koch from selling his medicine to doctors, they gave him a cease and desist order from advertising in any way to doctors. This prevented doctors from knowing about it and from using it to treat cancer patients and other diseases. It is estimated that in excess of 100,000 patients were cured of cancer between the years of 1917 when Dr. Koch cured his first cancer patient until 1951 when the FTC ordered him to stop advertising to doctors. His laboratories were unable to stay in business without the sales. Recently there are those who have attempted to duplicate his formula, but he and most of those who knew the details are now dead. Basically this cure for cancer and many other diseases has been lost.

Do you see why the MMS is so important at this time? It is a medicine that can be used by anyone and everyone can know the formula. Once out, and once it has been tested widely by the public, none of the alphabet soup agencies (FDA, FTC, AMA mostly) will have any way to stop it, and the pharmaceutical companies will be up a creek. It will be the dawning of the end of the tremendous cash flow for drugs that treat only the symptoms. If my strategy works and it does get to the public, it will be the beginning of many books of the same nature by others. The end of the tremendous suffering of mankind at the hands of medical and pharmaceutical people for money is in sight. With the Internet and modern technology, normal people can now know more than doctors used to know. We can no longer be kept in ignorance about medicine. The dawn of the age of information has already happened, but this is the dawn of the age of medical information to the average person. I hope it is. It is if you help. Had Dr. Koch's cure been used by all doctors, literally millions of people would not have suffered and died. They would have lived happy lives.

The other cancer-cure that I wanted to mention is the one developed by Royal R. Rife of San Diego, California. He started research somewhat later than Dr. Koch, but in the same era. His research started in 1920. He began by inventing a microscope that was quite different from the best standard microscopes. His best microscope had a magnification of 30,000, although his first ones were not that powerful. The problem was that in the scientific field it is well known that the most powerful non electronic microscope had only 2,500 powers.   The theory of light prevents anything more powerful than that because at that power the light waves theoretically cannot be amplified any more.

Rife, however, had his own theory of light microscopes. The electronic microscope cannot be used with small viruses because the light frequency that it uses destroys the virus.   Rife built many really tremendous microscopes over his lifetime; each new one was better than the one before. His microscopes were duplicated and some still exist to this day. They were so powerful that they could reveal the viruses that caused cancer. The microscopes used several different light sources of different frequencies. His microscope used the heterodyne principle of light frequency. That's where one frequency is converted to another frequency. This principle has been used in radio frequencies for many years and still is. Rife just learned to use it with light frequencies. No reason why he shouldn't, but his microscopes were destroyed and his books and plans were burned. Despite that fact literally hundreds of doctors used Rife's microscopes to identify and verify cancer.

The other thing that Rife did, after identifying the cancer virus, was design a device that killed the cancer virus in place? The theory that he used was simple and scientific. He used the theory of radio antennas. It is not a hard basic theory to understand. Each different frequency will cause a flow of electrical current in an exact precise length of metal. So if you have a wire of the right length connected to your radio, you can pick up the frequency that causes an electrical flow of current in that wire. You don't see the wire anymore in modern radios, but it's there somewhere.

So Rife figured, "We know that those little fellows can conduct electricity, so why not make a radio antenna out of them." He decided that all he needed to do was measure their size and then calculate the frequency that would cause an electrical current to flow in them the same as a TV or radio antenna. If he could cause an electrical current to flow in them that would kill them. A special Research Committee of the University of Southern California oversaw his laboratory work until the end of the 1930's. Follow-up clinics conducted in 1935, 1936 and 1937 by the head of the U.S.C. Medical Committee verified the results that he was getting. Independent physicians, utilizing machines that were duplicates of Rife's machine, successfully treated as many as 40 patients per day. A number of doctors continued to treat patients for up to 22 years, but the pressure became too great. When authorities found a machine in operation they either destroyed it on the spot or confiscate it for evidence.

Rife determined the precise frequency for herpes, tuberculosis, and other illnesses as well as cancer. His work was in Science magazines, medical journals, and later the Smithsonian Institution's annual report. Thousands were cured during the 1930's, and then the authorities struck. Rife began working with John Crane, and engineer. Rife's life work was in John Crane's lab when the authorities hit it. They destroyed everything, burned books and jailed John Crane. After that there were continuous problems with the authorities. The University no longer backed Rife and he simply had to quit.

Today there are numerous people throughout the world that have Rife frequency generators. Many do not work as they do not duplicate Rife's work closely enough, but many do work and cancer and other diseases are still cured with these frequency generators. There are even a few people who have his microscopes or good duplicates of his microscopes. They still work.

The question is how were these people stopped when they were curing people? How was the truth covered over so easily? There are two reasons. Both were greed. There were scientists who did not want their theories of cancer and other diseases questioned and there were the pharmaceutical companies who did not want their incomes decreased. Billions of dollars can exert huge amounts of pressure. The medical laws of this country have been shaped by the pharmaceutical companies. They have spent billions of dollars with at least two lawyers in Washington, D.C. for each representative and each senator. It all boils down to money, but the criminality of it is beyond belief. Millions suffer and die so that they can make money, and there was another reason. Many of the medical scientists were pushing their own favorite concepts that made then well known and they were mostly in with the pharmaceutical companies. That also boils down to money.

Hundreds of very important industries exist in the United States that do not spend billions of dollars influence Congress on making laws. There is no acceptable reason for the drug companies to be spending that huge amount of money to influence congress, but they do.

You can check my accuracy in these statements by going on the Internet and reading some of the thousands of documents that are available. Just go to Google or one of the other search engines and put in the various names of the people I have mentioned or just put in FDA Suppression. The Internet documents then point you towards the actual documents. The proof is all there. The FDA likes to dispute it, of course, and there is no money to dispute them. They have the billions to say you are wrong. In court, you don't have a chance to prove technology. They always bring up points of law and one never gets to the crux of the matter which is that the present technology is wrong. There is simply no proving anything. But the fact is, anyone who wants to dig can prove the points I give here, but smart lawyers won't allow it to be brought up in court.

This book about the MMS might be able to change some of the suffering and overcome some of the power of the pharmaceutical giants. If it is distributed widely enough, that will happen. Please help and join this crusade. All you have to do is send this book to as many people as possible. If you want to print it out and give it away, that's okay. If you are giving it away, give as many as you want. Give a thousand, or give a million, but if you are using it in a commercial way, then you need permission in writing from the Author. Keep in mind that all of the profit will be spent to more widely distribute this book or to bring the MMS to Africa. Now that's my promise, but I am not nor do I have, a nonprofit organization. I do belong to a nonprofit organization known as the Kinnaman Foundation. Donations can be sent to the Kinnaman foundation African/Americas project in care of Bill Myers, 814 Fruitdale Rd., Morgantown, Indiana 46160. Please join this crusade as all of us together can change the world.

Please don't believe the following statements, but please check it out. The facts are there and they can be verified. Take the time to verify it. It's important to you and your family.

One other thing you should know. <u>There are no incurable diseases.</u> Along with the MMS there are cures for every disease known. They are suppressed. Many were discovered years ago and now set unused. The stories and lies about the "Quacks" have prevented alternate medicine from using many of them and books have been burned. Why was it necessary to burn books and destroy microscopes and other valuable equipment if there was nothing that would work? By their actions they have proved something of value was there. With the public's help we can make this a better world where there are no incurable diseases. The answers are there, all we need to do is to prevent our government from suppressing the answers. The public has the power and we can do it. The MMS is not the only cure for many diseases, but it will give you a lot more confidence to see the MMS work. Your first step is to use some of it and see that it works. The second step is to start telling your neighbors and everyone you know. That's all we need. The world will change.

Help us defeat the FDA. You may not believe it, but the FDA has been suppressing all real cancer cures, and information concerning how vitamins prevent heart attacks and all other information or products that may in any way reduce the income of the large pharmaceutical medical drug companies.

Please don't take my word for it; become informed. Read the data available on the Internet. Just go to any search engine and put in "FDA Suppression." There is tremendous documentation starting back in the 1930's. They often put authors in jail and tell them that they will withdraw the accusations if the author will withdraw his claims. Once the author has lost all of his money and is tired of fighting he gives up. There are hundreds of medical facts that are suppressed right now that would save thousands of lives. There are many records of people who

have died under very questionable conditions when they have tried to
inform the people. Please don't write this off as a bunch of crazy
conspiracy nuts. Your life and the life of thousands are at stake. Isn't
that important enough to at least try it once on someone, or on you?
Spend a couple of hours.

Why do you suppose drugs in this world, especially in America, almost
always treat symptoms? That's no secret about drugs only treating
symptoms, most people know that already. Ask any person interested in
health. Medical drugs treat symptoms and all of the medical research by
pharmaceutical companies is directed towards treating symptoms, and
not towards finding the cause of the problem. Well, the reason is that if
you find the cause of a disease or health problem you can usually cure
the problem. In that case you cannot continue to sell the drug over and
over until the person dies. Billions of dollars are involved. Treating
symptoms does not cure or change the problem. Why do you reason that
there has been no significant advancement in Cancer technology in 100
years? With one or two minor exceptions the same treatments are still
used, more than 100 years later. The world has advance fantastically in
almost everything but cancer treatment and other disease treatments.
They refine the treatment, make the drugs more pure, make the needles
better, make the X-ray machines better, make the records better, and
make the timers better that time the treatment, but the treatment itself
does not change.

There is only one way that they could keep the same treatment for 100
years and that is to suppress every new concept that ever arose. They
have their own judges, their own laws, and they simply stop any real
improvements.

The pharmaceutical companies spend billions of dollars with at least two
lawyers for each Congressman and each senator and many law offices in
Washington, DC. They have tried again and again to suppress vitamins.
I don't have time to cover all of the data here. Please become informed
on this subject. The data and the proof are available. The truth cannot
be suppressed. Just read the thousands of documents available on the
Internet. They spent billions influencing Congress on the pretension of
public safety to prevent us from even having printed literature on
vitamins. Do you imagine that we would be much safer if we didn't

know about vitamins?   (I mentioned this before earlier in book 1, but it is important enough to mention again, and possibly you didn't read book 1.)

Now, the MMS is such a simple cure that it need not be relegated to doctors.   The public at large has the ability to treat themselves.   This means that the FDA is going to have a much harder time at suppressing this one.   The public, the sick and suffering have this one short window that will be open, we don't know for how long.   But this time the FDA cannot suppress a couple of doctors or arrest the author of a book.   (They can't find me.)   Luckily I am not tied to some expensive lab, and I can move around.   But they don't have to find me to stop it.   The billions of dollars behind them will definitely try, because ultimately a great part of those billions are lost if the MMS becomes well known.   Please, please take the attitude to error on the side of maybe I might just be telling the truth.

This is where you come in.   It is now resting on your shoulders.   I've done what I can do.   It's up to you, the readers of this book to spread the word to the world.   It can happen if you will tell your friends.   The more people that you get to read this book or the free download e-book, the more people you tell before the pharmaceuticals find out about it, the less likely they will be able to suppress it. Up to this point they are so convinced that I am a charlatan, that they have paid me no attention.   It's my only safe guard.   But when they start getting reports of people getting well and people being cured, it will be a different story.   (OK, I mentioned this in book 1, too.)

There is a point, I don't know how many people, but a point can be reached which I call the point of no return.   If we reach that point, the window can no longer be slammed in our face. That is when enough public individuals have learned the data, have used it, and know it works. Believe me; a few individuals won't do it.   It will take millions who know that it works.   Please join us.   Either use it, or just accept the idea that the public deserves to know.   Get as many people to download the free e-book (The Miracle Mineral Supplement of the 21st Century Book I) as possible (and also book II).   And when you successfully use the MMS to help someone or yourself, broadcast it widely.   We may only have a few months. You probably have less than 12 months to get it to the public. The elimination and prevention of suffering, misery and death of millions depends upon you. (Sorry to be so dramatic, but that is the fact.)   Have your friends download the free book at the www.miraclemineral.org Site or better still have them purchase this book or hard book for $19.95 at the same site.

Again, check Google and use "FDA Suppression" for your search and you will know that I am telling the truth.

Otherwise, you will know that what I say here is true when they begin their campaigns to prove the data in this book false. The problem that they will have is that anyone can try it. But that won't stop them, because they know that they can use fear to prevent millions from even considering it. That is why we need millions who have already tried it and know that it works. Join the crusade. Lives are at stake. Of course, if you don't tell your friends there will never be such a campaign from the FDA and pharmaceuticals. You may not know, but at this time, more than 55% of the American public have quit their family doctor and started using alternate medical answerer.

I apologize again for being so dramatic, and for repeating myself, but I am 74 years old, and in my years I have learned that people would rather hear the facts than someone "beating around the bush." And what I say three times will usually be remembered. My 4th grade teacher told me that.

 Remember, the MMS does not treat diseases, it aids the immune system.

There are millions of people who have such utter faith in modern medicine that they are not even willing to check the facts. In my 40 years in the health business I have watch a number of my friends die from cancer while being totally convinced that I was a confused man. They preferred to die rather than check my data. Two of my close relatives died rather than check my data. Please take the time to check modern alternate medicine data or test the MMS for yourself.

I look forward to hearing how you have used the MMS. Please write me at my address or my email. See the Copyright page for the email address.

Please, even if you don't write me, please record all of the times that you treat yourself or others and the results that you get. This can be very important as time goes by.

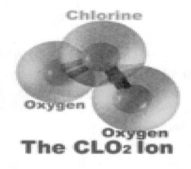

Chlorine

Oxygen

Oxygen

The CLO₂ Ion

Chapter 22

On The Mechanisms of Oxidation of Chlorine Oxides – An Overview

Note: Please see the last paragraph of chapter 10.

By Thomas Lee Hesselink, MD

Copyright © August 7th, 2007

DISCOVERY

Jim Humble, a modern gold prospecting geologist, needed to travel to malaria infested areas numerous times. He or his coworkers would on occasion contract malaria. At times access to modern medical treatment was absolutely unavailable. Under such dire circumstances it was found that a solution useful to sanitize drinking water was also effective to treat malaria if diluted and taken orally. Despite no formal medical training Mr. Humble had the innate wisdom to experiment with various dosage and administration techniques. Out of such necessity was invented an easy to use treatment for malaria which was found rapidly effective in almost all cases. [1]

References:
1. A Possible Solution to the Malaria Problem? Humble J Libertarian Times, May 9, 2005

MATERIALS AND METHODS

The procedure as used by Mr. Humble follows: A 28% stock solution of 80% (technical grade) sodium chlorite (NaClO2) is prepared. The remaining 20% is a mixture of the usual recipients necessary in the manufacture and stabilization of sodium chlorite powder or flake. Such are mostly sodium chloride (NaCl) ~19%, sodium hydroxide (NaOH) <1%, and sodium chlorate (NaClO3) <1%. The actual sodium chlorite present is therefore 22.4%. Using a large caliber dropper (25 drops per cc), the usual administered dose per treatment is 6 to 15 drops. In terms of milligrams of sodium chlorite, this calculates out to 9mg per drop or 54mg to 135mg per treatment. Effectiveness is enhanced, if prior to administration the selected drops are premixed with 2.5 to 5 cc of table vinegar or lime juice and allowed to react for 3 minutes. The acidified solution is then mixed into a glass of water or apple juice and taken orally. This can be taken on an empty stomach to enhance effectiveness but this often causes nausea. Nausea is less likely to occur if food is present such as one hour after meals. The vinegar (5% acetic acid) or lime juice (6 to 9% citric acid) neutralizes the sodium hydroxide and at the same time converts a small portion of the chlorite (ClO2-) to its conjugate acid known as chlorous acid (HClO2). Under such conditions some of the chlorous acid will oxidize other chlorite anions and gradually produce chlorine dioxide (ClO2). Chlorine dioxide appears in solution as a yellow tint which smells exactly like chlorine.

BENEFITS:

I first learned of Jim Humble's remarkable discovery in the fall of 2006. That sodium chlorite or chlorine dioxide could kill parasites in vivo seemed immediately reasonable to me at the onset. It is well known that many disease causing organisms are sensitive to oxidants. Various compounds classifiable as oxides of chlorine such as sodium hypochlorite and chlorine dioxide are already widely used as disinfectants. What is novel and exciting here is that Mr. Humble's technique seems: 1) easy to use, 2) rapidly acting, 3) successful, 4) apparently lacking in toxicity, and 5) affordable. If this treatment continues to prove effective, it could be used to help rid the world of one of the most devastating of all known plagues. [1, 2] Especially moving in me is the empathy I feel for anyone with a debilitating febrile illness. I cannot forget how horrible I feel whenever I have caught influenza. How much more miserable it must be to suffer like that again and again every 2 to 3 days as happens in malaria. Millions of people suffer this way year round. 1 to 3 million dies from malaria every year mostly children. Thus motivated I sought to learn all I could about the chemistry of the oxides of chlorine. I wanted to understand their probable mechanisms of toxicity towards the causative agents of malaria (Plasmodium species). [3] I wanted to check available literature pertaining to issues of safety or risk in human use.

References:
1. Current status of malaria control. Tripathi RP, Mishra RC, Dwivedi N, Tewari N, Verma SS Curr Med Chem. 2005;12(22):2643-59

2. Current status and progresses made in malaria chemotherapy.
Linares GE, Rodriguez JB Curr Med Chem. 2007; 14(3):289-314

3. An overview of chemotherapeutic targets for antimalarial drug discovery.
Olliaro PL, Yuthavong Y Pharmacol Ther. 1999 Feb; 81(2):91-110

OXIDANTS AS PHYSIOLOGIC AGENTS

I was already very familiar with most of the other known medicinally useful oxidants. Examples are: hydrogen peroxide, zinc peroxide, various quinones, various glyoxals, ozone, ultraviolet light, hyperbaric oxygen, benzoyl peroxide, artemisinin, methylene blue, allicin, iodine and permanganate. I had taught at numerous seminars on their use and explained their mechanisms of action on the biochemical level. Oxidants are atoms or molecules which take up electrons. Reductants are atoms or molecules which donate electrons to oxidants.

Low dose oxidant exposure to living red blood cells induces a change in oxyhemoglobin (Hb-O2) activity so that more oxygen (O2) is released to tissues throughout the body. [1] Hyperbaric oxygenation (oxygen under pressure): 1) is a powerful detoxifier against carbon monoxide; 2) is a powerful support for natural healing in burns, crush injuries, and ischemic strokes; and 3) is an effective aid to treat most bacterial infections.

Taken internally, intermittently and in low doses many oxidants have been found to be powerful immune stimulants. Exposure of live blood to ultraviolet light has similar immune enhancing effects. These treatments work through a natural physiologic trigger mechanism, which induces peripheral white blood cells to express and to release cytokines. These cytokines serve as an alarm system to increase cellular attack against pathogens and to down-regulate allergic reactions.

Activated cells of the immune system naturally produce strong oxidants as part of the inflammatory process at sites of infection or cancer to rid the body of these diseases. One such natural defense oxidant is hydrogen peroxide (H2O2). Another is peroxynitrate (-OONO) the coupled product of superoxide (*OO-) and nitric oxide (*NO) radicals. Yet another is hypochlorous acid (HOCl) the conjugate acid of sodium hypochlorite (NaClO).

References:
Decreased level of 2,3-diphosphoglycerate and alteration of structural integrity in erythrocytes infected with Plasmodium falciparum invitro.Dubey ML, Hegde R, Ganguly NK, Mahajan RC Mol Cell Biochem. 2003 Apr; 246(1-2):137-41

OXIDANTS AS DISINFECTANTS

Various strong oxidants are widely used as disinfectants. [4, 11, 12, 13, 28] All bacteria have been shown to be incapable of growing in any medium in which the oxidants (electron grabbers) out-number the reductants (electron donors). [29] Thus oxidants are at least bacteriostatic and at most are bactericidal. [27] Some oxidants such as iodine, various peroxides, or permanganate are applied topically to the skin to treat or to prevent infections caused by bacteria or fungi. Chlorine dioxide has been similarly used. [15]

Hypochlorites (ClO-) are commonly used as bleaching agents, as swimming pool sanitizers, and as disinfectants. Chlorine dioxide (ClO2) as well as ozone (O3) are effective disinfectants for public water supplies and are often used for that purpose. [9,14] Sodium chlorite (NaClO2) solutions have long been used as mouth washes to rapidly clear mouth odors and oral bacteria. Acidified sodium chlorite is FDA approved as a spray in the meat packing industry to sanitized meat. [1, 2, 8, 10, 26] Farmers use this to cleanse the udders of cows to prevent mastitis, [5, 6, 7] and to rid eggs of pathogenic bacteria. Chlorine dioxide kills many viruses. [16, 17, 18, 19, 20, 21, 22, 23, 24, 25] Acidified sodium chlorite is even useful to sanitize vegetables. [3] Some work has been done using dilute solutions of sodium chlorite internally to treat fungal infections, chronic fatigue, and cancer. Little however has been published in that regard.

References:
1. Effects of Carcass Washing Systems on Campylobacter Contamination in Large Broiler Processing Plants by M P Bashor, Master's Thesis, North Carolina State University, Dec 2002

2. Research Project Outline #4111, by C N Cutter, Penn State Univ, Nov 2005

3. Review - Application of Acidified Sodium Chlorite to Improve the Food Hygiene of Lightly Fermented Vegetables. by Y Inatsu, L Bari, S Kawamoto JARC 41(1 , pp 17-23, 2007

4. Antiseptics and Disinfectants: Activity, Action and Resistance. by G McDonnell & A D Russell Clinical Microbiology Reviews, pp 147-179, Jan 1999

5. Efficacy of Two Barrier Teat Dips Containing Chlorous Acid Germicides Against Experimental Challenge ... by R L Boddie, S C Nickerson, G K Kemp Journal of Dairy Science, 77 (10):3192-3197, 1994

6. Evaluation of a Chlorous Experimental and Natural Acid Chlorine Dioxide Teat Dip Under Experimental and Natural Exposure Conditions by P A Drechsler, E E Wildman, J W Pankey Journal of Dairy Science, 73 (8):2121, 1990

7. Preventing Bovine Mastitis by a Postmilking Teat Disinfectant Containing Acidified Sodium Chlorite by J E Hillerton, J Cooper, J Morelli Journal of Dairy Science, 90:1201-1208, 2007

8. Validation of the use of organic acids and acidified sodium chlorite to reduce Escherichia coli O157 and Salmonella typhimurium in beef trim and ground beef in a simulated processing environment. By Harris K, Miller MF, Loneragan GH, Brashears MM. J Food Prot. 69(8):1802-7, Aug 2006

9. Disinfectant efficacy of chlorite and chlorine dioxide in drinking water biofilms. Gagnon GA, Rand JL, O'leary KC, Rygel AC, Chauret C, Andrews RC Water Research, 39(9):1809-17, May 2005

10. Decreased dosage of acidified sodium chlorite reduces microbial contamination and maintains organoleptic qualities of ground beef products. Bosilevac JM, Shackelford SD, Fahle R, Biela T, Koohmaraie M. J Food Prot. 2004 Oct;67(10):2248-54

11. Treatment with oxidizing agents damages the inner membrane of spores of Bacillus subtilis and sensitizes spores to subsequent stress. Cortezzo DE, Koziol-Dube K, Setlow B, Setlow P J Appl Microbiol. 2004; 97(4):838-52

12. Mechanisms of killing of Bacillus subtilis spores by hypochlorite and chlorine dioxide. Young SB, Setlow P. J Appl Microbiol. 2003; 95(1):54-67

13. Inactivation of bacteria by Purogene. Harakeh S, Illescas A, Matin A. J Appl Bacteriol. 1988 May; 64(5):459-63

14. The inhibitory effect of Alcide, an antimicrobial drug, on protein synthesis in Escherichia coli. Scatina J, Abdel-Rahman MS, Goldman E. J Appl Toxicol. 1985 Dec; 5(6):388-94

15. Clinical and microbiological efficacy of chlorine dioxide in the management of chronic atrophic candidiasis: an open study. Mohammad AR, Giannini PJ, Preshaw PM, Alliger H. Int Dent J. 2004 Jun;54(3):154-8

16. Degradation of the Poliovirus 1 genome by chlorine dioxide. Simonet J, Gantzer C J Appl Microbiol. 2006 Apr; 100(4):862-70

17. Inactivation of enteric adenovirus and feline calicivirus by chlorine dioxide. Thurston-Enriquez JA, Haas CN, Jacangelo J, Gerba CP Appl Environ Microbiol. 2005 Jun; 71(6):3100-5

18. Mechanisms of inactivation of hepatitis A virus in water by chlorine dioxide. Li JW, Xin ZT, Wang XW, Zheng JL, Chao FH Water Res. 2004 Mar;38(6):1514-9

19. Virucidal efficacy of four new disinfectants. Eleraky NZ, Potgieter LN, Kennedy MA J Am Anim Hosp Assoc. 2002 May-Jun; 38(3):231-4

20. Chlorine dioxide sterilization of red blood cells for transfusion, additional studies. Rubinstein A, Chanh T, Rubinstein DB. Int Conf AIDS. 1994 Aug 7-12; 10: 235 (abstract no. PB0953). U.S.C. School of Medicine, Los Angeles

21. Inactivation of human immunodeficiency virus by a medical waste disposal process using chlorine dioxide. Farr RW, Walton C Infect Control Hosp Epidemiol. 1993 Sep; 14(9):527-9

22. Inactivation of human and simian rotaviruses by chlorine dioxide. Chen YS, Vaughn JM Appl Environ Microbiol. 1990 May;56(5):1363-6

23. Disinfecting capabilities of oxychlorine compounds. Noss CI, Olivieri VP Appl Environ Microbiol. 1985 Nov;50(5):1162-4

24. Mechanisms of inactivation of poliovirus by chlorine dioxide and iodine. Alvarez ME, O'Brien RT Appl Environ Microbiol. 1982 Nov; 44(5):1064-71

25. A comparison of the virucidal properties of chlorine, chlorine dioxide, bromine chloride and iodine. Taylor GR, Butler M J Hyg (Lond). 1982 Oct; 89(2):321-8

26. The Evaluation of Antimicrobial Treatments for Poultry Carcasses European Commission Health & Consumer Protection Directorate- General, April 2003

27. Role of Oxidants in Microbial Pathophysiology. R A Miller, B E Britigan Clinical Microbiology Reviews, and 10(1):1-18, Jan 1997

28. PURE WATER HANDBOOK Osmonics, Inc. Minnetonka, Minnesota

29. OXIDATION-REDUCTION POTENTIALS IN BACTERIOLOGY AND BIOCHEMISTRY L F Hewitt, 6th Ed, E. & S. Livingston Ltd., 1950

MALARIA IS OXIDANT SENSITIVE

>From November 2006 through May of 2007 I spent hundreds of hours searching biochemical literature and medical literature pertaining to the biochemistry of Plasmodia. Four species are commonly pathogenic in humans namely: Plasmodium vivax, Plasmodium falciparum, Plasmodium ovale and Plasmodium malariae. What I found was an abundance of confirmation that, just like bacteria, Plasmodia are indeed quite sensitive to oxidants. [15] Examples of oxidants toxic to Plasmodia include: artemisinin [16, 27, 36, 41], atovaquone [48], menadione, and methylene blue [29,47]. Also like bacteria and tumor cells, the ability of Plasmodia to live and grow depends heavily on an internal abundance of thiol compounds [38, 55]. Thiols are also known as sulfhydryl compounds (RSH). Thiols as a class behave as reductants (electron donors). Thus they are notoriously sensitive to oxidation and they are rapidly reactive with oxides of chlorine. This includes sodium chlorite (NaClO2) and chlorine dioxide (ClO2) the very agents present in Mr. Humble's solution. The products of oxidation of thiols using various

oxides of chlorine are: disulfides (RSSR), disulfide monoxides (RSSOR), sulfenic acids (RSOH), sulfinic acids (RSO2H), and sulfonic acids (RSO3H). None of these can support the life processes of the parasite. Upon sufficient removal of the parasite's life sustaining thiols by oxidation, the parasite rapidly dies. A list of thiols (RSH) upon which survival of Plasmodium species heavily depend includes: lipoic acid & dihydrolipoic acid [1, 2, 3, 5, 7, 8, 10, 11], coenzyme A & acyl carrier protein [6, 9, 12, 39, 43], glutathione [4, 19, 26, 32, 35, 37], glutathione reductase [33, 34, 42], glutathione-S-transferase [24, 30, 49, 50, 52, 53], peroxiredoxin [40, 56, 57, 58, 59, 60, 61, 62, 63, 65, 66, 67], thioredoxin [20, 21, 22, 25, 44, 64], glutaredoxin [31,45], plasmoredoxin [28], thioredoxin reductase [23, 46], ornithine decarboxylase and falcipain [13,14,17,18,51,54].

References:
1. The plasmodial apicoplast was retained under evolutionary selective pressure to assuage blood stage oxidative stress. Toler S Med Hypotheses. 2005; 65(4):683-90

2. Scavenging of the cofactor lipoate is essential for the survival of the malaria parasite Plasmodium falciparum Allary M, Lu JZ, Zhu L, Prigge ST Mol Microbiol. 2007 Mar; 63(5):1331-44;Epub 2007 Jan 22

3. Plasmodium falciparum possesses organelle-specific alpha- keto acid dehydrogenase complexes and lipoylation pathways. Günther S, McMillan PJ, Wallace LJ, Müller S Biochem Soc Trans. 2005 Nov;33(Pt 5):977-80

4. Characterization of the glyoxalases of the malaria parasite Plasmodium falciparum and comparison with their human counterparts Akoachere M, Iozef R, Rahlfs S, Deponte M, Mannervik B, Creighton DJ, Schirmer H, Becker K Biol Chem. 2005 Jan;386(1):41-52

5. The malaria parasite Plasmodium falciparum has only one pyruvate dehydrogenase complex, which is located in the apicoplast. Foth BJ, Stimmler LM, Handman E, Crabb BS, Hodder AN, McFadden GI Mol Microbiol. 2005 Jan; 55(1):39-53 Comment in: Mol Microbiol. 2005 Jan; 55(1):1-4

6. Fatty acid biosynthesis as a drug target in apicomplexan parasites. Goodman CD, McFadden GI Curr Drug Targets. 2007 Jan;8(1):15-30

7. The human malaria parasite Plasmodium falciparum possesses two distinct

dihydrolipoamide dehydrogenases. McMillan PJ, Stimmler LM, Foth BJ, McFadden GI, Müller S Mol Microbiol. 2005 Jan;55(1):27-38 Comment in: Mol Microbiol. 2005 Jan; 55(1):1-4

8. The human malaria parasite Plasmodium falciparum has distinct organelle-specific lipoylation pathways. Wrenger C, Müller S Mol Microbiol. 2004 Jul; 53(1):103-13

9. Apicoplast fatty acid biosynthesis as a target for medical intervention in apicomplexan parasites. Gornicki P Int J Parasitol. 2003 Aug; 33(9):885-96

10. Apicomplexan parasites contain a single lipoic acid synthase located in the plastid. Thomsen-Zieger N, Schachtner J, Seeber F FEBS Lett. 2003 Jul 17; 547(1-3):80-6

11. Biosynthetic pathways of plastid-derived organelles as potential drug targets against parasitic apicomplexa. Seeber F Curr Drug Targets Immune Endocr Metabol Disord. 2003 Jun; 3(2):99-109

12. A type II pathway for fatty acid biosynthesis presents drug targets in Plasmodium falciparum. Waller RF, Ralph SA, Reed MB, Su V, Douglas JD, Minnikin DE, Cowman AF, Besra GS, McFadden GI Antimicrob Agents Chemother. 2003 Jan; 47(1):297-301

13. Gene disruption confirms a critical role for the cysteine protease falcipain-2 in hemoglobin hydrolysis by Plasmodium falciparum. Sijwali PS, Rosenthal PJ Proc Natl Acad Sci U S A. 2004 Mar 30;101(13):4384-9

14. Plasmodium falciparum cysteine protease falcipain-2 cleaves erythrocyte membrane skeletal proteins at late stages of parasite development. Hanspal M, Dua M, Takakuwa Y, Chishti AH, Mizuno A Blood. 2002 Aug 1;100(3):1048-54

15. Double-drug development against antioxidant enzymes from Plasmodium falciparum. Biot C, Dessolin J, Grellier P, Davioud-Charvet E Redox Rep. 2003;8(5):280-3

16. Mechanism-based design of parasite-targeted artemisinin derivatives: synthesis and antimalarial activity of new diamine containing analogues. Hindley S, Ward SA, Storr RC, Searle NL, Bray PG, Park BK, Davies J, O'Neill PM J Med Chem. 2002 Feb 28;45(5):1052-63

17. Expression and characterization of the Plasmodium falciparum

haemoglobinase falcipain-3. Sijwali PS, Shenai BR, Gut J, Singh A, Rosenthal PJ Biochem J. 2001 Dec 1; 360(Pt 2):481-9

18. Characterization of native and recombinant falcipain-2, a principal trophozoite cysteine protease and essential hemoglobinase of Plasmodium falciparum. Shenai BR, Sijwali PS, Singh A, Rosenthal PJ J Biol Chem. 2000 Sep 15; 275(37):29000-10

19. Glutathione--functions and metabolism in the malaria parasite Plasmodium falciparum. Becker K, Rahlfs S, Nickel C, Schirmer RH Biol Chem. 2003 Apr; 384(4):551-66

20. The thioredoxin system of the malaria parasite Plasmodium falciparum. Glutathione reduction revisited. Kanzok SM, Schirmer RH, Turbachova I, Iozef R, Becker K J Biol Chem. 2000 Dec 22;275(51):40180-6

21. Thioredoxin networks in the malaria parasite Plasmodium falciparum. Nickel C, Rahlfs S, Deponte M, Koncarevic S, Becker K Antioxid Redox Signal. 2006 Jul-Aug;8(7-8):1227-39

22. Thioredoxin and glutathione system of malaria parasite Plasmodium falciparum. Muller S, Gilberger TW, Krnajski Z, Luersen K, Meierjohann S, Walter RD, MÃ¼ller S, LÃ¼ersen K Protoplasma. 2001;217(1-3):43-9

23. Thioredoxin reductase and glutathione synthesis in Plasmodium falciparum. Muller S, MÃ¼ller S Redox Rep. 2003;8(5):251-5

24. Glutathione S-transferase of the malaria parasite Plasmodium falciparum: characterization of a potential drug target. Harwaldt P, Rahlfs S, Becker K Biol Chem. 2002 May; 383(5):821-30

25. Plasmodium falciparum thioredoxins and glutaredoxins as central players in redox metabolism. Rahlfs S, Nickel C, Deponte M, Schirmer RH, Becker K Redox Rep. 2003; 8(5):246-50

26. Plasmodium falciparum-infected red blood cells depend on a functional glutathione de novo synthesis attributable to an enhanced loss of glutathione. Luersen K, Walter RD, Muller S, LÃ¼ersen K, MÃ¼ller S Biochem J. 2000 Mar 1;346 Pt 2:545-52

27. Proposed reductive metabolism of artemisinin by glutathione transferases in vitro. Mukanganyama S, Naik YS, Widersten M, Mannervik B, Hasler JA Free Radic Res. 2001 Oct;35(4):427-34

28. Plasmoredoxin, a novel redox-active protein unique for malarial parasites. Becker K, Kanzok SM, Iozef R, Fischer M, Schirmer RH, Rahlfs S Eur J Biochem. 2003 Mar; 270(6):1057-64

29. Methylene blue as an antimalarial agent. Schirmer RH, Coulibaly B, Stich A, Scheiwein M, Merkle H, Eubel J, Becker K, Becher H, MÃ¼ller O, Zich T, Schiek W, KouyatÃ© B Redox Rep. 2003;8(5):272-5

30. Glutathione S-transferase from malarial parasites: structural and functional aspects. Deponte M, Becker K Methods Enzymol. 2005;401: 241-53

31. Plasmodium falciparum possesses a classical glutaredoxin and a second, glutaredoxin-like protein with a PICOT homology domain. Rahlfs S, Fischer M, Becker K J Biol Chem. 2001 Oct 5; 276(40):37133-40

32. Characterization of the glyoxalases of the malaria parasite Plasmodium falciparum and comparison with their human counterparts. Akoachere M, Iozef R, Rahlfs S, Deponte M, Mannervik B, Creighton DJ, Schirmer H, Becker K Biol Chem. 2005 Jan;386(1):41-52

33. Glutathione reductase-deficient erythrocytes as host cells of malarial parasites. Zhang Y, KÃ¶nig I, Schirmer RH Biochem Pharmacol. 1988 Mar 1;37(5):861-5

34. Glutathione reductase of the malaria parasite Plasmodium falciparum: crystal structure and inhibitor development. Sarma GN, Savvides SN, Becker K, Schirmer M, Schirmer RH, Karplus PA J Mol Biol. 2003 May 9;328(4):893-907

35. Glutathione synthetase from Plasmodium falciparum. Meierjohann S, Walter RD, MÃ¼ller S Biochem J. 2002 May 1; 63(Pt 3):833-8

36. Effect of dihydroartemisinin on the antioxidant capacity of P. falciparum-infected erythrocytes. Ittarat W, Sreepian A, Srisarin A, Pathepchotivong K Southeast Asian J Trop Med Public Health. 2003 Dec;34(4):744-50

37. Ceramide mediates growth inhibition of the Plasmodium falciparum parasite. Pankova-Kholmyansky I, Dagan A, Gold D, Zaslavsky Z, Skutelsky E, Gatt S, Flescher E Cell Mol Life Sci. 2003 Mar;60(3):577-87

38. Thiol-based redox metabolism of protozoan parasites. MÃ¼ller S, Liebau E, Walter RD, Krauth-Siegel RL Trends Parasitol. 2003 Jul;19(7):320-8 Comment in: Trends Parasitol. 2004 Feb; 20(2):58-9

39. Recombinant expression and biochemical characterization of the unique elongating beta-ketoacyl-acyl carrier protein synthase involved in fatty acid biosynthesis of Plasmodium falciparum using natural and artificial substrates Lack G, Homberger-Zizzari E, Folkers G, Scapozza L, Perozzo R J Biol Chem. 2006 Apr 7;281(14):9538-46

40. Roles of 1-Cys peroxiredoxin in haem detoxification in the human malaria parasite Plasmodium falciparum. Kawazu S, Ikenoue N, Takemae H, Komaki-Yasuda K, Kano S FEBS J. 2005 Apr;272(7):1784-91

41. Evidence that haem iron in the malaria parasite is not needed for the antimalarial effects of artemisinin. Parapini S, Basilico N, Mondani M, Olliaro P, Taramelli D, Monti D FEBS Lett. 2004 Sep 24; 575(1-3):91-4

42. Kinetic characterization of glutathione reductase from the malaria parasite Plasmodium falciparum. Comparison with the human enzyme. Bohme CC, Arscott LD, Becker K, Schirmer RH, Williams CH Jr J Biol Chem. 2000 Dec 1;275(48):37317-23

43. Identification, characterization, and inhibition of Plasmodium falciparum beta-hydroxyacyl-acyl carrier protein dehydratase (FabZ). Sharma SK, Kapoor M, Ramya TN, Kumar S, Kumar G, Modak R, Sharma S, Surolia N, Surolia A J Biol Chem. 2003 Nov 14;278(46):45661-71

44. The thioredoxin system of Plasmodium falciparum and other parasites. Rahlfs S, Schirmer RH, Becker K Cell Mol Life Sci. 2002 Jun; 59(6):1024-41

45. Plasmodium falciparum glutaredoxin-like proteins. Deponte M, Becker K, Rahlfs S Biol Chem. 2005 Jan;386(1):33-40

46. Specific inhibitors of Plasmodium falciparum thioredoxin reductase as potential antimalarial agents. Andricopulo AD, Akoachere MB, Krogh R, Nickel C, McLeish MJ, Kenyon GL, Arscott LD, Williams CH Jr, Davioud-Charvet E, Becker K Bioorg Med Chem Lett. 2006 Apr 15;16(8):2283-92

47. Recombinant Plasmodium falciparum glutathione reductase is inhibited by the antimalarial dye methylene blue. FÃ¤rber PM, Arscott LD, Williams CH Jr, Becker K, Schirmer RH FEBS Lett. 1998 Feb 6;422(3):311-4

48. The multiple roles of the mitochondrion of the malaria parasite. Krungkrai J Parasitology. 2004 Nov; 129(Pt 5):511-24

49. The glutathione S-transferase from Plasmodium falciparum. Liebau E,

Bergmann B, Campbell AM, Teesdale-Spittle P, Brophy PM, LÃ¼ersen K, Walter RD Mol Biochem Parasitol. 2002 Sep-Oct;124(1-2):85-90

50. Glutathione S-transferases and related proteins from pathogenic human parasites behave as immunomodulatory factors. Ouaissi A, Ouaissi M, Sereno D Immunol Lett. 2002 May 1; 81(3):159-64

51. Reducing requirements for hemoglobin hydrolysis by Plasmodium falciparum cysteine proteases. Shenai BR, Rosenthal PJ Mol Biochem Parasitol. 2002 Jun;122(1):99-104

52. Plasmodium falciparum glutathione S-transferase-- structural and mechanistic studies on ligand binding and enzyme inhibition. Hiller N, Fritz-Wolf K, Deponte M, Wende W, Zimmermann H, Becker K Protein Sci. 2006 Feb;15(2):281-9;Epub 2005 Dec 29.

53. Cooperativity and pseudo-cooperativity in the glutathione S-transferase from Plasmodium falciparum. Liebau E, De Maria F, Burmeister C, Perbandt M, Turella P, Antonini G, Federici G, Giansanti F, Stella L, Lo Bello M, Caccuri AM, Ricci G J Biol Chem. 2005 Jul 15;280(28):26121-8

54. Cysteine proteases of malaria parasites. Rosenthal PJ Int J Parasitol. 2004 Dec;34(13-14):1489-99

55. The thiol-based redox networks of pathogens: unexploited targets in the search for new drugs. Jaeger T, Flohe L, Flohé L Biofactors. 2006; 27(1-4):109-20

56. Structural and biochemical characterization of a mitochondrial peroxiredoxin from Plasmodium falciparum. Boucher IW, McMillan PJ, Gabrielsen M, Akerman SE, Brannigan JA, Schnick C, Brzozowski AM, Wilkinson AJ, Muller S, Müller S Mol Microbiol. 2006 Aug; 61(4):948-59

57. 2-Cys Peroxiredoxin TPx-1 is involved in gametocyte development in Plasmodium berghei. Yano K, Komaki-Yasuda K, Tsuboi T, Torii M, Kano S, Kawazu S Mol Biochem Parasitol. 2006 Jul;148(1):44-51

58. Plasmodium falciparum 2-Cys peroxiredoxin reacts with plasmoredoxin and peroxynitrite. Nickel C, Trujillo M, Rahlfs S, Deponte M, Radi R, Becker K Biol Chem. 2005 Nov;386(11):1129-36

59. Expression of mRNAs and proteins for peroxiredoxins in Plasmodium falciparum erythrocytic stage. Yano K, Komaki-Yasuda K, Kobayashi T,

Takemae H, Kita K, Kano S, Kawazu S Parasitol Int. 2005 Mar;54(1):35-41

60. Crystal structure of a novel Plasmodium falciparum 1-Cys peroxiredoxin. Sarma GN, Nickel C, Rahlfs S, Fischer M, Becker K, Karplus PA J Mol Biol. 2005 Mar 4;346(4):1021-34

61. 2-Cys peroxiredoxin PfTrx-Px1 is involved in the antioxidant defence of Plasmodium falciparum. Akerman SE, Muller S, Müller S Mol Biochem Parasitol. 2003 Aug 31; 130(2):75-81

62. Expression profiles of peroxiredoxin proteins of the rodent malaria parasite Plasmodium yoelii. Kawazu S, Nozaki T, Tsuboi T, Nakano Y, Komaki-Yasuda K, Ikenoue N, Torii M, Kano S Int J Parasitol. 2003 Nov;33(13):1455-61

63. Disruption of the Plasmodium falciparum 2-Cys peroxiredoxin gene renders parasites hypersensitive to reactive oxygen and nitrogen species. Komaki-Yasuda K, Kawazu S, Kano S FEBS Lett. 2003 Jul 17;547(1-3):140-4

64. Thioredoxin, thioredoxin reductase, and thioredoxin peroxidase of malaria parasite Plasmodium falciparum. Kanzok SM, Rahlfs S, Becker K, Schirmer RH Methods Enzymol. 2002; 347:370-81

65. Molecular characterization of a 2-Cys peroxiredoxin from the human malaria parasite Plasmodium falciparum. Kawazu S, Komaki K, Tsuji N, Kawai S, Ikenoue N, Hatabu T, Ishikawa H, Matsumoto Y, Himeno K, Kano S Mol Biochem Parasitol. 2001 Aug; 116(1):73-9

66. Isolation and functional analysis of two thioredoxin peroxidases (peroxiredoxins) from Plasmodium falciparum. Krnajski Z, Walter RD, Muller S, Müller S Mol Biochem Parasitol. 2001 Apr 6;113(2):303-8

67. Thioredoxin peroxidases of the malaria parasite Plasmodium falciparum. Rahlfs S, Becker K Eur J Biochem. 2001 Mar; 268(5):1404-9

HEME IS AN OXIDANT SENSITIZER

Of particular relevance to treating malaria is the fact that Plasmodial trophozoites living inside red blood cells must digest hemoglobin as their preferred protein source. [8, 13] They accomplish this by ingesting hemoglobin into an organelle known as the "acid food vacuole". [3, 16] Incidently, the high concentration of acid in this organelle could serve as an additional site of conversion of chlorite (ClO2-) to the more active chlorine dioxide (ClO2) right inside the parasite.

Next falcipain (a hemoglobin digesting enzyme) hydrolyzes hemoglobin protein to release its nutritional amino acids. [4, 5, 6, 26, 27] A necessary byproduct of this digestion is the release of 4 heme molecules from each hemoglobin molecule digested. [1] Free heme (also known as ferriprotoporphyrin) is redox active and can react with ambient oxygen (O2), an abundance of which is always present in red blood cells. This produces superoxide radical (*OO-), hydrogen peroxide (H2O2) and other reactive oxidant toxic species. [2, 7, 9, 10, 11, 12, 14, 15, 20] These can rapidly poison the parasite internally.

To protect itself against this dangerous side-effect of eating blood protein, Plasmodia must continuously and rapidly eliminate heme. [18, 22] This is accomplished by two methods. Firstly, heme is polymerized producing hemozoin. [19, 21, 23, 24] Secondly, heme is metabolized in a detoxification process that requires reduced glutathione (GSH). [17, 25] Therefore any method (including exposure to oxidants) which limits the availability of reduced glutathione will cause a toxic build up of heme inside the parasite cells. Since sodium chlorite and chlorine dioxide readily oxidize glutathione heme detoxification is inhibited. As these are the exact agents used in Mr. Humble's treatment, the observed effect of killing Plasmodia should be expected.

References:
1. In vitro activity of riboflavin against the human malaria parasite Plasmodium falciparum. Akompong T, Ghori N, Haldar K Antimicrob Agents Chemother. 2000 Ja ; 44(1):88-96

2. Potentiation of an antimalarial oxidant drug. Winter RW, Ignatushchenko M, Ogundahunsi OA, Cornell KA, Oduola AM, Hinrichs DJ, Riscoe MK Antimicrob Agents Chemother. 1997 Jul;41(7):1449-54

3. Hemoglobin degradation. Goldberg DE Curr Top Microbiol Immunol. 2005; 295:275-91

4. Development of cysteine protease inhibitors as chemotherapy for parasitic diseases: insights on safety, target validation, and mechanism of action. McKerrow JH Int J Parasitol. 1999 Jun; 29(6):833-7

5. Cysteine proteases of malaria parasites: targets for chemotherapy. Rosenthal PJ, Sijwali PS, Singh A, Shenai BR Curr Pharm Des. 2002; 8(18):1659-72

6. Proteases of malaria parasites: new targets for chemotherapy. Rosenthal PJ Emerg Infect Dis. 1998 Jan-Mar;4(1):49-57

7. Hemoglobin metabolism in the malaria parasite Plasmodium falciparum. Francis SE, Sullivan DJ Jr, Goldberg DE Annu Rev Microbiol. 1997; 51:97-123

8. Plasmodium falciparum: inhibitors of lysosomal cysteine proteinases inhibit a trophozoite proteinase and block parasite development. Rosenthal PJ, McKerrow JH, Rasnick D, Leech JH Mol Biochem Parasitol. 1989 Jun 15; 35(2):177-83

9. Identification and characterization of heme-interacting proteins in the malaria parasite, Plasmodium falciparum. Campanale N, Nickel C, Daubenberger CA, Wehlan DA, Gorman JJ, Klonis N, Becker K, Tilley L J Biol Chem. 2003 Jul 25;278(30):27354-61

10. The redox status of malaria-infected erythrocytes: an overview with an emphasis on unresolved problems. Ginsburg H, Atamna H Parasite. 1994 Mar; 1(1):5-13

11. Redox and antioxidant systems of the malaria parasite Plasmodium falciparum. Muller S Mol Microbiol. 2004 Sep;53(5):1291-305

12. Origin of reactive oxygen species in erythrocytes infected with Plasmodium falciparum. Atamna H, Ginsburg H Mol Biochem Parasitol. 1993 Oct; 61(2):231-41 Erratum in: Mol Biochem Parasitol 1994 Feb;63(2):312

13. Intraerythrocytic Plasmodium falciparum utilizes only a fraction of the amino acids derived from the digestion of host cell cytosol for the biosynthesis of its proteins. Krugliak M, Zhang J, Ginsburg H Mol Biochem Parasitol. 2002 Feb;119(2):249-56

14. Oxidative stress in malaria parasite-infected erythrocytes: host-parasite interactions. Becker K, Tilley L, Vennerstrom JL, Roberts D, Rogerson S, Ginsburg H Int J Parasitol. 2004 Feb; 34(2):163-89

15. Clotrimazole binds to heme and enhances heme-dependent hemolysis: proposed antimalarial mechanism of clotrimazole. Huy NT, Kamei K, Yamamoto T, Kondo Y, Kanaori K, Takano R, Tajima K, Hara S J Biol Chem. 2002 Feb 8;277(6):4152-8
16. Acidification of the malaria parasite's digestive vacuole by a H+-ATPase and a H+-pyrophosphatase. Saliba KJ, Allen RJ, Zissis S, Bray PG, Ward SA, Kirk K J Biol Chem. 2003 Feb 21; 278(8):5605-12

17. A non-radiolabeled heme-GSH interaction test for the screening of antimalarial compounds. Garavito G, Monje MC, Maurel S, Valentin A, Nepveu F, Deharo E Exp Parasitol. 2007 Jan 23

18. Effect of antifungal azoles on the heme detoxification system of malaria parasite. Huy NT, Kamei K, Kondo Y, Serada S, Kanaori K, Takano R, Tajima K, Hara S J Biochem (Tokyo). 2002 Mar; 131(3):437-44

19. Malarial haemozoin/beta-haematin supports haem polymerization in the absence of protein. Dorn A, Stoffel R, Matile H, Bubendorf A, Ridley RG Nature. 1995 Mar 16;374(6519):269-71

20. Illumination of the malaria parasite Plasmodium falciparum alters intracellular pH. Implications for live cell imaging. Wissing F, Sanchez CP, Rohrbach P, Ricken S, Lanzer M J Biol Chem. 2002 Oct 4;277(40):37747-55

21. Plasmodium falciparum histidine-rich protein-2 (PfHRP2) modulates the redox activity of ferri-protoporphyrin IX (FePPIX): peroxidase-like activity of the PfHRP2-FePPIX complex. Mashima R, Tilley L, Siomos MA, Papalexis V, Raftery MJ, Stocker R J Biol Chem. 2002 Apr 26;277(17):14514-20

22. Chloroquine - some open questions on its antimalarial mode of action and resistance. Ginsburg H, Krugliak M Drug Resist Updat. 1999 Jun; 2(3):180-187

23. A physiochemical mechanism of hemozoin (beta-hematin) synthesis by malaria parasite. Tripathi AK, Garg SK, Tekwani BL Biochem Biophys Res Commun. 2002 Jan 11;290(1):595-601

24. Histidine-rich protein 2 of the malaria parasite, Plasmodium falciparum, is involved in detoxification of the by-products of hemoglobin degradation. Papalexis V, Siomos MA, Campanale N,

Guo X, Kocak G, Foley M, Tilley L Mol Biochem Parasitol. 2001 Jun; 115(1):77-86

25. Inhibition of glutathione-dependent degradation of heme by chloroquine and amodiaquine as a possible basis for their antimalarial mode of action. Ginsburg H, Famin O, Zhang J, Krugliak M Biochem Pharmacol. 1998 Nov 15; 56(10):1305-13

26. Hydrolysis of erythrocyte proteins by proteases of malaria parasites. Rosenthal PJ Curr Opin Hematol. 2002 Mar; 9(2):140-5

27. Cysteine protease inhibitors as chemotherapy for parasitic infections. McKerrow JH, Engel JC, Caffrey CR Bioorg Med Chem. 1999 Apr; 7(4):639-44

OVERCOMING ANTIBIOTIC RESISTANCE WITH OXIDATION

Now the issue of resistance of Plasmodium species to commonly used antiprotozoal antibiotics must be addressed. Quinine, chloroquine, mefloquine and other quinoline antibiotics all work by blocking the heme detoxifying system inside the trophozoites. [1, 2, 3, 4, 5] Many Plasmodial strains against which quinolines have repeatedly been used have found a way to adjust to this treatment and to acquire resistance. Recent research has shown, however, that the mechanism of this acquired resistance amounts to a mere upregulation of glutathione production and utilization. [6, 7, 8, 11, 19, 21, 22, 23] Recent research has also shown that oxidizing or otherwise depleting glutathione inside the parasite restores sensitivity to the quinoline antibiotics. [10, 12, 13, 15, 16, 18, 20] Therefore, some protocols combining the use of oxidants with quinolines are already showing signs of success. In this regard let us consider that no amount of intraplasmodial glutathione (GSH) could ever resist exposure to a sufficient dose of chlorine dioxide (ClO2). Note that each molecule of ClO2 can disable 5 molecules of glutathione.

10 GSH + 2 ClO2 -> 5 GSSG + 4 H2O + 2 HCl

Living things possess a recovery system to rescue oxidized sulfur compounds. It operates through donation of hydrogen atoms to these compounds and thereby restores their original condition as thiols. [9]2 [H] + GSSG -> 2 GSH A key player in this system is
the enzyme glucose-6-phosphate- dehydrogenase (G6PDH). Patients with a genetic defect of G6PDH, known as glucose-6-phosphate-dehydrogenase deficiency disease, are especially sensitive to oxidants and to prooxidant drugs. However, this genetic disease has a benefit in that such individuals are naturally resistant to malaria. They can still catch malaria, but it is much less severe in them, since they permanently lack the enzyme necessary to assist the parasite in reactivating glutathione. [14, 17]

Furthermore, G6PDH is profoundly sensitive to inhibition by sodium chlorate (NaClO3), another member of the chlorine oxide family of compounds. Sodium chlorate (NaClO3) is a lesser ingredient present in Jim Humble's antimalarial solution. Some sodium chlorate should also be produced in vivo by a slow reaction of chlorine dioxide with water under slightly alkaline conditions. The Plasmodia may attempt to restore its glutathione that is lost to oxidation. However, this will be difficult or impossible if G6PDH is inhibited by chlorate.

Rerences:
1. Inhibition of the peroxidative degradation of haem as the basis of action of chloroquine and other quinoline antimalarials. Loria P, Miller S, Foley M, Tilley L Biochem J. 1999 Apr 15; 339 (Pt 2):363-70

2. Quinoline antimalarials: mechanisms of action and resistance and prospects for new agents. Foley M, Tilley L Pharmacol Ther. 1998 Jul; 79(1):55-87

3. Quinoline antimalarials: mechanisms of action and resistance. Foley M, illey L Int J Parasitol. 1997 Feb; 27(2):231-40

4. Inhibition by anti-malarial drugs of haemoglobin denaturation and iron release in acidified red blood cell lysates--a possible mechanism of their anti-malarial effect? Gabay T, Krugliak M, Shalmiev G, Ginsburg H Parasitology. 1994 May; 108 (Pt 4):371-81

5. Chloroquine: mechanism of drug action and resistance in Plasmodium falciparum. Slater AF Pharmacol Ther. 1993 Feb-Mar;57(2-3):203-35

6. Regulation of intracellular glutathione levels in erythrocytes infected with chloroquine-sensitive and chloroquine-resistant Plasmodium falciparum. Meierjohann S, Walter RD, Muller S, Müller S Biochem J. 2002 Dec 15; 368(Pt 3):761-8

7. The malaria parasite supplies glutathione to its host cell--investigation of glutathione transport and metabolism in human erythrocytes infected with Plasmodium falciparum. Atamna H, Ginsburg H Eur J Biochem. 1997 Dec 15; 250(3):670-9

8. Is the expression of genes encoding enzymes of glutathione (GSH) metabolism involved in chloroquine resistance in Plasmodium chabaudi parasites? Ferreira ID, Nogueira F, Borges ST, do Rosario VE, Cravo P, do Rosyo VE Mol Biochem Parasitol. 2004 Jul; 136(1):43-50

9. Malaria parasite hexokinase and hexokinase-dependent glutathione reduction in the Plasmodium falciparum infected human erythrocyte. Roth EF Jr J Biol Chem. 1987 Nov 15;262(32):15678-82

10. A prodrug form of a Plasmodium falciparum glutathione reductase inhibitor conjugated with a 4-anilinoquinoline. Davioud-Charvet E, Delarue S, Biot C, Schwobel B, Boehme CC, Mussigbrodt A, Maes L, Sergheraert C, Grellier P, Schirmer RH, Becker K, SchwÃ¶bel B, MÃ¼ssigbrodt A J Med Chem. 2001 Nov 22;44(24):4268-76

11. Plasmodium falciparum glutathione metabolism and growth are independent of glutathione system of host erythrocyte. Ayi K, Cappadoro M, Branca M, Turrini F, Arese P FEBS Lett. 1998 Mar 13;424(3):257-61

12. The treatment of Plasmodium falciparum-infected erythrocytes with chloroquine leads to accumulation of ferriprotoporphyrin IX bound to particular parasite proteins and to the inhibition of the parasite's 6-phosphogluconate dehydrogenase. Famin O, Ginsburg H Parasite. 2003 Mar;10(1):39-50

13. Deletion of the parasite-specific insertions and mutation of the catalytic triad in glutathione reductase from chloroquine-sensitive Plasmodium falciparum 3D7. Gilberger TW, Schirmer RH, Walter RD, MÃ¼ller S Mol Biochem Parasitol. 2000 Apr 15; 107(2):169-79

14. Redox metabolism in glucose-6-phosphate dehydrogenase deficient erythrocytes and its relation to antimalarial chemotherapy. Ginsburg H, Golenser J Parassitologia. 1999 Sep;41(1-3):309-11

15. Potentiation of the antimalarial action of chloroquine in rodent malaria by drugs known to reduce cellular glutathione levels. Deharo E, Barkan D, Krugliak M, Golenser J, Ginsburg H Biochem Pharmacol. 2003 Sep 1; 66(5):809-17

16. Glutathione is involved in the antimalarial action of chloroquine and its modulation affects drug sensitivity of human and murine species of Plasmodium. Ginsburg H, Golenser J Redox Rep. 2003; 8(5):276-9

17. Plasmodium falciparum: thiol status and growth in normal and glucose-6-phosphate dehydrogenase deficient human erythrocytes. Miller J, Golenser J, Spira DT, Kosower NS Exp Parasitol. 1984 Jun; 57(3):239-47

18. Plasmodium berghei: dehydroepiandrosterone sulfate reverses chloroquino-resistance in experimental malaria infection; correlation with glucose 6-phosphate dehydrogenase and glutathione synthesis pathway. Safeukui I, Mangou F, Malvy D, Vincendeau P, Mossalayi D, Haumont G, Vatan R, Olliaro P, Millet P Biochem Pharmacol. 2004 Nov 15; 68(10):1903-10

19. Glutathione-S-transferases from chloroquine-resistant and -sensitive strains of Plasmodium falciparum: what are their differences? Rojpibulstit P, Kangsadalampai S, Ratanavalachai T, Denduangboripant J, Chavalitshewinkoon-Petmitr P Southeast Asian J Trop Med Public Health. 2004 Jun; 35(2):292-9

20. Double-drug development against antioxidant enzymes from Plasmodium falciparum. Biot C, Dessolin J, Grellier P, Davioud-Charvet E Redox Rep. 2003;8(5):280-3

21. Plasmodium berghei: analysis of the gamma-glutamylcysteine synthetase gene in drug-resistant lines. Perez-Rosado J, Gervais GW, Ferrer-Rodriguez I, Peters W, Serrano AE, PÃ©rez-Rosado J, Ferrer-RodrÃguez I Exp Parasitol. 2002 Aug;101(4):175-82

22. Glutathione-S-transferase activity in malarial parasites. Srivastava P, Puri SK, Kamboj KK, Pandey VC Trop Med Int Health. 1999 Apr; 4(4):251-4

23. Role of glutathione in the detoxification of ferriprotoporphyrin IX in chloroquine resistant Plasmodium berghei. Platel DF, Mangou F, Tribouley-Duret J Mol Biochem Parasitol. 1999 Jan 25;98(2):215-23

TARGETING IRON

While most available literature refers to redox imbalances causing depletion of necessary thiols. Other mechanisms of toxicity of the oxides of chlorine against Plasmodia should also be considered. Oxides of chlorine are generally rapidly reactive with ferrous iron (Fe++). This explains why in cases of overdosed exposures to oxides of chlorine such as sodium chlorite (NaClO2) there was a notable rise in methemoglobin levels. Methemoglobin is a metabolically inactive form of hemoglobin in which its ferrous iron (Fe++) cofactor has been oxidized to ferric (Fe+++). Many enzymes in living things employ iron as a cofactor including those in parasites. [8, 9, 10] Thus it is reasonable to expect that any damage to Plasmodia caused by oxides of chlorine is compounded by conversion of ferrous cofactors to ferric. [1, 2, 3, 4, 5, 6, 7]

References:
1. The plant-type ferredoxin-NADP+ reductase/ferredoxin redox system as a possible drug target against apicomplexan human parasites. Seeber F, Aliverti A, Zanetti G Curr Pharm Des. 2005; 11(24):3159-72

2. Ferredoxin-NADP (+) Reductase from Plasmodium falciparum Undergoes NADP (+)-dependent Dimerization and Inactivation: Functional and Crystallographic Analysis. Milani M, Balconi E, Aliverti A, Mastrangelo E, Seeber F, Bolognesi M, Zanetti G J Mol Biol. 2007 Mar 23;367(2):501-13;Epub 2007 Jan 09

3. Cloning and Characterization of Ferredoxin and Ferredoxin-NADP+ Reductase from Human Malaria Parasite. Kimata-Ariga Y, Kurisu G, Kusunoki M, Aoki S, Sato D, Kobayashi T, Kita K, Horii T, Hase T J Biochem (Tokyo). 2007 Mar; 141(3):421-428;Epub 2007 Jan 23

4. Reconstitution of an apicoplast-localised electron transfer pathway involved in the isoprenoid biosynthesis of Plasmodium falciparum. Röhrich RC, Englert N, Troschke K, Reichenberg A, Hintz M, Seeber F, Balconi E, Aliverti A, Zanetti G, Köhler U, Pfeiffer M, Beck E, Jomaa H, Wiesner J. FEBS Lett. 2005 Nov 21; 579(28):6433-8;Epub 2005 Nov 02

5. The plant-type ferredoxin-NADP+ reductase/ferredoxin redox system as a possible drug target against apicomplexan human parasites. Seeber F, Aliverti A, Zanetti G Curr Pharm Des. 2005;11(24):3159-72

6. Biogenesis of iron-sulphur clusters in amitochondriate and apicomplexan protists. Seeber F Int J Parasitol. 2002 Sep; 32(10):1207-17

7. Apicomplexan parasites possess distinct nuclear-encoded, but apicoplast-localized, plant-type ferredoxin-NADP+ reductase and ferredoxin. Vollmer M, Thomsen N, Wiek S, Seeber F J Biol Chem. 2001 Feb 23;276(8):5483-90;Epub 2000 Oct 30

8. Design, synthesis and antimalarial activity of a new class of iron chelators. Solomon VR, Haq W, Puri SK, Srivastava K, Katti SB Med Chem. 2006 Mar;2(2):133-8

9. Heme biosynthesis by the malaria parasite. Import of delta-aminolevulinate dehydrase from the host red cell. Bonday ZQ, Taketani S, Gupta PD, Padmanaban G J Biol Chem. 1997 Aug 29; 272(35):21839-46

10. Hemoglobin catabolism and iron utilization by malaria parasites. Rosenthal PJ, Meshnick SR Mol Biochem Parasitol. 1996 Dec 20; 83(2):131-9

TARGETING POLYAMINES

Other metabolites necessary for survival and growth in tumors, bacteria and parasites are the polyamines. [2] When these are lacking pathogens quit growing and die. [1] Polyamines are also sensitive to oxidation and can be eliminated by strong oxidants. When oxidized, polyamines are converted to aldehydes, which are deadly to parasites and to tumors. Thus any procedure which is successful to oxidize polyamines doe's double damage to the pathogen. Chlorine dioxide (ClO2) is known to be especially reactive against secondary amines. This includes spermine and spermidine, the two main biologically important polyamines.

References:
1. Targeting enzymes involved in spermidine metabolism of parasitic protozoa--a possible new strategy for anti-parasitic treatment. Kaiser A, Gottwald A, Maier W, Seitz HM Parasitol Res. 2003 Dec;91(6):508-16

2. Polyamines in the cell cycle of the malaria parasite Plasmodium falciparum. Bachrach U, Abu-Elheiga L, Assaraf YG, Golenser J, Spira DT Adv Exp Med Biol. 1988;250:643-50

SAFETY ISSUES
A remaining concern is safety. So far, at least anecdotally, the dosages of chlorine oxides as administered orally per Jim Humble's protocol have produced no definite toxicity. Some have taken this as often as 1 to 3 times weekly and on the surface seem to suffer no ill effects. To be certain if this is safe, more research is warranted for such long term or repeated use. The concern is that too much or too frequent administration of oxidants could excessively deplete the body's reductants and promote oxidative stress. One useful way to monitor this may be to periodically check methemoglobin levels in frequent users. Sodium chlorite, as found in municipal water supplies after disinfection by chlorine dioxide, has been studied and proven safe. Animal studies using yet higher oral doses have also proven safe. One case of extreme overdose in a suicide attempt caused nearly fatal kidney failure and refractory methemoglobinemia. Special precautions must be employed in cases of glucose-6-phosphate-dehydrogenase deficiency disease, as these patients are especially sensitive to oxidants of all kinds. Nevertheless, oral sodium chlorite (NaClO2) solutions may yet be found safe and effective in them, but

probably will need to be administered at lower doses.

MORE RESEARCH

It is hoped that this overview will spark a flurry of interest, and stimulate more research into the use of acidified sodium chlorite in the treatment of malaria. The above appreciated observations need to be proven more rigorously and published [8]. The biochemistry most likely involved suggests that other members of the phylum Apicomplexa should also be sensitive to this treatment. This phylum includes: Plasmodium, Babesia, Toxoplasma [2], Cryptosporidium [3], Eimeria [4], Theileria, Sarcocystis, Cyclospora, Isospora and Neospora. These agents are responsible for widespread diseases in humans, pets and cattle.

Chlorine dioxide has been proven to be cidal to almost all known infectious agents' in vitro using remarkably low concentrations. This includes parasites [1, 6, 7, 9, and 10], fungi [5], bacteria and viruses. The experiences noted above imply that this compound is tolerable orally at effective concentrations. Therefore extensive research is warranted to determine if acidified sodium chlorite is effective in many other infections. We may be on the verge of discovering the most potent and broad spectrum antibiotic yet known. Special thanks go to Jim Humble for his willingness to share his discovery with the world.

References:
1. Cysticidal effect of chlorine dioxide on Giardia intestinalis cysts. Winiecka-Krusnell J, Linder E Acta Trop. 1998 Jul 30;70(3):369-72

2. Toxoplasma gondii: the model apicomplexan. Kim K, Weiss LM Int J Parasitol. 2004 Mar 9; 34(3):423-32

3. Effects of ozone, chlorine dioxide, chlorine, and monochloramine on Cryptosporidium parvum oocyst viability. Korich DG, Mead JR, Madore MS, Sinclair NA, Sterling CR Appl Environ Microbiol. 1990 May; 56(5):1423-8

4. The effect of 'Alcide' on 4 strains of rodent coccidial oocysts. Owen DG Lab Anim. 1983 Oct;17(4):267-9

5. Glutathione, altruistic metabolite in fungi. PÃ³csi I, Prade RA, Penninckx MJ Adv Microb Physiol. 2004; 49:1-76

6. Characterization of an omega-class glutathione- S-transferase from Schistosoma mansoni with glutaredoxin-like dehydroascorbate reductase and thiol transferase activities. Girardini J, Amirante A, Zemzoumi K, Serra E Eur J Biochem. 2002 Nov; 269(22):5512-21

7. Thiol-based redox metabolism of protozoan parasites. MÃ¼ller S, Liebau E, Walter RD, Krauth-Siegel RL Trends Parasitol. 2003 Jul;19(7):320-8 Comment in: Trends Parasitol. 2004 Feb;20(2):58-9

8. Estimation of the total parasite biomass in acute falciparum malaria from plasma PfHRP2. Dondorp AM, Desakorn V, Pongtavornpinyo W, Sahassananda D, Silamut K, Chotivanich K, Newton PN, Pitisuttithum P, Smithyman AM, White NJ, Day NP PLoS Med. 2005 Aug;2(8):e204;Epub 2005 Aug 23 Erratum in: PLoS Med. 2005 Oct;2(10):390 Comment in: PLoS Med. 2006 Jan;3(1):e68; Author reply e69.
9. The parasite-specific trypanothione metabolism of trypanosoma and leishmania. Krauth-Siegel RL, Meiering SK, Schmidt H Biol Chem. 2003 Apr; 384(4):539-49

10. The synthesis of parasitic cysteine protease and trypanothione reductase inhibitors. Chibale K, Musonda CC Curr Med Chem. 2003 Sep; 10(18):1863-89

----

http://www.miraclemineral.org
http://bioredox.mysite.com
Additional references will be posted on the internet or made available upon request.

Thomas Lee Hesselink, MD

Hesselink's reference files & folders already incorporated: ClOx_DisinfectantEffects/*.*   ClOx_AntiParasiticEffects/ Apicoplast&Lipoic.txt,   Apicoplast.txt ClOx&AntiParasiticDisinfectant.txt,   MalariaSolution-JimHumble-LibertarianTimes.htm,   Plamsodium&AcidFoodVacuole.txt

Plamsodium&CysteineProteases.txt,   Plamsodium&GSHdependence.txt,
Plamsodium&Heme&GSH.txt Plamsodium&Peroxiredoxin.txt

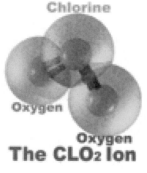

Chlorine

Oxygen

Oxygen

The CLO₂ Ion

Chapter 23

The MMS Adventures of a Grade School Teacher in Mexico

You may have wondered just what might really be done with the MMS, really! Well, read this:

I'm an elementary school teacher in Hermosillo Mexico in the state of Sonora. My name is Clara Beltrones. I first started using the MMS on May 25 of this year (2007). My youngest daughter's tonsils became swollen with white spots on them. I took her to the doctor and he prescribed penicillin and anti-inflammatory drops which I gave to her when we returned home. Within ½ hour her whole body started to swell with spots similar to those on her tonsils and she had problems breathing. I took her back to the same doctor who gave her a shot to bring the swelling down. I brought her home and in an hour nothing had happened. So I called Jim Humble and he said give her one drop of MMS and then another drop an hour later. In the first 15 minutes of the first dose, the swelling of her body went back to normal. I took her back to the doctor as I wanted him to see what was going on in her body. The doctor asked what I gave her, because the tonsils were half way down and the spots were gone. I decided not to say anything to the doctor. I came back home and gave her the second drop. This happened during the morning and by that afternoon, she was back to normal except she had a runny nose. The next day she was completely clear.

Even though I saw it work on my daughter I was still disbelieving of the MMS. However, on June 17 my aunt Patty Velez and her daughter Patty Souza came to see me and I thought to give it to them just to try it out. I then gave both of them six drops of MMS with the necessary lime drops and the 3 minute wait. When they drank it they both mentioned that they felt tingling in their whole body for about fifteen minutes. We waited an hour and they took a second dose of 6 drops. At that time they went home.

The next day I called to find out how they were doing. They pointed out that the daughter, Patty Souza, had not had her period for six months, plus she had not yet developed breasts. She had a large chest, but no breasts had shown. Yet, that morning breasts about the size of a small lime had begun to develop. At that time I suggested the daughter take another dose on Thursday which was 4 days later. When I called on Thursday she mentioned that her large chest had formed into full size breasts and she now had her period for the first time in six months. She now says that she feels less nervous and that she is losing a lot of the weight that she needs to lose. She was taking pills from a psychiatrist for depression which she no long feels that she needs to take. Her mother also experienced change. She said that she felt much energized and for the first time she was able to sleep through the whole night. She mentioned that she was taking pills prescribed by a psychiatrist for depression and anxiety and pills to go to sleep and pills to wake up in the morning. The first night she was able to sleep and did not take the pills. The second day the back pain and leg pain that she had been experiencing for many years was gone. She also stopped taking the pills for depression and anxiety because she no longer needs them. She is a nurse and understands the need or no need for such pills. It's now two months later and both the mother and daughter are still doing well.

On June 26 my daughter Alejandra age 5 woke up very swollen in her entire body. She could hardly see out of her eyes. She had a pain on her lower right side of her stomach and she was throwing up because of the extreme pain. I took her to the emergency room and they admitted her and did a blood test, urine test, and X-rays and all came out positive to acute appendicitis. They began to program her for an operation immediately as an emergency. I decided to see about having her operation at a local private hospital. They started doing the paperwork for the transfer; in the meantime she was in observation. I went to the car, got my bottle of MMS and a lime that I had thought to bring in the car in case I might need it, and prepared her a 6 drop dose. I had her drink it like she was drinking a glass of water. The doctor noticed that the swelling on her body began to reduce and the pain was almost gone in about 20 minutes. So they kept her in observation and after 3 hours of paper work and observation there was no longer any swelling or pain. So the doctor asked me if I gave her anything and I said nothing. He asked several times but knowing doctors I decided it best to say nothing. The doctor decided to have another set of tests. The blood test, urine test, and the X-rays all came out negative for appendicitis. I asked for the results of the tests, but the doctor would only allow me to have the second set of tests which I now have at home. When we came home she had a severe pain in her stomach and she run to the restroom and had much water and green stuff come out. That was the end of it. I did not give her a second dose.

On July 6 I visited Liz Chan who complained of back pain, leg pain, and that she has not been able to sit down because she gets cramps in her legs. She has had the cramp problem since she was 18 when she had her tonsils removed. At that time she began having rheumatoid arthritis and varicose veins. So I decided to give her six drops with the lime and 3 minutes wait and then a similar dose after one hour. After the first dose in about 15 minutes her lower back pain went away and she was able to sit down and stand up with no problem. The next morning she called and said she had no pain and she was able to sit up with no problem. She was amazed with the results. On the third day of taking the six drops each night her varicose veins were still the same size but the pain was gone. She felt a lot of energy. On August 8 she told me she had lost 10 pounds of weight and on August 9th she got diarrhea for a whole day and I had her take lemon aid and salt to overcome any dehydration. On August 10 she went camping and she was able to walk over 4 miles without pain or tiring. During the process she noticed that the fungus that had been on the bottom of her foot for over 5 years had disappeared. She also feels that her skin is in much better condition. Also she has noticed that all cramping before her period is now gone.

Martha, a lady that owns a small grocery store near my house one morning complained about a pain in the neck caused by lying wrong. I had her come to my house and gave her the two six drop doses at one hour between each dose. The pain in her neck went away on the first dose. Now she keeps a MMS bottle in her store and treats people in the neighborhood and those who bring products to the store. For example, one person who had a tooth ache she had him wash his mouth with 15 drops of MMS, activated with lime, the 3 wait and with water added. The pain went away immediately. She began treating her mother who suffers from emphysema. The disease was so bad that the doctors could give her no hope. She also has rheumatoid arthritis. When I saw her the first time she was laying with oxygen and not able to move. On the first dose of 6 drops she vomited white stuff. With the second dose after an hour she felt OK and went to sleep with no need for oxygen. The next day she felt so good that she wanted to go outside. She was able to get up from bed with no help. There was still pain but it was less than 50% of what it was according to her evaluation. On the third day it was raining and yet the pain was even less and she was able to walk around the house with the help of a walker. She takes the 6 drops every night and now she plans to start increasing the number of drops. It is now 8 days later, and she has said what she likes about the drops is that they make her vomit a lot of mucus every other day and that she always feels much better after vomiting. Now she only uses oxygen now and then. Martha (the daughter) personally takes drops every time she feels nervous and anxious and that calms her down right away.

My mother suffered from both acid reflux and hemorrhoids which caused her lower intestines to become inflamed for many years. The first time she took the MMS she took a full 15 drops with the vinegar instead of lime. She said she felt nothing from the drops, but the second day she got diarrhea and she took another 15 drops. She vomited for about 3 hours and the only thing she took was lemonade with salt to hydrate her body. She felt very week. The third day she didn't take any drops but she felt good with a lot of energy. She was afraid to eat, but she did eat a little fruit for breakfast and nothing for lunch. At dinner she went ahead and had a stake with a lot of salsa. She had no problem with digestion and she noticed no burning problem. After that she took 6 drops for about 2 months and one day she decided that she needed to clean herself out. She then went to 10 drops and then to 11 drops and then she began vomiting bright orange material and she felt weak and remained in bed with diarrhea. The next day she took 12 drops and after an hour she threw up dark green material only 4 times that day. Finally the throw up material was orange again and she began feeling better and had one meal. On the third day she awoke feeling really great with lots of energy and has been feeling good ever since. She continues to take the MMS and she has lost 6 pounds so far. Her stomach is much smaller in size now.

There's one other case I would like to tell you about. My son, Carlos, who is 12 years old has had Attention Deficit Disorder (ADD) all of his life. I have always paid to have him attend special schools. This year the tuition is $2000 US. A cost not easily obtained in Mexico. The

ADD often comes with poor conduct and poor social abilities. And that was especially in the case with Carlos. It was hard for me, his mother, to keep him doing his chores. He did not get along with the other children and he was what I considered a continuous problem. And then one evening a couple of months ago I started him off, the same as everyone else, with a 6 drop dose, of course with the lemon juice, three minute wait and then added juice. He took the second similar dose one hour later, and has been taking 6 drop doses every evening. After about two weeks his attitude began to change. He began being nicer to me, and to the other children. There has been no fighting incidents and Carlos has become a very well behaved child and seems quite appreciative of other people. He hasn't started to school yet, but I am anxious to see how his grades will be.

-- I hope you have as good results as I have had. Clara Beltrones.

Note from the Author: As you can see here Clara has been using a little different protocol than I have suggested in this book in that I usually suggest starting at 2 drops of MMS or less. However, it is hard to argue with success. Clara has now treated more than 45 people using the six drop first dose and she always waits an hour before giving them a second dose. In discussing the cases with her, she almost always notices quite a bit of burping within 15 minutes or so. Most of the people here in this desert city of Hermosillo vomit white or colored mucus within the first several hours, often after they go home from taking the two 6 drop doses. She always warns them that they will probably vomit at first and so far they have all agreed to go ahead and take the 6 drop doses. All the cases that Clara has treated has reported feeling really great, or better than they have felt for years. There has been a positive result from everyone, and many of them have gotten positive results with their loved ones.

If you look at protocol number 3 at the end of Chapter 10 you will notice that I have added the 6 and 6 protocol. This protocol seems to work very good in many cases. Please read the protocol and use it when it seems warranted.

Good fortune and Good luck.

The Author

Notes: Please use these extra pages to write notes concerning you use of MMS. It might become very valuable to you as time passes. Please keep records.

Notes:

Notes:

Notes:

Notes:

Notes:

Notes:

Notes:

Notes: